Authentic Cariño

Authentic Cariño

Transformative Schooling for Latinx Youth

Marnie W. Curry

Foreword by Angela Valenzuela

TEACHERS COLLEGE PRESS

TEACHERS COLLEGE | COLUMBIA UNIVERSITY
NEW YORK AND LONDON

Published by Teachers College Press,® 1234 Amsterdam Avenue, New York, NY 10027

Copyright © 2021 by Teachers College, Columbia University

Cover photo of "Beautiful Struggle" mural by Deborah Sherman. The mural was created by students from Oakland High School's Visual Arts Academy Magnet Program, who were mentored by Tara Asciutto Ashton and Keith "K-Dub" Williams.

Library of Congress Cataloging-in-Publication Data

Names: Curry, Marnie W., author.
Title: Authentic Cariño : transformative schooling for Latinx youth / Marnie W. Curry.
Description: New York, NY : Teachers College Press, [2021] | Includes bibliographical references and index.
Identifiers: LCCN 2021034671 (print) | LCCN 2021034672 (ebook) | ISBN 9780807766323 (hardcover) | ISBN 9780807766316 (paperback) | ISBN 9780807780718 (ebook)
Subjects: LCSH: Transformative learning—California. | Hispanic American high school students—Social conditions—California. | Low-income high school students—California. | Social justice and education—California.
Classification: LCC LC1100 .C88 2021 (print) | LCC LC1100 (ebook) | DDC 371.829/68073—dc23/eng/20211006
LC record available at https://lccn.loc.gov/2021034671
LC ebook record available at https://lccn.loc.gov/2021034672

ISBN 978-0-8077-6631-6 (paper)
ISBN 978-0-8077-6632-3 (hardcover)
ISBN 978-0-8077-8071-8 (ebook)

Printed on acid-free paper
Manufactured in the United States of America

Este libro está dedicado a Güero quien modeló el amor y la paz y a los educadores quienes le enseñaron y quienes han seguido luchando la lucha hermosa en su memoria.

And also to Steve, Finn, and Sam for their endless cariño. Los quiero mucho.

Contents

Contents

Foreword

It has been well over 20 years since I researched and wrote about authentic caring in my book, *Subtractive Schooling*. Marnie Curry's beautifully written ethnography of Molina High School (MHS) in Northern California is a timely and important extension of my work. In *Authentic Cariño: Transformative Schooling for Latinx Youth*, she tells the story of a vibrant community school that is the antithesis of Seguín High School (pseudonym) in Texas, where I conducted my 3-year ethnography. Unlike the Mexican youth I documented at Seguín, who contended with uncaring teachers whose assimilationist practices disregarded students' heritage cultures, languages, and desire for *educación*, Curry documents a school in which staff assiduously and lovingly fostered students' moral, social, academic, and personal development. Anchored in a grounded analysis of MHS's schooling practices, Curry advances a theory of authentic *cariño* that illuminates the transformative possibilities of learning when it is anchored in its key constituent components of familial, intellectual, and critical care. She argues that empowering expressions of care entail the integration of these three dimensions. Through her engaging account of how authentic cariño saturated MHS classrooms and public spaces, and spilled outwardly into the community, she illustrates the kind of additive schooling for which the students and families of Seguín hungered, but rarely received.

I found myself deeply moved while reading about MHS educators, families, community members, and youth collaborating in culturally sustaining ways to learn together and uplift one another. Curry's counter-narrative provided an opportunity for me to step back and better understand my own involvement over the last 8 years with Academia Cuauhtli (Nahuatl for "Eagle Academy"), a Saturday school in Austin, Texas, where Nuestro Grupo ("Our Group") organizers have embodied authentic cariño with impressive results, including the retention over an 8-year time period of all its teachers that participate in the academy.

While our *escuelita* (little school) exhibits all of the forms of *cariño* manifest at MHS, I take the opportunity to briefly capture the practice of *cariño* among Nuestro Grupo members as this has proved vital to our sustainability. We are an intergenerational group that exemplifies familial *cariño*, exhibiting what we term a "relational ecology," where we take care of not solely our students and parents at Academia Cuauhtli, but each other as well. Several of us, for example, have our partners, adult children, as well as undergraduate and graduate students as actively involved members. Despite the inevitable movement of students and community members that move on, the remaining core group remains, providing a sense of not only continuity, but a deep sense of family and belonging.

Reminiscent of how MHS teachers began their meetings with team-building icebreakers and how they concluded meetings with public testimonies of affirmation to colleagues, *floricanto* is an important practice in our weekly, Wednesday evening, meetings that help build trust and caring. We understand *floricanto* to be our ancestors' instructions on how to live lives filled with gratitude by sharing in each others' accomplishments, trials, and well-being through various forms of expression, including storytelling, poetry, and song. We never begin a meeting without some form of sharing, a practice that helped us all to endure the trying months of the pandemic with a deep and abiding sense of strength, purpose, and wholeness.

Intellectually, Nuestro Grupo has become a pathway into the masters and doctoral program in the College of Education at UT Austin. Over the length of our existence, we have nurtured at least 20 students, many of them who now have masters and doctoral degrees either in educational leadership and policy or curriculum and instruction. We collaborate in research, write policy briefs and reports, engage in community and legislative advocacy, and deliver presentations throughout the state and country, in such areas as ethnic studies, high-stakes testing, bilingual student assessment, transgender rights, culturally relevant pedagogy, and immigrant rights. For graduate students, this provides them with a community—similar to Curry's description of a "network of care"—that helps them to navigate the rigors of graduate school.

Critical cariño is an explicit aspect of our reason for being. Nuestro Grupo's intergenerational representation of university faculty, coupled with community elders seasoned in the world of policy—whether at the school board, city council, State Board of Education, or Texas State Legislature—students learn how to be agents of change. Not only have we been influential in high-profile struggles surrounding ethnic studies and student assessment, but we also saved two schools from school closure and successfully lobbied the AISD school board for ethnic studies that is today taught in every high school districtwide. When our children's families were targeted for deportation by Immigration Customs Enforcement, we participated in marches and brought legal resources to our parents so that they could be informed of their rights while providing them with a safe space at our community center.

Our curriculum for the students reflected this crisis by focusing on student voice and helping them know how to defend themselves against discrimination. Throughout the pandemic, we have been an ongoing resource to 40 families, assisting them with their digital needs, providing school supplies, helping them with rental assistance, food, and averting eviction, particularly in the aftermath of the epic winter storm that left Austin's most vulnerable families, like those we serve, without work. These unexpected and significant challenges organically transformed us into a wraparound service provider, one fundraiser at a time.

Just as I found Marnie's book a helpful companion for reflecting on all that we in Nuestro Grupo do and in the spirit in which it is done, I believe that others—teachers, administrators, policy makers, youth workers, teacher educators, curriculum developers, and community organizers—will also find much here to guide and deepen their work. This kind of reflection is especially urgent as schools reopen following the COVID-19 pandemic, the racial strife of the last year and a half, and for us, our deadly winter storm. We return to classrooms knowing that low-income, culturally and linguistically diverse youth have endured disproportionate suffering and trauma during this crisis. In the face of the staggering challenges that lie ahead, I believe that examples such as MHS and Academia Cuauhtli show how caring for children's full humanity is not only possible, but imperative. Indeed, they are testaments to the power of a curriculum and pedagogy grounded in authentic *cariño* to heal and transform individuals and communities. Now more than ever, we must infuse authentic *cariño* into our schools in order to press forward toward a pluralistic, multiracial democracy where "liberty and justice" prevail for all. For this reason, I genuinely welcome *Authentic Cariño: Transformative Schooling for Latinx Youth* and hope that readers will be inspired to use it as resource to advance additive, as opposed to subtractive, schooling.

—*Angela Valenzuela*, PhD

Acknowledgments

This book would not exist without the many opportunities that led me to educational research and placed me at Molina High School with the right people at the right time. I cannot possibly thank each teacher, student, mentor, scholar, and friend who influenced me, but I am deeply grateful for the vast reservoir of love, skills, and understanding that I have accrued during my life. Because the energy and wisdom of many individuals suffuse the words assembled here, I say *un enorme gracias a todos por todo*!

The themes explored in this book have been germinating in my consciousness for decades. As a Dartmouth undergraduate, I had the good fortune to study moral development with Andrew Garrod, who introduced me to Carol Gilligan. Her "ethic of care" seeded my interest in authentic cariño. During those years, I also read Moraga and Anzaldúa's (1981/1983) *This Bridge Called My Back* under the able tutelage of Carla Freccero. These experiences coupled with teacher credential courses and mentorship from Faith Dunne and Becky Langrall awakened me to social inequity and catapulted me into a career in education.

During my master's program, University of Wisconsin-Madison professors Michael Apple, Anne Egan-Robertson, Mary Louise Gómez, Carl Grant, Herb Kliebard, Gloria Ladson-Billings, and Ken Zeichner sharpened my research and deepened my interest in culturally responsive and critical pedagogy. My University of California-Berkeley (UCB) doctoral professors, Bruce Fuller, Norton Grubb, and Dan Perlstein, and especially my dissertation committee, Judith Warren Little, Maryl Gearhardt, and Christina Maslach, refined my understanding of school organizations, education policy, and the conditions necessary for teachers' optimal work. The collegial support of the UCB Working Lives of Teachers Research Group—Maika Watanabe, Rebecca Cox, Lora Bartlett, Lani Horn, Judith Kafka, Jennifer Russell, James Nagle, Sandra Park, Jean Wing, Kim Bancroft, Julia Aguirre, and Janice Bissell—immeasurably enriched my scholarship. Also at UCB, Paul Ammon, Sarah Freedman, David Pearson, and Linda Tredway provided important opportunities for me to apply my learning through the Principal Leadership Institute and Project IMPACT (Inquiry Making Progress Across Communities of Teachers). In the latter, a cast of talented facilitators—Elisa Salasin, Sarah Altschul, Dan Appel, Soung Bae, Jeanette

Bicais, Amy Bloodgood, Erica Boas, Elizabeth Boner, Mary Alice Callahan, Katie Herrick, Betina Hsieh, Kim Jaxon, Suzy Loper, Alexis Martin, Sharita Martin, Agnus Mazur, Thomas Philip, Eric Rose, Elisa Stone, Kathryn Young, and Bissa Zamboldi—collaborating with a formidable posse of dedicated K–12 teachers showed me the transformative possibilities of educators caring deeply for their students.

Along the way, many educators, including Kristin Buras, Gail Brewer, Jamal Cooks, Coni Cullimore, M. J. Curry, Dave Donahue, Elyse Eidman-Aadahl, Peggy Estrada, Phyllis Goldsmith, Suzy Kisch, Linda Kroll, Tom Levine, Harriet MacLean, Tom Malarky, Rob Mueller-Owens, Kris Palmer, Anna Richert, Ray Schultz, Diana Elena Moran Thundercloud, Joyce Welch, and Judy Young enriched my development. Additionally, my reading of Jeff Duncan-Andrade, Gloria Anzaldúa, Lilia Bartolomé, Dolores Delgado Bernal, Shawn Ginwright, bell hooks, Mary Louise Keating, Betina Love, Becky Thompson, and Angela Valenzuela deepened my appreciation for activist scholars who demand better opportunities for multiply marginalized youth.

I am most indebted, though, to the staff, students, families, and community partners who welcomed me into MHS and taught me so much. Their cooperation allowed me to uncover the power of authentic cariño. Their generosity reminds me that the pages that follow are not mine to claim; they came through me, but exist only because of the incredible kindness of the MHS community. As an expression of my gratitude, all royalties from this book will be shared between MHS and a peace-making college scholarship in honor of Ernesto.

While this book is solo authored, it came to fruition through the Schools Organized for Latinxs' Educational Success (SOLES) study, spearheaded by Betty Achinstein and Rodney Ogawa and funded by the William T. Grant Foundation. Betty's and Rod's expertise, guidance, and encouragement have sustained me this last decade. Their feedback continually sharpened my analysis and prose. The SOLES team's collaboration stands out as a life highlight, and I am forever grateful for the intellectual stimulation and joy that emerged from my interactions with Steven Z. Athanases, Luciana C. de Oliveira, Ana María Villegas, Paulina Moreno, Marina Castro, Serena Padilla, Jose Rosario, Everett Au, Adriana Escarega, Etmae Brinkers, Mercedes de la Riva, Reynaldo Rodriguez, Victor Lagunes, and Naficeh Dastgheyb. The ongoing support of University of California-Santa Cruz made this book possible.

A special gracias goes to the artists who contributed to making the cover of this book vibrate with warmth and community spirit. Back in 2009 I periodically passed an eye-catching mural near my home. Crafted by students within Oakland High's Visual Arts Academy Magnet Program under the mentorship of Tara Asciutto Ashton and Keith "K-Dub" Williams, its "Beautiful Struggle" message became a touchstone of inspiration for my writing. I am supremely honored to have this mural appear on the cover. The cover was further enhanced by the collective brilliance of TCP's creative team, the photography of Deborah Sherman, and my graphic designer diva friends Sunshine at SunDesign Studios and Susan at SJWeeksDesigns.

During the final stages of going to press, my accountability partner Susan Haworth checked in with me daily and kept me motivated. Cate Sundling, my teacher buddy turned editor, brought her enthusiasm, grammatical prowess, and generosity to the task and accompanied me over the finish line. The guidance of Brian Ellerbeck, Lori Tate, and the anonymous reviewers at Teachers College Press also strengthened this book. Although this volume is the culmination of multiple collaborations, I take sole responsibility for the interpretations herein.

Beyond the professional sphere, I have been blessed by the support of family and friends whose faith in me has helped me stay the course. I wish to thank in particular my parents Bill Curry and Dozie Sheahan, my brother Quentin, as well as my entire extended family, especially Jeanie, Tom, Cricket, Courtney, Gaga, Grandfather, Gommy, G, Gigi, Meme, Sandy C., Shelley, Cybelle, Mason, Greg, Armida, Sandy G., Dan, Meg, Scott, Spencer, Madee, Elizabeth, Kyle, and my granddaughters Cayley, Annabelle, and Hannah. On the friend front, I am grateful for Kobbe, Lynne P., Archie, Eleni, Fritz, Ginny, Darcy, Patti, Anne, Dan, Pier, Muata, Noreen, Andrea, and Lynne C-S. A big gracias is also due to my Peruvian "framily," especially Juan Carlos, Nelly, Pierina, Vicky, Ursula, Eddy, Silvana, and Carlos. On the spiritual front, I give a deep bow to the Oakland Center for Spiritual Living and the congregants who prayed for this book's successful completion.

Finally, I thank my husband Steve and sons, Finn and Sam. For years, they have tolerated long hours of writing and put up with "the book," which seemed at times a figment of my imagination. They comforted me when a computer crash obliterated the first draft of the manuscript and encouraged my persistence through nightly dinner conversation. I owe this book to their steadfast cariño.

CHAPTER 1

Welcome to the Beautiful Struggle

When Ms. Barrett, a new English teacher, arrived at Molina High (MHS)[1] for her first day, Mr. Trung, a science teacher, greeted her with the words, "Welcome to the beautiful struggle!"[2] At that moment, Ms. Barrett sensed she had landed at a special school. Attesting to the truth of this epiphany in a commencement address 8 years later, Ms. Barrett recounted years of struggle, victories, setbacks, and progress at MHS. Waxing proudly about the school's success at building "a community so empowered and bold and ambitious," she counseled graduates to "find strength [from MHS] . . . a place that fights the good fight, a community that celebrates its members and remembers its losses—a home that loves you." Rosa, the salutatorian, echoed Ms. Barrett. She praised MHS's "passionate teachers" for creating a "second home" where students were cared for "academically as well as emotionally." She credited MHS staff for supporting her to become a first-generation college scholar and expressed regret about leaving the comforts of a school where "there is constant banda and mariachi music blasting in the teen center . . . where the janitor quizzes us on the five steps of being a successful student . . . [and where] a crowd of students of color [surrounds us daily]."

These tributes hint at the ways in which MHS was indeed a special school. During my 4 years investigating this community, I came to appreciate how MHS adults cared holistically for the urban youth of color who graced the school's hallways and classrooms. MHS teachers worked diligently to ensure that students felt cared for, seen, challenged, and supported. Observing their beautiful struggle to make schooling transformative, I saw how MHS educators embodied *authentic cariño*[3]—a potent combination of familial, intellectual, and critical care—that pervaded their interactions with youth and contributed to a culture of engaged learning.

In Spanish, "cariño" translates to caring, affection, or love, but the word also conveys qualities of tenderness and earnestness that defy easy translation. These semantic nuances are important because they speak to a kind of care and human connection seldom associated with bureaucratic organizations such as schools. Bartolomé's (2008) description of authentically cariñoso educators as fierce advocates compelled by "armed love" and

1

political clarity to fight for healthy, liberating, affirming, and academically rigorous schools aptly captures the spirit of MHS staff. These educators built robust relationships with students and families and consciously wove what they called a "network of care" to ensure students were supported by adult allies committed to their success in school and life.

The title for this introductory chapter, "Welcome to the Beautiful Struggle," conveys how MHS adults conceived their work as an arduous, worthy struggle undertaken with authentic cariño to combat social inequity and injustice. Oriented in this manner, MHS educators pushed back against the harsh economic, social, and political realities of urban life by immersing youth in an environment saturated with authentic cariño. Their collective care made MHS a place in which students' humanity, intelligence, and agency were honored and amplified. To introduce the school more fully, I invite readers into a vignette that illustrates how MHS established itself as a place where authentic cariño prevailed.

EMBRACING STUDENTS WITH AUTHENTIC CARIÑO FROM DAY ONE

Imagine this. Students returning from summer vacation gather for a first period, opening-day town hall assembly. The gymnasium bleachers fill up as clusters of students locate their spots under graffiti-style banners indicating sections for freshmen, sophomores, juniors, and seniors. Professionally dressed teachers stand near the doorways welcoming students, occasionally exchanging hugs and fist bumps, while also urging them to get seated. Rap music blares from an amplifier. Nearby, several students and staff adjust a projection screen and queue up a laptop PowerPoint presentation. At 8:15, the lights dim and Principal West's[4] voice booms through the microphone, "Welcome back, Molina High! I am going to throw out a good morning to each class, and I want you to throw it back." A call and response exchange follows. When prompted, each grade shouts in unison, "Good morning Mr. West!" As West moves up the grades, students' voices crescendo. After teasing the freshmen for a lackluster performance and telling them "You gotta work on that," West launches into his remarks.

"It's really wonderful to see you again. We are celebrating our 10th anniversary this year, and, as you probably know, the whole reason our school exists is to interrupt injustice and inequity for the underserved communities in our city. Our mission is all about engaging you in transformative learning experiences related to science, health, and medicine so that you can go to college and have a successful career. This summer, I reconnected with several MHS graduates who have gone on to medical school. If they can do it, you can too. Those of you who attended this town hall last year may remember that I talked about graduation rates for students of color.

"I'd like to ask all the Black and Latino males up in the bleachers to stand up." The gym buzzes as these students rise. He points from the far end of the bleachers to somewhere near the middle. "Now, I'd like those of you from here to here to sit down. Those who just sat down represent the 57% of Black and Latino males in our city who drop out of high school before ever graduating. When I talk about being a dramatically different kind of school, what I am telling you is that our goal is to make sure everyone in this gym graduates. If you know this part of my presentation, please roll with me. These slides show how the drop-out rate happens." A slide displaying the silhouetted, stylized shapes of 100 kids of color appears on the screen. With a click, the slide transforms and half of the silhouettes disappear to represent the high school dropout rate. With each click, the disappearances continue until the penultimate slide displays eight silhouettes signifying the students who graduate from 4-year colleges. The last slide features one lone silhouette, representing the one who obtains a graduate degree. "What does that mean? Seven thousand kids drop out in the United States each day. If you convert it into dropouts per hour, every 26 seconds, a kid drops out. Right while I've been talking, 12 kids have dropped out of high school.[5]

"Some of you might be thinking, 'Who cares about graduation? I can make some money working for my dad.' But look at these numbers. If you drop out, you'll make $17,000 a year compared to a high school graduate, who will make $26,000. If you finish college, you can bump that number up to $52,500 per year. That's a lot of money that can go back into your community. So, every day you're in class matters. Malcolm X recognized this when he said, 'Education is our passport to the future, for tomorrow belongs only to the people who prepare for it today.' On that note, let's introduce the staff who will be helping you get those passports and graduate."

Mr. Simmons, a veteran mathematics teacher, takes the microphone and becomes the master of ceremonies. In a dramatic voice, he invites students to guess which staff member he is describing as he reads short, often humorous, biographical blurbs. "This staff member went to the Santa Cruz Boardwalk this summer where he ate funnel cake, a fried Twinkie, ice cream, and cotton candy. He then rode roller coasters for 2 hours and puked. He'll also teach you how to mutate bacteria in 9th-grade biology." Students laugh, applaud, and shout, "Mr. Trung!" Mr. Trung jogs out, slapping the upheld hands of colleagues assembled in a high-five gauntlet line. "Up next, this staff member moved to the United States at 18 from Colombia, and she learned to run really fast to hide from *la migra* (immigration police). She is now 40 going on 13, and everyone in her house is Mexican but her. She is the loudest voice on staff with the most passion for fun." The students scream, "Luz!" and she too runs the gauntlet. "Okay, this staff member is trying to buy a house in the neighborhood so she can be closer to MHS. She prides herself on saying she has taught just about every student here!" Students holler guesses and Ms. Barrett charges forward. After the final introduction, Mr. West interrupts. "The state of California may have gutted school funding, but can you see how many people are still standing before you to make sure you get out of here and graduate? Stand up, and give them a round of applause." Students rise clapping and hooting. A sense of solidarity pervades the gym.

A series of icebreakers follow in which audience volunteers participate in games such as musical squares (a cooperative version of musical chairs) to see which class has the most spirit and talent. Interspersed with these playful activities are brief presentations. Fifteen leadership students introduce themselves and share a jointly created digital movie featuring scenes from MHS events. The gym quiets as R. Kelly's "I'm the Greatest" fills the air, and images of youth playing pool in the teen center, of teachers and students arm-in-arm during field trips, and of robe-clad seniors clutching diplomas at graduation flash and fade away. In another presentation, Luz, the extended day program (EDP) coordinator, boasts about the superintendent calling her over the summer to congratulate her on having the best after-school program in the district because of its high attendance, superior academic supports, high parent satisfaction, and caring staff. She closes with her signature mantra: "Reading, writing, and math are revolutionary!" Eliciting audience participation, she hollers, "What did I say? Reading and writing and math are?" and the students scream back "Revolutionary!" It's clear from their quick reply that they are familiar with this call-and-response ritual.

The morning also includes ceremonies to recognize student and school accomplishments. Students who completed summer internships in local hospitals are applauded, and MHS's districtwide achievement awards are announced. Plaques for being the school with the best community partnerships and outstanding community engagement, the highest district attendance, and the biggest academic gains for Latinx[6] and Black students on the California Standards Tests are proudly unveiled.

As the assembly winds down, Mr. West tells the audience, "There's one thing I have to settle before we leave. Conrado and Octavio, come on down." Two young men stride forward. One carries a chair and a rolled-up towel. Mr. West puts his arm around Octavio. "Last year, Conrado and I had a bet. If Conrado was able to get a 3.5 GPA,[7] I told him I would dye my hair pink. Octavio here made me the same bet, but he didn't hold up his end. And so now you have the privilege of watching Conrado dye my hair, and then I get to do Octavio's!" Conrado unfurls his towel to reveal a can of hot pink spray hair dye. He motions Mr. West to sit, drapes the towel around his principal's shoulders, and sprays. Students and staff have their cell phones stretched forward to video the moment. Octavio takes his turn, and when his hair glows fluorescent pink, Mr. West motions toward Octavio and says, "This is my brother right here. I do this because I am serious about each of you doing your personal best. And by the way, I want to renew this same bet for this year."

Next, César, an EDP coach, comes forward. "If I can get your respect. Thank you so much. In true MHS fashion, I am going to lead you in the unity clap. Where did it come from? Farm workers, African Americans, Filipinos, even poor White folks. Some thought that they couldn't show their unity and come together, but they created the United Farm Workers' Movement. Some of you have done this before. It starts off slow like you as freshmen and then it's going to gain momentum. Everybody stand up please. This unity stomp is dedicated to MHS. We're going to use what God has blessed us with. Start out slow." The gym thunders with feet pounding the bleachers and hands clapping. César shouts, "¡*Si se puede*!" (Yes, we can!) and the students chorus back, "¡Si se puede!" César ends with the proclamation, "¡*Que viva Molina High*!" (Long live MHS!).

As a relative newcomer to MHS feverishly inputting fieldnotes into my laptop, I typed a personal note to myself as the gym emptied. "I am teary. The energy, camaraderie, joy, and love in this room are palpable." In many ways, this note marks the moment I began to wonder about MHS's culture of cariño. How was this energy and feeling created? How deeply did this cariño penetrate school structures, classrooms, and surrounding communities? How did students respond to it? Over the next few years, I set out to answer these questions and examine the ways in which MHS's enactment of institutional care might provide new insights to improve schooling for marginalized youth.

WHY THIS CASE STUDY MATTERS

One thing that struck me after that 1st day and in subsequent observations was how MHS differed starkly from Seguín High, the Texas high school documented in Angela Valenzuela's (1999) pioneering ethnography, *Subtractive Schooling*. Valenzuela depicted a school where "each weekday, for 8 hours a day, teenagers inhabited a world populated by adults who did not care—or at least did not care for them sufficiently" (p. 3). Her analysis exposed the subtractive processes by which a bureaucratic school system blocked the academic success of Mexican youth by divesting them of important social and cultural resources. In contrast, MHS surrounded students each weekday, and often on weekends, for 8 hours a day and often more with adults who cared for them profoundly. This institutional enactment of authentic cariño merits attention for several reasons.

First, Latinx students are the fastest growing segment of the U.S. school population, now comprising 28% of school-age children ages 5–17 nationally (NCES, 2018) and 54% in California (http://www.ed-data.k12.ca.us). By 2060, one in three children in U.S. K–12 classrooms will be of Hispanic origin (U.S. Census Bureau, 2017), and the United States will be a majority "minority" country. Given these demographics, the ability of schools to serve this population successfully has major implications for our nation's well-being. We need quality schools for Latinx youth if they are to participate fully in our democracy and economy.

Second, U.S. schools have historically underserved Latinx youth, many of whom continue to confront the subtractive practices Valenzuela chronicled decades ago. Disproportionally, Brown and Black students attend underfunded, overcrowded, hyper-segregated, dilapidated schools staffed with underqualified teachers (Betts et al., 2000; Orfield et al., 2012). This "educational debt" (Ladson-Billings, 2006) has exacted a toll on student performance. While achievement metrics have long been faulted for racial and linguistic biases and their role in exacerbating inequality, these indicators provide an imperfect but sobering portrait of what some scholars have deemed the "Latino education crisis" (Gándara & Contreras, 2009). Student results on the National Assessment of Educational Progress reveal that the White–Hispanic[8] achievement gap for 12th graders has not changed significantly since 1992 in reading and since 2005 in math (NCES, 2016). While Latinx students' high school graduation and college enrollment rates have hit record highs (Gramlich, 2017), the degree to which Latinx students leave school prepared to thrive in college remains questionable. According to 2015 results, only a minority of Hispanic high school ACT test-takers met college readiness attainment benchmarks (ACT, 2016).[9]

College remedial course-taking patterns parallel these data. Indicators from the California State University system show that, in 2016, 37% of first-time entering Latinx freshmen needed remediation in math, while 29% needed remediation in English, compared to the respective 15% and 11% remedial rates for Whites (CSU, 2016). Given that remedial enrollment correlates with low persistence and degree attainment (Bailey, 2009), the fact that a third of Californian Latinx college goers arrive underprepared represents a serious problem. Overall, these stubborn and stagnant achievement patterns point to the inadequacy of accountability-driven reforms that have prevailed in the 21st century and underscore the need for new approaches to nurture the intellectual engagement and academic success of low-SES Latinx students.

By offering a portrait of a school institutionalizing such new approaches, this book seeds hope in a time when both public schools and low-income, nondominant communities of color are under attack. Highly visible incidents of police brutality against Brown and Black youth have exposed institutional racism, unmasking the ways in which the ethnic and racial identities of these youth are interrogated, incriminated, and imperiled. Additionally, the xenophobia unleashed by the 2016 U.S. presidential election has enveloped Latinx teenagers in a world in which 24 hours a day the specter of hate looms over them (Rogers et al., 2017). These socially toxic conditions are exacerbated by the push toward neoliberal, market-oriented educational remedies, as well as by federal gestures to truncate funding for free lunch and after-school programs. These trends have left public schools that serve economically distressed Latinx youth further beleaguered. The stress borne out of these realities harms the health and well-being of both individuals and communities. Against this backdrop, the status quo of "impersonal, irrelevant, and lifeless" schooling (Valenzuela, 1999, p. 22) for Latinx youth is unacceptable.

Finally, and more broadly, this book illuminates a school community struggling to address a crisis of societal isolation and alienation (Putnam, 1995), a crisis felt perhaps most acutely in urban neighborhoods in which concentrated poverty coupled with the threat of violence has bred fear and distrust and thus impeded social networks from flourishing (Ginwright, 2010). Gripped by the relentless press of individualism, meritocracy, and materialism, many Americans, not just urban dwellers, have disconnected from each other and from public institutions. This erosion has taken its toll on our collective psyche and has been linked to cynicism, emptiness, loneliness, and civic disengagement, as well as the ascendency of private interests over public interests. Educators at MHS opposed these trends and strove to cultivate a generation of "community ready" young adults, eager and willing to care for each other and prepared to invest their minds and hearts into revitalizing their communities, their nation, and the world. This case study, then, invites readers to view schooling as a challenging yet often joyful moral enterprise wherein students, educators, and community members can approach learning as a "beautiful struggle" toward building a more caring and just world.

WHAT DOES IT REALLY MEAN TO CARE?

Practitioners and scholars have long recognized the importance care plays in the educational process. bell hooks (2003) sums up this position when she asserts that "at its best, teaching is a caring profession" (p. 86). This commonly held view of caring as an essential part of supportive (and therefore constructive) student–teacher relations belies the complexity of enacting care in classrooms and suffusing care into bureaucratic schools. A proliferation of terms—natural care, ethical care, aesthetic care,[10] critical care, soft care, hard care, rhetorical care, revolucionista care, and authentic care—attests to the messy theoretical state of the construct. Indeed, even Nel Noddings (1990), the philosopher most often associated with care theory, has conceded that "the language of caring is dangerous. It has an ambiguous ring and a deeply flawed history" (p. 125). In a similar vein, Valenzuela (1999) concluded *Subtractive Schooling* by lamenting that "it is entirely accurate to say that we do not yet know what it really means to care" (p. 267). Given this murkiness, these next sections examine the evolution of care theory as a way to uncover the nuances of care and situate authentic cariño within existing scholarship.

First-Wave Care Theory: Explicating an Ethic of Care

Noddings (1984) posits that care involves four qualities: engrossment, displacement of motivation, commitment, and confirmation. According to her, a caregiver becomes engrossed when she is fully attentive and receptive to the one being cared for. Engrossment is not to be confused with a projective display of empathy whereby a caregiver attempts to imagine or objectively discern the needs, feelings, and circumstances of another; rather, as Noddings conceived it, engrossment entails the caregiver intuitively receiving the other into the self and seeing and feeling *with* the other. In doing so, the caregiver suspends personal interests, gives primacy to the one being cared for, and commits to responding to the particular needs of the cared for. This commitment focuses on seeing and confirming the cared for's "best self" (1984, p. 67). Such individualized attention means that caring relations hinge on flexible, contingent actions (or inaction) to nurture the wholeness of another within specific contexts. As such, "there is no recipe for caring" (Noddings, 1992/2005, p. 17).

Noddings (1992/2005) argues that schools guided by a robust ethic of care would not focus exclusively on academic achievement; rather, they would prioritize students' growth as healthy, competent, moral people to ensure that they develop the capacity and desire to care for others. Such a caring orientation would necessitate revamping school bureaucracies, including the "hierarchical structure of management, the rigid mode of allocating time, the kind of relationships encouraged, the size of schools and classes, the goals of instruction, modes of evaluation, patterns of interaction, [and] selection of content" (Noddings, 1988, p. 221). Noddings advocates for smaller schools, peer-to-peer support structures to promote learning communities, and continuity of place, people, purpose, and curricula.

Noddings (1988) urges teachers to develop funds "of knowledge about the particular persons with whom they are working" and use that knowledge to construct with students a curriculum centered on topics students deem meaningful (p. 221). She anticipates that such a curriculum would focus on themes of care: care for self, intimate others, strangers and distant others, animals, plants and the living environment, objects and instruments, and ideas (Noddings, 1992/2005). Noddings further suggests that schools embrace Freire's (1970/2005) pedagogy of the oppressed and cultivate "reflective examination of one's own life—life as an individual, as a member of a particular race, as a member of an economic class, [and] as a member of any particular group" (Noddings, 1992/2005, p. 136). She also recommends the inclusion of ethnic and gender studies to promote nondominant students' sense of solidarity as well as their understanding of cultural heritage, political action, and oppression theories (Noddings, 1992/2005, pp. 116–117).

Second-Wave Care Theory: Expanding Toward Authentic Care

Noddings' seminal scholarship provided important insights into the dynamics of caring relations, but her theory's heavy reliance on the dyadic intimacy of the mother–child relationship as experienced within the private sphere of a traditional heterosexual, Eurocentric, middle-class family elicited a range of critiques.[11] In contrast to the "ahistoricism, cultural bias, and obliviousness to systemic power relations" (Thompson, 1998, p. 527) embedded in mainstream care theories premised on Gilligan (1982) and Noddings (1984), a new scholarship emerged with a sharpened focus on how race, class, gender, and ethnicity shape the enactment of care. Championed by Black critical scholars (Beauboeuf-Lafontant, 2002; Ginwright, 2010, 2016; hooks, 2003; Ladson-Billings, 1994; Walker, 1993; Ward, 2000) and Latinx critical scholars[12] (Antrop-González & De Jesús, 2006; Bartolomé, 2008; Delgado Bernal et al., 2006; Moraga & Anzaldúa,1983; Rolón-Dow, 2005; Sosa-Provencio, 2019; Valenzuela, 1999), this second wave of care theory employed feminist, womanist, and mujerista[13] lenses to reframe care as a holistic, communal undertaking grounded in culture, spirit, and politics. The liberating ethics of care advanced by these scholars share a set of core values that converge in authentic care. Because authentic care is foundational to my conception of authentic cariño, I elaborate these core values to orient readers toward the mindset with which MHS educators approached their work.

Care and justice are indivisible. Rather than dichotomizing care and justice, authentic care embraces both. These orientations are not an either–or proposition. Students from historically oppressed subordinate groups stand to benefit from both the just distribution of educational opportunities and resources (teachers, facilities, materials, etc.) as well as from affirmation and nurturance from caring educators (Walker & Snarey, 2004). In short, the White-defined split between care and justice does not square with the realities faced by marginalized communities of color.

Care demands political clarity. Because schools exist within a society that differentially structures opportunities for children on the basis of race, ethnicity, and class, schools are inherently political institutions. For teachers aspiring to enact authentic care, political clarity entails recognizing oppressive structures and ideologies and grappling with how macroeconomic and sociopolitical realities impact day-to-day life, especially the schooling experiences of subordinated groups. Armed with this awareness, caring educators seek to interrupt inequity through pedagogy and activism (Bartolomé, 2008; Beauboeuf-Lafontant, 2002). Political clarity also means preparing students to become democratic citizens who exercise their rights and participate fully in political processes in order to build vibrant and just communities.

Care attends to and affirms ethnoracial identity. Eschewing a color-blind expression of care, educators who cultivate authentically caring relations with students recognize the centrality of race and ethnicity in everyday life. Such teachers understand the corrosive and pervasive nature of racism, as well as how the intersecting matrix of race, ethnicity, class, culture, identity, phenotype, gender, history, language, citizenship, and immigration status complicates and enriches students' identities. Seeking to help youth develop healthy cultural identities, these educators are "identity workers" (Gutiérrez, 2013), who interrogate and reject deficit scripts that construct marginalized students and their families as damaged, deviant, and/or lacking (Dabach et al., 2017). In classrooms, they center "questions of otherness, difference, and power" (Valenzuela, 1999, p. 25) and honor community cultural wealth (Yosso, 2005) by connecting youth to ancestral wisdom, heritage traditions, and liberation struggles. Importantly, these educators recognize that what *counts* as care "is likely to vary from one culture or situation to another" (Thompson, 2003, p. 27) and proceed in ways that are culturally congruent and sustaining.

Care nourishes wholeness and encompasses bodymindspirit.[14] Guided by the belief that well-being encompasses the fullness of the human experience and includes psychological, emotional, spiritual, and physical wellness, authentic care strives to "feed people in all their hungers" (Moraga, 1983/2000, p. 132). Within this paradigm, Western dichotomies of mind versus body, cognition versus emotion, subject versus object, rationality versus spirituality, and male versus female dissolve because, as Anzaldúa asserts, we are each *un amasamiento*, a mixture of selves kneaded together. Being whole, therefore, involves claiming and nurturing all of "the splintered and disowned parts" because *"todas las partes de nosotros valen"* (all parts of us matter) (Anzaldúa, 1987/2012, p. 110).[15] Authentic care, then, transpires when embodied, flesh-and-blood persons show up in vulnerability to be fully present to one another. Rooted in an awareness that inner wellness precedes outer change (Anzaldúa, 1987/2012; Ginwright, 2016; hooks, 1994), authentic care seeks to heal the psychic wounds inflicted by racism and poverty while also nourishing the capacity to dream, create, and love. Authentic care aims to ensure that every person has a life rich with meaning, purpose, and joy.

Care transforms individuals, communities, and organizations. While authentic care theory acknowledges the transformative power of intimate, interpersonal enactments of care, it extends further by conceiving care as a "communal responsibility" focused on the "liberation of all" (Beauboeuf-Lafontant, 2002, pp. 72 and 76). This stance manifests in the belief that the "welfare of the family, the community, and the tribe is more important than the welfare of the individual" (Anzaldúa, 1987/2012, p. 40). It is this conviction that undergirds the Latinx cultural construct of *educación* that stresses the importance of learning to act morally with integrity, respect, and responsibility to preserve the dignity and humanity of all (Valenzuela, 1999, p. 21). Within this expanded view, care is impoverished unless it is anchored to a commitment to the uplift of all. For this reason, robust expressions of authentic care involve a collective struggle to transform communities and reshape institutions to advance the common good. In this manner, schools may exhibit "institutional care" by adopting explicit policies, practices, and organizational cultures designed to meet the psychological, sociological, and academic needs of *all* students (Walker, 1993).

Educators who exhibit authentic care embrace these five values, allowing them to guide decisions in ways that profoundly transform the quality and substance of human relationships and the learning that transpires within schools.

AUTHENTIC CARIÑO

Building on first- and second-wave care theories, authentic cariño is a synthesized, theoretical model that elaborates how authentic care can be cultivated and institutionalized in schools. My choice to use the Spanish "cariño" rather than the English "care" reflects my desire to decenter Eurocentric maternal connotations of caring in favor of culturally and politically informed forms of care. For me, the term "cariño" with its sonorous tilde-carrying "ñ" brings a softness into the mouth that conveys a level of reverence and fondness that is absent in the single-syllabic and antiseptic English word "care." While phrases such as "health care," "Medicare," and "in-home care" conjure images of care delivered by bureaucratic systems or in monetary exchanges, cariño evokes a sense of human connection anchored in "an unapologetic and radical love" for youth and their communities (Ginwright, 2016, p. 38).

Importantly, the use of "cariño" is not meant to imply that all Latinxs embrace a single, uniform ethic of care. Rather, this term signals my rejection of essentializing, color-blind conceptions of care that ignore "the cultural specificity of what counts as caring or the political issues that matter in the lives of students of color" (Rolón-Dow, 2005, p. 87). Additionally, my use of Spanish does not restrict cariño-based practices to only Latinx students. In actuality, the infusion of authentic cariño into schools stands to benefit *all* students, but seems especially essential for

Figure 1.1. A Model of Authentic Cariño

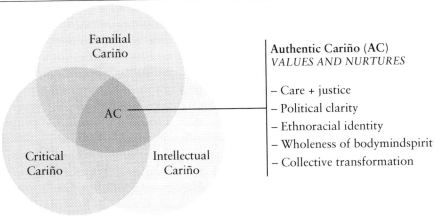

Familial
Cariño

AC

Critical
Cariño

Intellectual
Cariño

Authentic Cariño (AC)
VALUES AND NURTURES

– Care + justice
– Political clarity
– Ethnoracial identity
– Wholeness of bodymindspirit
– Collective transformation

the well-being and academic success of historically underserved and/or marginalized youth.

As noted earlier, authentic cariño draws on the five values of authentic care and unfolds at the nexus of three expressions of care: familial, intellectual, and critical. As Figure 1.1 demonstrates, authentic cariño is achieved only when all three forms of cariño are present.

Familial Cariño

Familial cariño emphasizes a relational orientation toward learning in which educators genuinely care about students' entire well-being and work to establish safe and affirming learning environments (Cooper, 2013, 2014). Reflecting Latinx cultural values of *personalismo* and *familismo* (Andrés-Hyman et al., 2006), familial cariño underscores the importance of forging bonds between educators and students anchored in reciprocity, trust, respect, and connectedness. Supportive peer-to-peer relations are especially nurtured in order to address the "'social de-capitalization' or limited presence of academically oriented networks" among nondominant youth (Valenzuela, 1999, p. 31). Ideally, familial cariño also includes ties to students' biological families. While the metaphor of school as *familia* may evoke patriarchy for feminists, familial cariño within this model highlights how schools can embrace and share in nonoppressive ways the family's role in *educación* by taking seriously the role of fostering students' moral, social, and personal development.

In the town hall vignette presented earlier, familial cariño surfaced in several ways. By devoting the 1st hour and a half of the academic year to an all-school assembly, MHS demonstrated the high value it placed on being together in community. The class competitions promoted solidarity among grade-level peers, while the closing unity clap honored the totality of MHS—its entire community, its legacy, and its spirit. Another indicator of familial cariño emerged in the staff introductions that allowed students to see teachers not as distant, authoritative figures, but as real people interested in connection. The faculty's high-five gauntlet ritual coupled with the students' standing ovation suggested a community united by a desire to achieve success. Meanwhile, the student-made welcome film replete with pictures of students and staff arm-in-arm and interacting in familial ways was reminiscent of a family photo album in which cherished memories are preserved for future generations to revisit. Finally, the playfulness and affection evident in Mr. West's teasing of the freshmen, the team-building games, and the hair-dying ceremony also suggested how MHS harnessed revelry to build trusting, reciprocal relations.

Intellectual Cariño

Intellectual cariño involves educators caring deeply about developing students' intellects. Within this arena, analytical, argumentative, and metacognitive thought command center stage because these Habits of Mind (HOM) enable students to understand the world and make meaning and change (Meier, 1995; Sizer, 1984, 1992). Educators who embody intellectual cariño recognize the identity-shaping dimensions of thinking and learning. Thus, they attend to students' cognitive, affective, cultural, social, and spiritual selves as they design and implement academically challenging, transformative, and expanded learning activities. Their pedagogy features high academic expectations, asset-based orientations toward nondominant youth, cultural relevance, college advocacy, and Socratic reflexivity. Additionally, intellectually cariñosa teachers take students' ideas seriously and encourage dialogic discourse, eliciting multiple perspectives and the co-construction of knowledge. They display a special kind of pedagogical mindfulness and presence that involves contingent and responsive attention to students as learning interactions unfold, while also staying attuned to the broad array of skills, knowledge, and habits students must develop to succeed in college and beyond. Schools that embrace intellectual cariño exemplify cultures of engaged learning (Athanases et al., 2016) in which adults and youth derive pleasure and satisfaction from investigating, creating, debating, and problem-solving.

In the context of the town hall, Principal West's emphasis on "transformative learning experiences" represented an expression of intellectual cariño because learning and transformation were celebrated as paths to achieve economic prosperity and community uplift. Similarly, Luz's call and response chant declaring "reading, writing, and math are revolutionary" highlighted how intellectual work at MHS was not associated with numbing drill and skill classwork but rather framed as empowering activity to help youth revolutionize their lives and society at large. Evidence of intellectual cariño in action surfaced in the leadership students' use of technology over the summer to craft the digital welcome movie. By using their minds collaboratively to develop a thoughtful product, they reached and influenced a real audience. Other indicators of intellectual cariño emerged in references to 3.5 GPAs, climbing CST achievement scores, and the superior academic support offered in EDP.

Critical Cariño

Critical cariño, the third component of authentic cariño, refers to caring undertaken with historical and political consciousness of students' communities. Fueled by a desire to interrupt inequity and promote social justice, schools infused with critical cariño challenge students to examine how race, ethnicity, social class, and gender shape history and day-to-day living. Critical cariño pedagogies strive to develop students' critical consciousness in an effort to dramatically interrupt the dominant social order. Additionally, they involve explicit attention to cultures of power with an aim toward helping students master dominant discourses while still valuing and sustaining their home cultures. In alignment with critiques of narrowly defined conceptions of resistance (Hidalgo & Duncan-Andrade, 2009; Mehan et al., 1994; Solórzano & Delgado Bernal, 2001; Valenzuela, 1999), critical cariño appreciates both those who strive to overcome societal barriers through the pursuit of socially accepted paths (college and careers) and those who choose to engage in overt political action to transform oppressive power relations. Educators who embody critical cariño recognize the developmental challenges that nondominant students face as they negotiate multiple and often conflicting social systems and contexts. In some instances, this work means attending to the complex trauma students have experienced as a result of poverty and violence as well as to students' internalized oppression (shame and hatred of ethnic/racial identities). The enactment of critical cariño, therefore, involves "radical healing" (Ginwright, 2010) aimed at reconnecting youth to inner resources in ways that amplify their capacity to care, love, hope, and participate in struggles for justice.

At the opening day town hall, critical cariño came across in several ways. Symbolically, the graffiti-inspired class banners and rap music honored local youth culture, while references to Malcolm X, running from la migra, and the United Farm Workers' movement made clear MHS's social justice commitments. Mr. West's explicit and extended focus on inequitable graduation rates required students to confront head-on the harsh injustice of an education system that fails Brown and Black youth. The adamancy with which West recited the school's mission ("The whole reason why our school exists is to interrupt injustice and inequity for the underserved communities in our city") and the pride he displayed as he lauded MHS graduates who had gone on to medical school communicated to students the stakes and promise of being serious about their education. Recalling this PowerPoint presentation in a focus group, Camila, a junior, said, "Mr. West motivated us because he talked about the Latino and African American dropout rate and how they're helping us. I feel like it opens your eyes." By opening students' eyes to inequity and urging them to resist failure and strive for success, the staff exemplified critical cariño, reframing schooling as a liberatory EDP.

Subsequent chapters examine each dimension of authentic cariño in greater detail. Before delving further, though, I must first explain how I arrived at MHS.

THE STUDY

This book evolved from a larger research project examining organizational structures and instructional interactions associated with Latinx students' engagement in academically challenging work. Principal investigators Betty Achinstein and Rod Ogawa initiated the Schools Organized for Latinxs' Educational Success (SOLES) study with a grant from the William T. Grant Foundation.[16] Weary of "damage-centered" research (Tuck, 2009) focusing on why and how schools fail students of color, Betty and Rod designed a success-centered study to investigate schools that were serving Latinx youth well. They assembled an ethnically and linguistically diverse team that included myself as well as two researchers from other universities supported by a talented pool of graduate and undergraduate students. In total, we numbered 16, with more than half overall Latinx and several bilingual. Seeking to uncover insiders' views and document richly textured portraits of educational practice, we conducted a comparative case study of three high schools. By closely examining the inner workings of schools and analyzing the relationships and dynamics within our sites, we sought to generate theories that would support the success of Latinx youth.[17]

The choice to study MHS emerged from a snowball sampling process. We turned to individuals within our professional networks to nominate publicly funded high schools in California (the state with the highest Latinx population in the United States) that were (a) situated in urban, high-need areas, (b) serving predominantly Latinx students, (c) adhering to explicit missions to advance the education of youth from nondominant cultural and linguistic communities, and (d) exhibiting promising indicators of success, such as college-going rates, course completion rates for admission into California universities, achievement scores, retention, honors, or community collaboration.

The first phase of research unfolded from 2011 to 2013. As the SOLES team's designated lead researcher at MHS, I generally spent 1 to 2 days a week there during the 2011–2012 school year. Thereafter, I visited 1 to

2 days a month. At the project's end, we shared findings with MHS staff in a member-check meeting. The staff's enthusiastic response to the theme of authentic cariño prompted me to embark independently on a second phase of research (2013–2015) to better understand authentic cariño. Across both phases of research, ethnographic methods documenting insiders' views and meanings predominated. The final data set included 45 semi-structured interviews with leaders, teachers, students, parents, and community partners; a faculty survey; school documents; listserv communication; student work samples; and over 300 hours of formal observations of classroom, school, and community activities (of which 50 hours were video recorded).

Data analysis involved a battery of interpretive processes. Most were iterative and dialogical, some were exactingly systematic, and others were disorderly, yet productive. During the initial collaborative phase, our team undertook joint, weekly review of data (reading fieldnotes and transcripts, viewing video records, and discussing emerging insights). We utilized NVivo, a qualitative data analysis software package, to systematically code interviews. We also applied two classroom observation instruments developed by other researchers to examine learning interactions (Hilberg et al., 2003; Pianta et al., 2006). Throughout the study, we drafted and discussed analytic memos addressing (a) school history and normative social structures; (b) school resources, including physical, social, human, and multicultural capital; (c) instruction; (d) successful outcomes; and (e) underlying tensions.

In the second phase, I reread the full data corpus to discern the structures, processes, and features associated with authentic care. The NVivo project expanded to include observation fieldnotes and new codes, including familial, intellectual, critical, and institutional cariño. After generating summary reports for each of these, I identified patterns and themes and wrote memos to clarify emerging understandings. These memos explored topics such as interpersonal care, peer-to-peer care, performance-based assessments, learning as pleasure, care dilemmas, and adult allies.

During this second phase, I read widely, seeking to discover how MHS overlapped with and diverged from trends discussed by other care theorists. I also periodically consulted SOLES teammates and study participants to elicit input. Throughout both phases, I reflected on how being a White, economically privileged woman, former high school English teacher, and teacher-educator shaped my interpretations. Spurred by my commitment to ethical and reciprocal relations with participants (Curry, 2012), I organized the library, volunteered as a writing coach, chaperoned field trips, provided support to a teacher seeking National Board Certification, witnessed and scored student exhibitions, and attended community gatherings. These activities fortified my understanding of the school as well as my friendships with MHS staff and students.

THE SCHOOL

The campus of Molina High School sits blocks away from the heart of its city's Latinx district, which features a busy commercial strip populated by taquerias, fast-food vendors, pawn shops, discount clothing stores, beauty salons, bodegas, a transit hub, and more. Colorful public mosaics and murals by Latinx artists adorn walls and planters along this route, where annual celebrations of Diá de los Muertos and Cinco de Mayo attract massive crowds. The surrounding neighborhoods feature a mix of single-family homes and apartment buildings, some with well-tended gardens, some with graffiti-sprayed walls, most with security bars mounted to protect windows. Drugs, gangs, and poverty encroach on residents' daily lives, and safety concerns constrain students' freedom to congregate and play outside. MHS parents worried about the threat of violence and shootings as their children commuted to school and navigated the city. During this study, Latinxs (mainly Mexican, but also Guatemalans and El Salvadorians) comprised the majority of this census tract (51%); African Americans (18%) and Asians (19%) also figured prominently. The median annual household income was $38,000. Educational attainment reflected limited education opportunities with 38% of adults over 25 years of age without high school diplomas, 42% with high school degrees, and 20% with advanced degrees. For decades, the city's school district had struggled with leadership crises, budget shortfalls, and legal battles related to its poor treatment of nondominant populations.

Against this backdrop, a grassroots coalition of parents and educators, frustrated with the dismal state of their schools and inspired by the small schools' movement (Meier, 1995), established MHS in 2001. Grounded in commitments to community-based organizing and political activism, this coalition adopted a bold mission to interrupt inequity for underserved students. MHS's founders aspired to graduate a cadre of bilingual, college-bound youth who would diversify local health care institutions and improve public health. To reach this goal, MHS focused on transformative learning linked to bioscience, medicine, and health. Students at MHS were expected to fulfill University of California and California State University A–G course requirements.[18] Congruent with a career academy model, all upperclassmen participated in mandatory internships in local hospitals, public health settings, or community-based organizations on a weekly basis throughout the school year. Adopting a whole-child orientation, MHS educators emphasized personalization and rigorous, project-based academics to strengthen students' Habits of Life, Mind, and Work (Figure 1.2).

Recognizing the importance of community–school relations, MHS conceived itself as a "full-service community school" and partnered closely with several community-based organizations (CBOs), including an award-winning EDP, a county-funded onsite health clinic, a school-based counseling center staffed by graduate school interns, and a college counseling center.

Figure 1.2. MHS Habits of Successful Students

Life	Mind	Work
• Empathy	• Inquiry	• Focus
• Courage	• Perspective	• Organization
• Integrity	• Evidence	• Revision
• Curiosity	• Logical reasoning/analysis	• Cooperation
	• Reflection/metacognition	• Effort

These entities coordinated their services to ensure that a robust "network of care" supported students' success and fulfillment in college, career, and life.

Visitors to the campus immediately sensed MHS's social justice commitments and its community/heritage roots. Take for instance the vibrantly colored mural of lush, earthy scenery framing the main stairway. Its imagery featured an Intricate, round Aztec calendar beaming rays that enveloped a tree whose roots ended in brown hands that extended to rest on the shoulders of an Indigenous woman. Surrounded by butterflies and flowers, this woman stood beside a chocolate-skinned young man reading a book entitled *Opening Minds*. These figures seemed to symbolize the power residing in book learning undertaken in conjunction with ancestral wisdom.

The hallways at MHS also imparted strong messages about the school's identity. Hand-painted portraits of activists and rebels—Gandhi, César Chávez, Rosa Parks, Leila Khaled, Barack Obama, and Tiburcio Vásquez—adorned the doors, while bulletin boards advertised internship opportunities, highlighted seniors' college acceptances, and displayed student work. One such display posted student letters written to Elie Wiesel regarding the book *Night* arranged around a letter of reply from the author commending students for understanding "the destructiveness of hate and the evil of any kind of prejudice." These decorative touches communicated MHS's interest in immersing students in a visually pleasing and affirming environment.

During the years of this study, student enrollment in grades 9–12 averaged 277.[19] Of these, 93% were eligible for free/reduced lunch, 82% were Latinx (predominantly second-generation Mexicans), and 28% were emergent bilinguals (EBs).[20] The district determined enrollment by lottery. Of incoming freshmen, 7% tested as proficient in math and 17% in English; on average, the remainder entered 2 years behind grade level. Despite these incoming achievement levels, MHS students regularly outperformed district and state peers. As Table 1.1 displays, MHS's Latinx students demonstrated commendable achievement on indicators such as college preparatory coursework completion, graduation rates, and high school exit exams. Particularly noteworthy is that MHS Latinx students completed A–G requirements at more than double the rate of their peers across the state (69% versus 31%).

Table 1.1. Latinx Students' Academic Achievement at MHS, Local District (LD), and State (CA)

Year (n)	% Graduates with A–G[a]			% Cohort Graduation Rate[b]			% Passing CAHSEE/ Math[c]			% Passing CAHSEE/ ELA[c]		
	MHS	LD	CA	MHS	LD	CA	MHS	LD	CA	MHS	LD	CA
2014–5 (240)	88	62	35	82	52	79	76	63	80	91	62	80
2013–4 (234)	80	53	32	75	59	77	82	62	80	77	56	78
2012–3 (228)	90	56	29	83	54	76	88	61	79	73	57	78
2011–2 (225)	19[d]	54	28	68	56	74	85	65	78	89	63	77
M	69	56	31	77	56	76	83	63	80	83	60	79

a. 12th-grade graduates who completed all the courses required for University of California (UC) and/or California State University (CSU) entrance with a grade of "C" or better.

b. Students in a 4-year cohort who graduated in 4 or fewer years with either a traditional diploma, an adult education diploma, or passage of the California High School Proficiency Exam (CHSPE).

c. 10th-grade students who passed the California High School Exit Exam (CAHSEE) when they took the exam for the first time.

d. MHS adopted an "A–G for all" and a "no D" policy in 2010–2011; the class of 2012 was "grandfathered" and exempted from these requirements.

Source: https://www.ed-data.org and local district website. n = total MHS students grades 9–12 identified as Hispanic during that school year. All values rounded to the nearest tenth in order to preserve anonymity.

This college-preparatory focus translated into high rates of college enrollment with more than 80% of graduates pursuing postsecondary education.

MHS's teachers were instrumental in achieving these outcomes. The faculty of 17 had an average of 6 years teaching experience and was predominantly prepared in university teacher education masters/credential programs with a smaller subset trained through alternative pathways. Racially, teachers identified as 47% White, 30% Asian, 18% biracial (African American/Mexican and East Indian/White), and 5% Latinx. Roughly half of the teachers were Spanish–English bilinguals. Teachers collaborated every Wednesday following an early student release, as well as during three annual off-site, multiday retreats. They exhibited a strong esprit de corp. Testifying to this, Mr. Keo, a veteran math teacher, noted, "We trust each other. We can challenge each other. We have fun together, and we're also very serious. We have a pretty similar mission and vision. It's kind of rare to have that, one singular-mindedness."

PREVIEW OF CHAPTERS

In the following chapters, I elaborate authentic cariño by examining each component in depth, sharing ethnographic portraits of care enactment, and exploring tensions that arose as educators strove to embody authentic cariño. Chapter 2, "Familial Cariño: Deeply Knowing and Supporting Students," documents how school reformers' calls to personalize instruction coupled with pressure from students' families to honor their culture (*educación, familismo,* and *personalismo*) prompted MHS to prioritize familial cariño and forge relations of mutual respect between educators and students as well as among peers. To clarify the nature of familial cariño, this chapter examines three distinctive features of the construct, specifically its life-affirming, healing-centered, and authentic qualities. To illustrate how MHS institutionalized familial cariño, I examine two complementary organizational structures. One, known as the "network of care," ensured students' connection to multiple support resources. The second focused on the "Habits of Life," a set of norms deemed essential for the development of healthy social identities and relationships.

The centerpiece of the chapter is an examination of annual rite of passage rituals known as "firewalks" held at the end of the school year to help sophomores and seniors honestly and publicly assess their academic and personal growth. By tracing the progression of Leticia, a student who stumbled through her sophomore firewalk yet managed to prevail in her senior firewalk, the chapter demonstrates how these rituals strengthened peer-to-peer academic networks and nurtured students' healthy identity development, reflexivity, and agency. Chapter 2 also addresses some of the complications that accompanied familial cariño, specifically the challenge of knowing when intensive care becomes crippling, invasive, or unsustainable.

Chapter 3, "Intellectual Cariño: Cultivating Engaged Pensadoras," opens with an overview of intellectual cariño. Next, it examines four core normative beliefs about learning and thinking that anchored MHS's culture of engaged learning. These widely held beliefs emphasizing the importance, power, complexity, and pleasure of learning meant that students consistently encountered adults across MHS who took their teaching and students' thinking seriously. Guided by these beliefs, the faculty functioned as a community of learners designing and maintaining an expansive learning ecology focused on nurturing students' HOM and constructing "transformative learning experiences." This chapter illustrates how MHS educators enacted intellectual cariño within classrooms as well as in other settings, among them academic rites of passage, internships, town halls, and a special end-of-the-year interlude known as "post-session." Chapter 3 concludes with an exploration of the tensions that emerged as master schedule modifications threatened to erode the school's commitment to detracked, heterogeneous instruction for all students.

Chapter 4, "Critical Cariño: Nurturing Strong Sociocultural Identities, Political Awareness, and Civic Engagement," reacquaints readers with critical cariño as a form of care that (a) affirms students' home and community contexts, (b) acknowledges the ways race/ethnicity, social class, gender, and sexual orientation shape students' lives, (c) centers social justice through pedagogies of liberation and critiques of social oppression, and (d) seeds hope and transformation. The chapter examines four core instructional strategies—narrative, controversy, community engagement, and collective action—through which MHS enacted critical cariño and fostered students' community cultural wealth, especially their aspirational, navigational, resistant, and social capital (Yosso, 2005). Next, I outline how three organizational structures—the mission, curricular autonomy, and community partnerships—ensured that these pedagogies flourished across the school. This chapter also explores three challenges MHS encountered as it embraced critical cariño. First, the school existed within neoliberal contexts that complicated MHS's social justice efforts. Second, Black youth at times felt marginalized in a Latinx majority school. Third, educators with varying levels of critical consciousness around issues of race and economic inequality sometimes disagreed about how to empower youth. Overall, this chapter argues that despite these challenges MHS's enactment of critical cariño on an institutional level fostered students' community readiness and community well-being.

Chapter 5, "Authentic Cariño: Braiding Together Familial, Intellectual, and Critical Care," emphasizes the integrative and holistic nature of authentic cariño by revisiting examples from prior chapters and mapping the ways in which familial, intellectual, and critical cariño converged to yield authentic cariño. Chapter 5 also draws attention to how school–community boundary crossing, dialogic engagement, and embodied activity enhanced authentic cariño. To illustrate the power residing within robust enactments of authentic cariño, I recount the story of MHS's Peaceful City Campaign, a sustained, multiyear movement to combat gun violence and promote peace in surrounding neighborhoods following the homicides of several youth. I argue that students' immersion in authentic cariño over their 4 years of high school dramatically reframed their relationship with school, learning, and themselves.

Finally, the book's conclusion, "Seguir Adelante—Moving Onward," revisits Valenzuela's 1999 admission that "we [do] not yet know what it really means to care" in schools and examines how the case of MHS advances our understanding of what it means to create schools anchored in authentic cariño. Among the lessons discussed are the importance of (a) simultaneously promoting interpersonal and institutional cariño, (b) adopting a whole-child orientation that honors students' cultural integrity and bodymindspirits, (c) attending to both inner healing and outward community engagement, and (d) advancing college and community readiness. The conclusion also explores the challenges schools face to institutionalize authentic cariño more broadly. Chief among these are the demands authentic cariño places on educators, the dangers of handicapping youth by accustoming them to intensive supports that may not be readily available in the real world, and the constraints posed by oppressive structures and systemic inequities. To assist educators to cultivate authentic cariño in their own contexts, the chapter ends with a set of reflection questions to guide those wishing to move this work forward.

In its totality, *Authentic Cariño: Transformative Schooling for Latinx* offers a compelling account of how committed educators working in partnership with community members confronted inequity and injustice. By caring deeply about Latinx students' development as thinkers, sense makers, change agents, and human beings, MHS supported many students to maintain healthy ethnic identities and to see themselves as thoughtful, problem-solving citizens, capable of uplifting their communities and contributing to broader social justice movements. In these subtractive times, MHS offers a valuable counterstory that elucidates how schools can cultivate hope and embolden youth to join the beautiful struggle rather to give in to despair and apathy.

CHAPTER 2

Familial Cariño

Deeply Knowing and Supporting Students

Nos sentimos como familia. Todos nos conocemos. Nos apoyamos. Es lo que siento—unidad, comunidad. Eso es la misión que he mirado siempre desde yo llegué aquí la primera vez. (We feel like family. We all know each other. We all support each other. That is what I feel—unity, community. That's the mission I've always seen since I got here the first time.)

—Magdalena, parent volunteer/liaison

We feel like a family. Honestly, for me, when I walk into MHS, it's like walking into my own house. When I see anybody at MHS, it's like I'm seeing somebody who is really close to my life and to my heart. There is no question that our organization will do whatever needs to be done for this school at any point. We will be there for them.

—Dolores, citywide faith-based community organizer and MHS founder

What I fell in love with at MHS is the family attitude. These teachers love these kids. It's not just the teachers. The kids love each other. There is a sense of community and responsibility.

—Luz, extended day program director and CBO partner

The family unity of MHS makes us special. A lot of our students see our school as a second home. You can see that right away because they don't want to leave the school. . . . I care a lot for my kids. I see my students as my own. I feel their pain sometimes, and I feel like I always want to protect them, and I always want to create a very safe environment.

—Mr. Avila, Spanish teacher

The teachers support you a lot. They're almost like another parent or aunt or uncle or any family member. . . . They don't give up on you. They really don't.

—Carmen, 11th-grade student

When we started this school, we said we wanted to create a school that was family where each of you were to be known by the adults in the community. . . . I come to this place every day with tremendous love for you.

—Principal West, town hall remarks to students

A family ethos permeated the organizational culture of MHS. In interviews, a cross section of MHS community members highlighted the school's familial atmosphere as one of its signature strengths. According to Principal West, personalization was "ingrained in the vision of the school" from its inception and was "the thing that we've held true to the most." This emphasis reflected both the input of founding families who yearned for a community school where their children would be safe and supported,[1] as well as the influence of small school advocates who championed personalization as an essential foundation to increase relevance and rigor in student learning (Meier, 1995; Sizer, 1984, 1992). At MHS, these commitments yielded familial cariño and meant that educators, students, staff, administrators, families, and community partners genuinely cared for one another. Familial cariño involved building robust interpersonal relationships grounded in mutual understanding, trust, and reciprocity, which nurtured the well-being of youth and the MHS community.

Mr. Keo, a veteran math teacher in his 7th year at MHS, noted that the school intentionally embraced the familial values of students' cultures and reproduced them through structures, norms, and traditions such as advisory, class trips, Habits of Life, and holiday celebrations. By cultivating relations of mutual respect between educators and students, as well as among peers, MHS aligned itself with *educación, familismo,* and *personalismo,* cultural values held by its predominantly Latinx student body. While Latinx families are extremely heterogeneous in their ethnic, national, linguistic, socioeconomic, and cultural identities, these three values seemed especially resonant with MHS's students. Valenzuela (1999), explaining the importance of educación, stresses that the term is conceptually broader than its English cognate. It encompasses the family's role in nurturing moral, social, and personal responsibility to ensure that children live lives of integrity and dignity (Bridges et al., 2012; Valenzuela, 1999). Valenzuela (1999) contends that schools have failed Latinx youth by being "systematically blind to the experiences of the 'other's' history and culture, and especially their folk understandings of education" (p. 263). She argues that schools must stop elevating book learning and bureaucratic efficiency over educación and instead construct cultures of authentic care that embrace students and families as "valued and respected partners" (p. 99).

MHS partnered with students and families by adopting practices aligned with familismo and personalismo. Familismo stresses connection, loyalty, and solidarity, as well as the obligation to support the well-being of nuclear and extended family members (Andrés-Hyman et al., 2006; Cauce & Domenech-Rodríguez, 2002). Anzaldúa (1987/2012) explains that, within Mexican culture, "The welfare of the family, the community, and the tribe is more important than the welfare of the individual. The individual exists first as kin—as sister, as father, as *padrino* [godparent]—and last as self" (p. 40). Complementing familismo, personalismo reflects the importance of warm, friendly relationships (Cauce & Domenech-Rodríguez,

2002; Santiago-Rivera, 2003). Within Latinx communities, these relational orientations manifest in the tradition of *compadrazgo,* wherein individuals become fictive kin through choice or baptismal rituals conferring upon them the status of *compadre* (godfather) or *comadre* (godmother) (Cauce & Domenech-Rodríguez, 2002; Keefe, 1984). Similar to the African American tradition of "other mothering" (Thompson, 1998, 2003), compadrazgo represents a form of communal caring that encourages shared participation in child-raising to ensure the survival, uplift, and well-being of all community members. By weaving these values into its culture and cultivating relations of trust and care, MHS founders sought to know students deeply and leverage that knowledge to enhance students' academic and personal development.

FAMILIAL CARIÑO: LIFE-AFFIRMING, HEALING-CENTERED, AND AUTHENTIC

Before elucidating how MHS institutionalized familial cariño, I wish to clarify several of its distinctive features. First, in using the qualifier "familial," I highlight how schools can replicate in nonoppressive ways the family's role in nurturing children's well-being. While patriarchal family arrangements have buttressed horrific domination and oppression (sexism, heterosexism, racism, xenophobia, classism, imperialism, etc.), families remain important socializing agents. Because most of us are born into and raised by families, it is within this setting that our consciousness develops as we relate with intimate others. Therefore, I use the qualifier "familial" in accordance with (and deep appreciation for) mujerista scholars (Delgado Bernal, 2006; Delgado-Gaitan, 1994; Sosa-Provencio, 2019; Yosso, 2005) who advocate for pedagogies of home that immerse students in cultural, ancestral, and spiritual ways of knowing in order to promote educational success. This mujerista stance underlies familial cariño and orients it toward social relations that are life affirming. Equally important, familial cariño is not a compensatory care aimed at filling a void left open by purportedly "bad" homes or "substandard" parenting. Familial cariño in schools honors students' biological families and views parents as partners.

Second, familial cariño is distinct from popular movements promoting social emotional learning (SEL) and trauma-informed care (Thomas et al., 2019; Weissberg & Cascarino, 2013). While familial cariño shares these movements' concern for psychosocial development, youth welfare, and the importance of caring, responsive school environments, it diverges from SEL and trauma-informed care approaches by adopting an explicit "healing-centered" orientation. Ginwright (2016, 2019), the scholar pioneering this approach, characterizes "healing centered engagement" as "a non-clinical, strength-based approach that advances a holistic view of healing and re-centers culture and identity as a central feature in well-being" (2019, p. 3). Criticizing SEL and trauma-informed approaches because of their apolitical, individual, and sometimes deficit lenses (see also Perry, 2016), Ginwright argues that the toxicity of poverty, violence, and racism is a collective experience for marginalized communities and therefore cannot be adequately addressed through interventions with individuals. A healing-centered framework concentrates on building collective awareness and action to "address the social conditions that threaten social emotional health in the first place" (2016, p. 8). By grounding itself in a healing-centered foundation, familial cariño is a culturally responsive expression of care that aims to vitalize young people's sense of identity, meaning, and purpose.

Finally, familial cariño transpires when humans authentically connect with their hearts. If offered in response to a prescribed policy, it risks backfiring (Phillippo, 2012). As Ms. Ruiz, MHS's college counselor, explained, youth are "very smart. They understand when you are being 'fake or real' and if it's not coming from a place of love, heart, and support—a place of 'I *really* do care,' then it's not going to be real to them." Students are astute enough to detect fakeness when expressed in "false empathy" and "rhetorical care." Duncan (2002) describes false empathy as "a response to the plight of oppressed individuals or groups by privileged individuals who visualize themselves in the places of members of oppressed groups and ask what they, the privileged, would want if they were oppressed" (p. 137). Despite good intentions, such efforts often miss the mark because would-be carers fail to comprehend how the oppressed would actually respond. Such miscalculations may exacerbate the marginalization of underserved youth. Echoing this point, Toshalis (2012) warns that the language and postures of care can conceal inequitable power relations by presenting "the carer as compassionate, personally connected, and committed" and positioning "the cared-for as needy, deficient, and defective" (p. 5). He contends that such "infantilizing and paternalistic forms of care . . . preserve the injurious hierarchies of teacher and learner, middle class and poor, White and Black (and Latino, and Asian, etc.), normal and abnormal, privileged and oppressed . . . [and thereby] enact symbolic violence" (p. 19). Against this backdrop, familial cariño requires educators to forge genuine bonds with students grounded in sincerity, vulnerability, and reciprocity. Maintaining healthy relationships that promote youth agency rather than dependency demands that educators regularly reflect and vigilantly guard against the ego trap of being "the savior." For White teachers in particular, this self-reflexivity involves interrogating racial privilege and wrestling with questions of otherness, difference, and power.

Having outlined familial cariño as a construct, the remainder of this chapter examines how MHS organized itself to allow familial cariño to flourish schoolwide, not just in a few isolated classrooms. I begin with two key strategies MHS employed to institutionalize familial cariño. Next, to illuminate familial cariño's enactment, I spotlight one student's participation in rites of passages designed to promote communal truth telling, academic success, and healthy identity development. Finally, I explore several tensions that arose as educators immersed students in familial cariño.

INSTITUTIONALIZING FAMILIAL CARIÑO

Convinced that knowing students well and cultivating a family environment was "huge in supporting all kids to learn," Principal West and his staff embraced personalization as a core value. To make personalization a reality, MHS adopted two complementary strategies. One involved a "network of care" ensuring students' connection to multiple support resources. The other focused on instilling the "Habits of Life"—a set of norms deemed essential for the development of healthy social identities and relationships. By intertwining these strategies and enacting explicit school policies to meet the psychological, sociological, and academic needs of students as individuals and as a group, MHS infused familial cariño into its organizational DNA. This accomplishment merits attention because it represents the fruition of what Walker (1993) calls "institutional care," whereby care permeates the culture of a whole school and is not arbitrarily available only to those students fortunate enough to be affiliated with particularly caring teachers or special programs.

A Network of Care

The "network of care" model conceived by Luz and referenced in school documents, staff retreats, and accreditation reports was a purposely coordinated web of people, programs, and policies woven together to provide students access to the resources they needed to thrive. One flyer distributed to visitors displayed this system of supports (Figure 2.1). Featuring six components—adult allies, education, peer networks, families, know systems, and health—this thoughtfully orchestrated network conveyed MHS's identity as a full-service community school committed to nurturing the whole child (Dryfoos, 2002).

To unpack the system's dynamic complexity, the next section illustrates each component by providing empirical examples and clarifying its connection to familial cariño. While I describe components separately, the web functioned as a cohesive whole. Principal West explained that he worked closely with Luz, the EDP coordinator and community programs director, to ensure that the components were "virtually seamless in their integration." The resulting tight coordination distinguished MHS from "Christmas tree schools" (Bryk et al., 1998) in which special programs run by external partners are suspended like dazzling ornaments around a school, but operate superficially on the periphery, unconnected to efforts to advance a school's mission.

Adult Allies.[2] Given their central role in infusing authentic cariño into each sphere of the network and coordinating those spheres, adult allies occupied the center of the web. At MHS, teachers and other adults embraced

Figure 2.1. The Network of Care

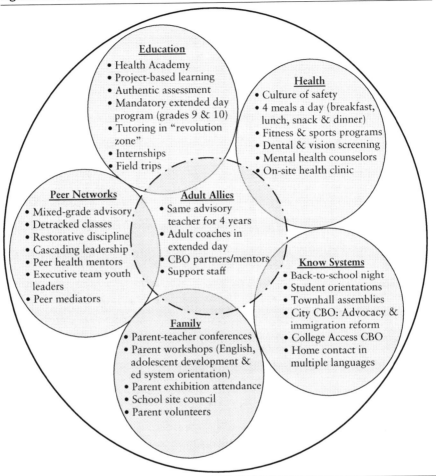

the expectation that they would be allies, caring for youth beyond academics and extending familial cariño to all students. Speaking at a staff retreat, Principal West noted that originally the school had envisioned every student being well known by one adult, but over time the vision had expanded. "We switched from one teacher to multiple teachers [because] that's a system."

To attract educators receptive to the ally role, MHS adopted hiring procedures involving a committee of administrators, teachers, students, and parents who vetted candidates. Principal West explained the behavior-based interview and demonstration lesson process:

The first part is to define [to candidates] the behaviors that are standard at the school. It will sound like, "At MHS, we value personalization with students. Tell me about a time when you developed a close personal relationship with a student and used that to further their academics." . . . In this way, the interview process defines who we are at the school. It gets people set up, and I've found that you can really tell an awful lot about people when they start BS'ing around those questions. . . . By the end of the day, you know if somebody's heart is in the work. You've seen if they have chops because they also have to come in and teach in front of a group of students.

Ms. Clark, a humanities teacher, linked this process to MHS's success attracting staff with "an orientation toward liking teenagers" and a sense of responsibility for "students' overall well-being and social-emotional development." This orientation emerged robustly in teachers' 4.9 mean response (scaled 1–5, 5 = very important) to the survey prompt "How important is it that Latinx students at MHS develop socially and emotionally?" as well as their strong agreement (4.8 mean response) to the prompt "Teachers in this school take a genuine interest in the personal development of their students." These responses highlight how MHS educators valued familial cariño and sought to forge positive adult–youth relationships.

Adult allies were most visible in advisory, a structure considered the bedrock of MHS's culture. (See Figure 2.2 for teachers' definition of advisory.) Advisory involved one to two teachers working with a mixed-grade cohort of 16–20 students over the entirety of their high school careers. The job description specified that advisors be "academic champions," setting

Figure 2.2. Teachers' Notes Defining Advisory

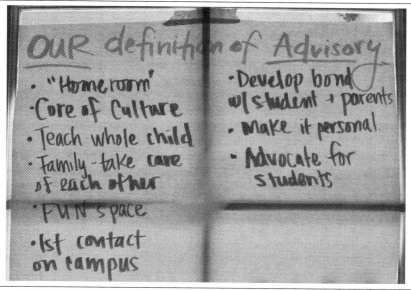

high expectations, developing strong relationships with advisees, and acting as first communicators with advisees' families. Advisors also carried the responsibility of tracking advisees' graduation and college preparation, coordinating interventions if necessary, and building community within the cohort.

During the August retreat, teachers discussed the purpose and structure of advisory to prepare new staff. This review outlined advisors' responsibility to meet with advisees each morning during a 5-minute check-in and specified activities for the four 45-minute advisory periods held each week. While each advisory developed its own personality and traditions, all advisories followed the same schedule, devoting Mondays and Thursdays to silent sustained reading, Tuesdays to study hall, and Fridays to community building. The last of these often involved sharing circles in which youth discussed the highs and lows of their lives, receiving affirmation from listeners. The continuity embedded in these weekly, year-in and year-out routines and in having a stable advisory cohort guided by the same adult(s) made this space one in which youth knew each other well and felt supported.

Students repeatedly reported the importance of advisors, citing the myriad ways these adults nurtured a culture of familial cariño. Advisors set the stage early by calling incoming 9th-grade advisees in August, welcoming them, and answering questions. At the start of school, advisors facilitated community-building activities and assisted their cohorts to create bulletin boards showcasing photos of advisory members with names, birthdays, goals, and favorite music, hobbies, and quotes. Over time, these boards expanded with photos of the advisory engaged in ice breakers, costume and sports competitions, and holiday celebrations. Some advisories created T-shirts designed by students with members' names prominently listed. These overtures communicated to students not only that they had an adult ally supporting them, but that they were integral to their advisory family and belonged at MHS.

Over the course of 4 years, advisors developed deep bonds of *confianza* (mutual trust) with students, helping them navigate difficulties and pursue growth opportunities. Students' willingness to disclose their struggles to advisors underscored how these relationships were rooted in genuine connection. Mr. Tran, a 1st-year math teacher, shared that one of his advisees confided in him concern for a peer whose drug habits seemed increasingly risky. Mr. Tran intervened and connected the struggling student to mental health services. Mr. Tran noted how the interpersonal connections he had nurtured in advisory allowed students to overcome the "teenage cult of not being a snitch" and feel comfortable approaching him. Another advisor, Mr. Avila, discovered that an advisee's grades were plummeting due to distress over her father's deportation. Mr. Avila connected this student with a counselor and organized an academic credit recovery plan. In another case, Ms. Dupont, who had counseled a pregnant advisee not to drop out, beamed recalling how this student had proudly crossed the commencement stage with her full belly to receive her diploma.

In one noteworthy instance, a distraught student called his advisor, Ms. Chin, on a weekend to confess that he was overly high on marijuana, agitated, and scared. She picked him up, comforted him while the high waned, and then drove him home to broker a conversation with family. Together, they got him into rehabilitation. Subsequently, with her encouragement, he devoted his senior project to examining the impact of marijuana on health and communities and also became a middle school peer mentor steering younger students away from marijuana. By helping students surmount personal challenges in ways that promoted overall well-being and academic success, advisors exemplified familial cariño. The magnitude of their influence surfaced at commencement when advisors proudly presented diplomas to "their" seniors and graduates publicly acknowledged their advisors with special "shout outs" such as "Thank you to Ms. R, my advisor and second mom" and "If it wasn't for my advisors, I wouldn't be on this stage. Thank you!"

In addition to helping students overcome personal issues and succeed academically, advisors connected youth to extracurricular enrichment opportunities. Some teachers hosted after-school running, book, and mountain bike clubs, while others worked in the EDP offering programs such as boxing, digital journalism, self-defense, drama, and STEM. Additionally, advisors frequently exchanged notices of internships, college access programs, scholarships, essay competitions, and community cultural events on the staff listserv for public announcement in advisory. Such messages often spawned email chains or hallway conversations in which advisors discussed grooming specific students for particular opportunities and nudged each other to press would-be applicants to apply.

One popular opportunity was Summer Search (https://www .summersearch.org/), a program aimed at enhancing college preparation and life success, for which advisors annually nominated 30–40 sophomores, of whom roughly a third secured spots. Mr. Avila said this recruitment showed teachers' desire to "move the entire person" and encourage youth to "be fearless and go out of their normal comfort zone." In some instances, when students gained admission to programs with tuition fees beyond their means, advisors set up and publicized online donation platforms to secure funding.

In focus groups, several students recounted how an advisor had urged them to apply for extracurricular programs. Linda shared:

> If it wasn't for my advisors and all of the teachers here pushing me to do Summer Search, I would have never done it. I would have never

experienced what I experienced in the summer. I would never have
fallen in love with Costa Rica. It's their support and their time in
trying to help you get into good programs, even though you don't feel
like you want to. I feel like they give you the fire, but it's really up to
you to take it. Whether you want to do it or not, they're still gonna
push you. . . . I joined Summer Search because I didn't want to
disappoint them. [*Laughter.*] I thought that going into Summer Search
was gonna be miserable for me, but then, I ended up enjoying it.

This student's testimony is remarkable in part because she admits
feeling obligated to go to Costa Rica because she didn't want to "disappoint" the adult allies who had invested their time and "fire" into providing her the opportunity. This dynamic illustrates the reciprocal nature of
familial cariño. In addition, it underscores how advisors transmitted vital
resources that enabled youth to extend social networks and build capacity. Given that MHS students live in economically distressed barrios affording diminished access to the social networks that connect middle- and
upper class children to agents holding institutional influence (Stanton-
Salazar, 2001), the effort to link students to different networks and enrichment opportunities constituted a significant way in which advisors
enacted the adult ally role.

In addition to teachers, a wide cast of janitors, after-school coaches, sec-
retaries, youth development workers, counselors, parent volunteers, health
clinicians, community organizers, and local political representatives also
served as allies. Rosa's fond recollection of "the janitor [who] quizzes us
on the five steps of being a successful student" (Chapter 1) hints at the way
all MHS adults invested themselves in supporting students and enveloping
them in familial cariño. From Ms. Garcia, the bilingual front office manager,
who greeted students with "*Buenos días, mi hijo. ¿Qué puedo hacer para
ti hoy?*" (Good morning, my son. What can I do for you today?), to EDP
coach César, who coordinated a young men's empowerment group, MHS
offered multiple sources of adult support.

Principal West proudly underscored this aspect of the school by sharing student survey results (Figure 2.3) showing that the vast majority of
students agreed that they were cared for, respected, and supported by
MHS adults. While there were a few students who indicated not feeling
deeply connected to their advisors and one instance where a family said
an advisor had failed to apprise them of a child's poor grades, overall,
evidence of adult allies playing an influential role in the network of care
abounded.

Education. Within the sphere of education, familial cariño surfaced in
teachers' efforts to know students well and leverage that knowledge to pro-
pel rigorous academics. Ms. Barrett launched the school year by writing

Figure 2.3. Student Survey Responses Regarding Adult Allies at MHS

I agree (strongly agree) that in my school this year . . .	Student response Agree (Strongly agree) (n = 135)
There is at least one adult who really cares about how I am doing in school.	98% (58%)
The adults here respect me.	98% (58%)
People here notice when I'm good at something.	95% (41%)
There is at least one adult who would be willing to help me with a personal problem.	94% (52%)

students a letter introducing herself as a "White teacher" from a "different background" who was committed to honoring students' experiences, communities, and strengths. She invited students to respond and share what excited and scared them about high school, as well as details about their interests, hobbies, and summer activities. "Tell me anything you think I should know about you in order to be a good teacher for YOU." One student, Francisco, wrote back:

> I'm so glad you're my English teacher because you speak Spanish and thats [sic] good for me because this is my 3rd year learning English. Learning English has been hard for me because I am very shy when we need to speak. . . . Something I'm scare [sic] about high school is that most of my teachers don't speak Spanish.

In her reply, Ms. Barrett explained that more than half of MHS teachers spoke Spanish, provided him a list, and assured him that "If you ever want to talk to anyone in Spanish, we're here." Francisco replied, "That just makes me feel so good." Given Anzaldua's (1987/2012) claim that "ethnic identity is twin skin to linguistic identity—I am my language. Until I can take pride in my language, I cannot take pride in myself" (p. 81), Ms. Barrett's exchange with Francisco and others like him showed that she valued students as cultural beings and was available to support them in their native language. Her efforts represent healing-centered engagement because she affirmed Francisco's identity and communicated to him the school's interest in his well-being.

Efforts to understand students and honor their lived experiences also appeared in curricular endeavors. One highly anticipated 11th-grade project revolved around a 6-week American immigration unit that involved pairs of students crafting digital stories to capture the immigration experience of a family member or friend. The project entailed interviews, transcripts, voiceovers, revisions, and audiovisual selections to convey meaning, mood, and themes. The final stories, showcased in an annual Academy Award–style evening attended by an overflow crowd of students, staff, parents, and siblings, recounted among many topics harrowing border crossings with duplicitous coyotes, transitions from agrarian to city lives, the challenges of learning English, and the dangers of living undocumented. During these exhibitions, the audience exhibited high engagement, offering enthusiastic applause after each presentation. A strong sense of community permeated the event, confirming the presence of familial cariño. Importantly, these digital testimonios also provided an opportunity for the MHS community to build collective awareness of oppressive social conditions, thereby incubating interest in transforming inequitable systems. In this regard, the immigration films were culturally sustaining expressions of care in which youth declared that their lives and communities mattered. In doing so, they strengthened their solidarity as a family and signaled their concern for the well-being of all members.

Mr. Behari, one of the humanities teachers orchestrating the unit, explained that he started each year with the theme of immigration to elicit students' "buy-in," personalize the curriculum, and connect with families. He introduced the project by telling students, "We all have stories that are valuable, and we'll start with your stories because your stories are probably the most valuable out of all the stories that we're going to study." He elaborated that "all learning, it starts from you, from your heart. What do you care about? What are you passionate about?" He stressed to students the importance of tapping into "human connection—that connection, like a shared humanity between you and your experience and everybody else's experience—that's something to be highlighted." These remarks reflect how MHS teachers viewed curriculum as a vehicle to connect students not only to big ideas, but to themselves, their peers, and the broader community. Through annual celebrations like the Immigration Film Festival and letter writing exercises like Ms. Bartlett's, MHS wove familial cariño into students' academics.

The education component of the network of care benefited also from the presence of the EDP, operated by the CBO Community Action (CA). During enrollment, students and families committed to participate in CA's after-school activities, which included leadership development, recreation, community impact projects, academic interventions for struggling students, and study halls called "Revolutionary Time" to underscore the liberatory potential of academic achievement. Luz trained the EDP team to stay focused on MHS's mission of providing "transformative learning experiences" and urged coaches to prioritize "high-engaging academics." The program garnered high accolades from teachers, students, families, district officials, and external evaluators. Ms. Barrett credited EDP with shifting students' homework completion from "pathetic" to "soaring" levels. One external evaluation noted high levels of "mutual respect," "camaraderie," and familial cariño. "The students and the staff respond very positively to each other, and appear to want to be a part of the program. The atmosphere is warm and seems family-like."

Another educative arena in which familial cariño flourished was a 13-day period called "post-session" that concluded the school year. Designed to fulfill art or physical education requirements, these mini-courses involved students and teachers playing together in something akin to summer camp. Pairs of teachers developed curriculum around their passions—art as a cultural expression, surfing as a way to appreciate marine ecology, biking or hiking as a way to see nature, dancing as a form of self-expression, etc. These innovative settings strengthened emotional connections among teachers and students. Ms. Clark explained that post-session "gives kids opportunities to step far outside their comfort zones and connect with teachers in different ways. . . . It gives students connections and opportunities to meet with teachers that they might not ever have." Mr. Behari noted his appreciation for the bonds he developed with students during post-session. "You get to know the kids on a more personal level. You have fun. You're on the bus for hours with them. You're in a hotel with them. You see them in a completely different light." These remarks illustrate how post-session allowed educators to see students in their full humanness and cultivate relations that transcended instrumental motives (e.g., eliciting academic growth or classroom cooperation).

Students praised post-session, describing it as an "awesome free vacation" that enabled them "to learn about each other and trust each other" in ways that made them feel "like a big family." Camila, a junior, shared her appreciation for how post-session created space for self-reflection. "You just get time for yourself. They even give you some time to reflect back on your life; what have you done?" Ms. Grace, a life skills teacher, testified to the "spiritual connections" of post-session, noting how she saw students use art as a vehicle to "liberate themselves from the identities that have been imposed upon them" and "figure out who they are." In these ways, post-session provided another avenue for MHS to cultivate familial cariño and fortify the network of care. When the district pressed MHS to relinquish post-session, teachers fought mightily. Describing these instructional weeks as "our heart," teachers agreed to teach more minutes each day without extra pay in order to preserve this tradition.

Peer Networks. The camaraderie and peer encouragement evident during post-session and the Immigrant Film showcase reflect the strong social emotional bonds students enjoyed at MHS. Committed to overcoming the "'social de-capitalization' or limited presence of academically oriented networks" among students of color (Flores-Gonzáles, 2002; Valenzuela, 1999), MHS actively promoted peer-to-peer support structures as a vital component of the network of care. This orientation underpinned the school's decision to detrack classes as much as possible. Recounting a "disastrous" experiment to offer AP classes, Principal West explained that the initiative failed because "it created two separate communities and two separate identities . . . [which] was not healthy for the school." The choice to jettison AP classes reflected familial cariño because educators realized how curricular tracking generated harmful status hierarchies that undermined the school's commitment to nurturing all students' wholeness, well-being, and academic progress. Guided by an awareness of the crucial role of peer relationships in students' academic engagement and moral development, MHS rejected the segmentation of youth into college-bound or general education tracks and opted instead to have "kids working cooperatively in groups, heterogeneously, on integrated projects." With this approach, MHS sought to build a cohesive learning community committed to all students' success.

Peer relations benefited from a host of initiatives. A restorative discipline program enabled students who transgressed school norms to reflect on their actions and make amends to the community. In one instance, a restorative circle of three students and 11 adults, following a physical fight between two young women, involved two hour-long sessions to explore the conflict. Ultimately, the circle developed a plan for the students to collaborate on an antibullying campaign on Facebook to heal the community. Another structure to bolster peer-to-peer care was the training of 15 youth health mentors who offered guidance about sexually transmitted diseases, nutrition, and drug use. Student leaders also designed a variety of school-wide programs such as town hall assemblies and advisory competitions to promote school unity and student engagement.

By far the most impactful peer-to-peer support occurred through advisory. Advisors encouraged co-advisees to see one another as brothers and sisters. Friday community circles provided a space to nurture healthy social identities and promote reflection. During Women's History month, youth in advisory circles shared stories of grandmothers, mothers, aunts, sisters, and other women who had inspired and encouraged them. Students opened up their lives for others to see and expressed a collective sense of gratitude for the community resource of caring women. This session exemplified a pedagogy of the home (Delgado Bernal, 2006) because it centered students' biological kin and celebrated how these women through their labor, *consejos* (advice), and *cuentos* (stories) had provided guidance, preserved community memory, and imparted survival strategies to navigate a hostile world. Such opportunities epitomized familial cariño's emphasis on affirming students' cultures, identities, and sense of existential meaning.

Interadvisory challenges such as the "Nerd Bowl" (a hybrid Family Feud–Trivial Pursuit game that aimed to make "being smart cool"), the

"Egg Olympics" (an activity in which students built contraptions to race an egg across a finish line), and the "March Madness Basura Ball Tournament" (a homegrown, coed game involving elaborate passing rules and sinking a ball into a trash can) strengthened advisory bonds and ignited boisterous, good-hearted competition. In emails coordinating these activities, advisors engaged in playful pregame banter. Some bragged about their advisory's prowess ("Better bring your A-game, because we're out to prove that a little bit of strategy goes a long way!"), while others jovially predicted victory ("Good luck! . . . but you will all ultimately lose to us! Bring your Kleenex and be prepared to weep.") After the March Madness playoff, Ms. Clark proclaimed on the listserv, "There was so much sweat, laughter, and fun being had on a Friday afternoon. Watching it was really powerful." Ms. Whitmore replied effusively:

> I know we always talk about these activities in terms of what they do for our kids and our school culture, but I for one think they make ME a better, happier, more job-satisfied teacher. Maybe it was a lot of the endorphins, but I was feeling SO in love with our school coming away from the games. And my advisory's love for one another just skyrockets.

The impact of adults and youth playing together in a sustained fashion added a vibrancy and joy to MHS that uplifted the community and generated solidarity.

The interpersonal connections nurtured through advisory community circles and playful competitions provided an important foundation for peers to support one another academically. Students tutored one another during study hall. Ms. Wang, a science teacher, recounted how a struggling emergent bilingual student frequently spent study hall paired with a classmate who translated physics concepts and terminology from English into Spanish. This translanguaging[3] exchange allowed both students to tackle a challenging course. Students also rehearsed important presentations in advisory and received moral support from co-advisees at culminating academic exhibitions. Speaking of the intentionality behind this arrangement, Principal West explained, "When seniors do their defenses, 11th grade co-advisees assess them so that they know what's expected of them the following year. Ninth graders are also there to see what the future holds for them." In this way, MHS encouraged older students to model academic excellence to younger co-advisees and facilitated occasions for youth to validate each other's intellectual development. When a student's public defense concluded with a round of "grow and glow" feedback, the observations and praise offered from student to student contributed to an affirmative environment of familial cariño.

Family. A fourth element of the network of care involved partnering with parents to support students' well-being. Ms. Garcia, whose own children attended the school, acted as the first point of contact for families when arriving on campus. Her warm demeanor and ability to speak with most parents in their preferred language immediately heralded MHS as a welcoming place. Home–school connections benefited also from mandatory parent conferences held each fall during a week of minimum days. During these sessions, advisors, students, and parents reviewed academic progress, accomplishments, and upcoming steps toward graduation and college. For seniors and struggling students, a second parent conference occurred in the spring.

In one fall conference, Ms. Clark facilitated the consultation mostly in Spanish with Violeta, a junior, and her mother. Although Violeta had a 3.4 GPA, held a coveted internship at a children's hospital, and was proud of her immigration digital story, her mother expressed concern that her daughter's academic interest seemed to be waning. She reported that Violeta had complained about being bored in school. Ms. Clark digested these concerns and shared her observations that Violeta seemed less happy than in previous years. During this conversation, the trio discussed self-esteem, college goals, academic frustrations, online school report cards, and family dynamics. At one point, Violeta's mother, lamenting that her daughter was spending too much time in front of a mirror criticizing herself, counseled her daughter on the importance of self-love. (*Yo me quiero mucho. Si no me quisiera mucho yo ya estuviera por los suelos.* I love myself a lot. If I didn't love myself, I would be depressed.) Reminiscent of the efforts of other Latina mothers seeking to teach their daughters to *valorarse y valerse por si misma* (value themselves and be self-reliant) within a society that denigrates and oppresses Brown bodies (Villenas & Moreno, 2001), this exchange prompted Ms. Clark to ask Violeta, "Are you okay, or are you just telling us you are okay?" While Violeta was reticent to respond, both adults demonstrated a sincere concern for Violeta's changing demeanor and communicated their support. As the conference ended, Ms. Clark reminded Violeta that she wanted to see her at morning check-ins and that she was going to be keeping a close eye on her. This glimpse into one conference reveals how teachers partnered with parents to nurture students' psychosocial development and academic success.

Beyond conferences, MHS also encouraged parents (or a significant adult selected by the student) to attend culminating exhibitions, especially sophomore and senior defenses. After these presentations, when audience members and community panelists shared feedback with students, parents' comments were usually the most poignant. Often delivering remarks in Spanish, parents teared up as they expressed pride in their child's hard work and intelligence, and then finished by hugging their child. This involvement gave parents the opportunity to affirm their child's intellectual development and thereby strengthen child–parent bonds.

Parents had other opportunities to deepen their ties with MHS. The EDP offered an evening parent academy that included sessions on (a) the U.S. educational system (grading, pedagogy, curriculum, college, testing, etc.), (b) adolescent development and parent–child relationships, (c) community activism (how to influence school board and city council, advocate for change, and raise funds), and (d) English and computer literacy. A group of mothers also prepared food for students staying after school. Participating parents received acknowledgment at an annual banquet during which Principal West and Luz distributed "comadre" and "compadre" awards for those with 20 hours or more of service and/or parent academy attendance. By invoking compadrazgo and using terms of endearment reserved for godparents, MHS tapped into cultural mores and validated the trusting bonds these parents formed with each other and the school as they involved themselves in their children's schooling. Commenting on the impact of parent participation, Luz noted that "kids behave better because parents are there, [and] parents are taking on ownership of school." Through these relationships with parents MHS bolstered familial cariño and enriched the educación of students.

Know Systems. Committed to keeping students and families informed regarding school policies, educational opportunities, community developments, and cultural history, MHS viewed communication as vital to the network of care. The school communicated messages to families in the home language through multiple channels—robocalls, newsletters, student handbooks/planners, an online grade portal, and a website. Beyond these fairly standard modes of communication, MHS infused familial cariño into informational events by making them opportunities for community building. For example, the *Noche de Regreso a la Escuela* (Back-to-School Night) kicked off with a well-attended potluck dinner. Explaining the cultural importance of offering food at such events, Luz said, "We're *familia*. At the table we all sit down. . . . We feed each other." Through this meal and the conversations that flowed during this informal segment of the evening, MHS created a warm, intimate environment congruent with families' cultural practices and positioned itself as a family-centered place rather than an impersonal bureaucracy. To further promote face-to-face interaction and fortify the network of care, Back-to-School night featured a passport game in which parents received verification stamps for chatting with their students' advisors and teachers and visiting informational stations set up by community-based partners. At the end of the evening, parents submitted completed passports into a raffle and the winner received a 100-dollar grocery gift card. This game not only incentivized relationship building, but also added an element of pleasure and levity to an event that could have been conducted as a dull formality.

One of the organizations presenting themselves at Noche de Regreso a la Escuela was the College and Beyond Support Consortium (CBSC), which operated a school-based college counseling center run by Ms. Ruiz, a bilingual Latina who was the first in her family to graduate college. Throughout the year, Ms. Ruiz and her team of five Latinx university undergraduate students visited 9th-and 10th-grade advisories to introduce college options, conducted one-on-one guidance sessions with each junior and senior at least twice, and held evening and weekend events to help students and parents gain knowledge about college admission and financial aid. Alma, a junior, explained, "Ms. Ruiz helps you apply for colleges. She informs you from where you are at now to where you want to go to. She'll make a plan for you, which I really like." Benicio, an undocumented junior, elaborated, "CBSC checks up on our credits and grades and if we're eligible to go to college, what are the next steps. Ms. Ruiz actually lays it out for us, what path should we take, which is very good." This support distinguished MHS from schools such as Seguín High, where Valenzuela (1999) documented how Latinx students were "insufficiently socialized into an understanding of the tools and knowledge they would need to reach [college]" (p. 151). Encouraged to pursue college and become well informed about their options, MHS students benefited from the familial cariño of their college counselors who advocated for their future success.

Another mechanism for expanding students' knowledge of their school, community, and cultural heritage surfaced in student-organized town hall assemblies celebrating occasions such as the start of school, Día de Los Muertos, Chinese New Year, and Latinx, Women's, and African American history months. Ms. Howard, a humanities teacher, described town halls as "some of the most powerful and beautiful things that we do at this school because kids work together . . . to create something cool to celebrate home culture and diversity." Observations of multiple town halls revealed how these forums intensified familial cariño by expanding students' understanding of themselves and each other, reinforcing a collective commitment to social justice, and showcasing the creative talents of youth.

During the Latinx History town hall, for example, students entered a gym decorated with student-created posters featuring inspirational quotes from Latinx notables (see Figure 2.4). The gathering launched with the unity clap and featured a program that included accounts of immigration, the 1968 East LA student walkouts, the Farm Workers' movement, and the independence struggles of Central and South American countries. Spoken word poetry, salsa dance performances, and a presentation by MHS student activists involved in passing the 2011 California Dream Act also captured the audience's attention. An MHS alumna returned from college to share an original poem testifying to the sacrifices her family had made to send her to university and her desire to remain anchored in her home community while pursuing her degree.

César, whose Chicano parents were United Farm Worker union organizers, sang "El Hijo del Pueblo" (The Son of the People) with lyrics

Figure 2.4. Student Posters Made for Latinx Heritage Town Hall

declaring *"orgullo haber nacido en el barrio más humilde alejado del bulli-cio de la falsa sociedad"* (pride to have been born in the most humble neigh-borhood away from the bustle of false society). Echoing this sentiment, Luz reminded students:

> We are poor. We are immigrants, some without license or papers. *[The crowd whoops loudly for several seconds responding to this statement.]* We are refugees. We don't speak English well, but we are trying to read and write as much as we can. The difference is that we have cultura. We have a culture—the culture of Molina High!

These presentations catalyzed collective awareness of historical struggles, solidarity within the school community, and cultural pride. By attending to students' lives and cultural identities, town halls promoted healing-centered engagement and magnified familial cariño.

Health. The final component of the network care involved MHS's attention to students' physical and mental health. The school offered qualifying students breakfast, lunch, snack, and dinner. By satisfying youths' literal hunger, MHS demonstrated an awareness that basic needs must be met if students are to succeed in school. Student success was further bolstered by a partnership with a psychology graduate school that placed clinical interns on campus to provide therapy and group counseling. Principal West stressed the importance of these services given the chronic trauma many MHS students experienced as they contended with poverty and violence. He reported that 35% of students accessed counseling services.

An onsite health clinic added another layer of support. Operated by a nonprofit whose mission was to help clients improve and maintain their physical, mental, emotional, social, and spiritual well-being in culturally respectful ways, the clinic offered students and their families integrated medical, dental, and vision care. Funded by the county health department and several grants, the clinic employed two bilingual nurse practitioners, two program directors, and a secretary. Doctors rotated in for appointments weekly. Over the course of 1 year, over 200 students received dental and vision screening and 88 youth (a third of MHS's student body) accessed the clinic for appointments. Testifying to the clinic's impact, Andrea Baranoski, a clinic director, recalled the transformation of a student with debilitating asthma. With close monitoring, the condition became manageable, and this student not only improved her school attendance but also formed positive relationships with clinic staff, who persuaded her to become a peer health educator. MHS's attention to students' health represented an important form of familial cariño. Because limited access to quality health care is a structural inequity that not only prevents low-wealth communities from thriving, but actually "cause[s] psychological, emotional, spiritual, and physical harm to individuals and communities" (Ginwright, 2016, p. 6), these efforts to meet students' medical and nutritional needs were an important demonstration of how MHS nurtured the bodymindspirits of youth to promote their overall well-being.

The convergence of all six components of the network of care—adult allies, education, peer networks, families, know systems, and health—fostered a schoolwide environment of familial cariño that affirmed students individually and collectively. Youth understood that the school was fully committed to their success and welfare. This knowledge encouraged them to engage fully as learners and see themselves as valued MHS community members. Students' engagement gained additional vitality through MHS's second personalization thrust—the Habits of Life.

Habits of Life

While the network of care established avenues for the expression of care, the Habits of Life specified the qualities of a caring person and provided an aspirational ideal for members of the MHS family to embody (see Figure 1.2). In alignment with educación, the Habits of Life communicated familial cariño by signaling the school's desire for students to develop healthy identities and become conscious, ethical, contributing individuals who cared for themselves and others. MHS's student handbook urged each student to be "a positive member of the community" by embodying four Habits of Life—empathy, courage, integrity, and curiosity. These Habits were posted in classrooms, invoked in advisory circles and town halls, and referenced as norms during class trips and restorative justice sessions.

Empathy. Principal West explained that empathy involved being "able to walk in someone else's shoes" and demonstrating the capacity "to care for other people and understand where they're coming from." One memorable display of schoolwide empathy occurred in response to the 2013 attack of an agender California teen whose skirt was set on fire by another teen while riding on a bus.[4] Members of the LGBTQ Club organized a "Skirts for Sasha Day" and encouraged all community members to wear skirts as a display of their respect for the victim, Sasha Fleischman, and their support for LGBTQ people. The listserv that day swelled with posts from teachers swapping photos of students and teachers posing arm-in-arm in skirts. Empathy also surfaced in campaigns to raise burial funds for families who lost children to gun violence and in an all-school field trip to see the documentary "Bully" (Hirsch, 2011), followed by advisory discussions focused on interrupting bullying and protecting victims. Through such activities, MHS reinforced familial cariño by helping students affirm, lift, and protect those who have been harmed by violence or disrespect. Given that many youth exposed to socially toxic environments cope by becoming numb and disconnected to themselves and their surroundings (Ginwright, 2016), MHS's emphasis on empathy encouraged students to reconnect with their inner intelligence and uncover ways to heal wounded bodymindspirits. In this manner, the habit of empathy was deeply life-affirming.

Courage. Courage was characterized as "approaching obstacles with fearlessness, confidence, and tenacity." Principal West told students that courage was imperative because "you are going up against a system that is not set up to support you. It requires some level of fearlessness and risk-taking in order to get to the place where you're ultimately going to become successful." One way MHS nurtured fearlessness was through activities designed to stretch students. As Hector, a junior, said, "You get pushed a lot to go out of your comfort zone and actually try new things here." Overnight, multiday, class camping trips transported students beyond familiar surroundings to explore the natural world in places such as California's Point Reyes National Seashore and Yosemite. MHS adults organized these adventures to develop students' courage. Asked to journey into environments in which chupacabras might lurk, undertake strenuous hikes, participate in team-building activities such as trust falls, and engage in conversation dyads requiring vulnerability, students had to push through fear and self-doubt. Mr. Trung noted that many students "have a lot of fears about leaving their home and school cultures and going to a different space. . . . By having them take risks, purely by such exposure, students actually can construct a lot of their own identity and where they belong." MHS students rose to these challenges. In multiple settings—camping trips, final exhibitions, town hall performances, and post-sessions—I witnessed adults and students encouraging struggling or nervous students to overcome fear and summon the courage to tackle a daunting task. Surrounded by the network of care and familial cariño, students transcended limiting beliefs and stretched themselves toward bigger visions of themselves.

Integrity. MHS defined integrity as "being honest, responsible, and trustworthy." Mr. West viewed integrity as difficult to promote in a society that glamorizes figures who achieve success through cut-throat competition, cheating, and lying. In defiance of these norms, MHS encouraged students to stand up for what was right even when it was unpopular and to do the right thing even when no one was looking. Luz pointed to the instance of a stolen computer and how students collaborated to identify the culprit, ultimately compelling him to return it and take responsibility. "The kids by themselves decided to do this and this is where integrity comes in." Another instance of integrity occurred off campus when a female student was physically threatened by gang members in a park and several MHS young men defended her. Afterward, these male students explained that they couldn't "be indifferent." The theme of "not being indifferent" resurfaced in a focus group when Anna, a senior, responded to the question "How has MHS shaped how you think about life?" She shared that MHS had taught her to "not be indifferent" and "to use your voice to say what you feel. Don't go with the flow. Go where you believe is right." By cultivating this ethic of doing what's right, MHS deepened students' attention to acting in ways likely to advance self-determination and justice; this focus foregrounded familial cariño's emphasis on building communal relations that uphold human dignity.

Curiosity. The final Habit of Life was curiosity, which the Student Handbook explained as "having passion, vision, and a deep thirst for knowledge and learning." Mr. Behari, a lead teacher on the professional development committee, championed this habit above all others. "More important than anything, you're building kids who want to learn. . . . If you love to learn, everything else will figure itself out. If you want to succeed . . . you've got to love digging in, diving into ideas, thinking about them, debating them." While this habit overlapped considerably with MHS's Habits of Mind and was cultivated mainly in classrooms, it also emerged in efforts to encourage students to learn about the lives of peers, teachers, community members, and others. Advisory community circles allowed students to explore the beliefs, histories, and views of co-advisees. Similarly, an activity during the Yosemite trip nurtured curiosity by having sophomores approach strangers to learn where they came from and what they thought about the United States and the National Park. Through such experiences, MHS expanded learning outside classrooms and underscored the importance of seeking to understand others, for without such understanding, authentic care is impossible.

Overall, the Habits of Life operated as a moral compass guiding students in a positive direction and fortifying a caring community. Principal West, crediting the Habits for being "the launching point to establish the culture," highlighted their power in helping students reflect on discipline infractions. Recalling a hallway incident during which a student made a racist comment, West reported:

> I don't think he did it in a mean-spirited way. It was more in a frustrated kind of way, but he didn't understand the implications of his comments. Empathy allows me an entry point. "Hey, here at MHS, man, one of the big principles is empathy. I want you to walk in his shoes and tell me how he might have felt with the experience that you created for him. You created this experience for him. You have to take responsibility. I need you to show some integrity and to be fearless and stand up and accept the responsibility for what you did to him by using those words.

In instances such as this, MHS adults invoked the Habits of Life to encourage students to care for others. Summarizing the importance of the Habits of Life, Mr. Behari claimed that they were the key to ensuring that each student became "not just a thinker, but a person who understands others, who cares about others, who wants to learn for the sake of learning, who tells the truth and has integrity and doesn't back down from a challenge."

FIREWALKS: SCHOOLWIDE RITUALS THAT EXEMPLIFY FAMILIAL CARIÑO

Thus far, this chapter has outlined the contours of familial cariño and identified structures enabling its institutionalization. For readers hungering for a more intimate portrayal of familial cariño's enactment, we journey now into an annual rite of passage known as the firewalk (Curry, 2016). Designed to encourage students to live the Habits of Life, Mind, and Work, firewalks were formal milestone ceremonies held at the end of the school year in which sophomores and seniors publicly assessed their academic and personal growth before a circle of peers and adults. Testifying to their impact, Esperanza, a junior, described firewalks as "a big part of our school that's good."

> [Firewalks] change the way you see yourself and the way you do things. . . . They make you realize things that you don't really see. . . . I didn't really care about my grades. I just thought, "Whatever. School's school." I think the firewalk helped me a lot to just see, I really do need school to be someone in life.

Esperanza's remarks suggest how the reflection and peer feedback embedded in these rituals heightened both students' self-awareness and sense of being supported by a school family.

Firewalks occurred in a classroom with 12 to 16 chairs configured in a circle. In separate ceremonies, firewalkers, seated in the center, described their progress, struggles, strengths, weaknesses, achievements, goals, and embodiment of the Habits of Life. Following these remarks, audience members (sophomore Yosemite trip companions or, for seniors, advisory peers) spent 20 minutes or more posing "brutally honest" questions to elicit firewalkers' views of who they were and who they were becoming. After this phase, a predesignated lead student asked circle members if they believed the firewalker had demonstrated sufficient emotional vulnerability, honesty, responsibility, and metacognition to proceed into junior year or graduation. If in agreement, the audience rose to their feet and each circle member spoke an affirmation before celebrating the firewalker's success. If audience members doubted a firewalker's readiness, they remained seated, aired concerns, and through dialogue constructed a remediation plan. As a grade promotion and graduation requirement, firewalks involved the entire community determining students' academic fate. On a handful of occasions, poor performances resulted in students being held back and having to repeat a semester.

For Leticia, a bright student, self-described tomboy, and passionate soccer player, firewalks were an emotional experience. During her sophomore firewalk, Letty confessed ambivalence about school. Saddled with responsibilities for cooking, cleaning, caring for an ill uncle, and providing childcare, she acknowledged neglecting school work. Citing these distractions, she admitted that her GPA had dropped to 1.8, down from 3.8 her freshman year. Despite these circumstances, she expressed relief that she had aced the California High School Exit Exam (CAHSEE) on the first try and that her test-taking prowess had enabled her to scrape by with mostly passing grades. As an introvert, she said the prospect of being surrounded by people for 4 days during Yosemite had scared her. She was glad, though, that she went. The hikes, rainbows, and waterfalls were unforgettable. Wrapping up her introduction, Letty stared downward and mumbled, "To be honest, I'm not sure school is going to get me anywhere. I have no papers, my family has no money, and my family needs my help. I'm not even sure it's worth trying anymore."

Sensing Letty's fragility, her firewalk circle launched the question period with inquiries seemingly aimed at illuminating her strengths. When asked about something she was proud of, Letty recalled that her math teacher had written her a *palanca*[5] telling her she was "brilliant." When asked about her favorite assignment, Letty identified a personal narrative written for humanities class that allowed her to uncover inner pain and self-hatred and appreciate her mother's unconditional love. She blushingly reported that her narrative was one of 15 selected from the sophomore class for broadcasting on the local public radio's "My Voice Matters" series. The conversation eventually shifted toward tougher questions. "You said you don't do your homework. Are you passing all your classes?" "What steps are you taking to make sure you don't fail?" "What would happen if you told your parents that you need to do homework and can't do all they are asking you to do at home?" Letty's peers ultimately commended her for her honesty but refused to stand given concerns over missing work in two classes and poor time management as evidenced by her choice to squander precious free time on Facebook. The circle indicated they would stand for her later in the week if she completed outstanding assignments and spoke with teachers and advisors about her struggles.

Before disbanding, a tearful Letty received encouragement. One peer promised, "I have your back 100%. If you need help with any subject, I will give it to you. . . . We love you very much." Another student said, "In Yosemite, you pushed me to reach the top of Nevada Falls. Before that hike, our class promised not to leave any sophomore behind, that we were gonna graduate together. If I made it to Nevada Falls, you can do this." Mr. Avila, the facilitator, offered some final words. "We all fall down and then we get up. . . . A lot of students struggle here with difficult homes. . . . There's a way to get out of the house, go to college, get away from the problems. . . . You have the power in your hands." As the period ended, Mr. Avila sighed and concluded, "We'll leave it like this. Remember the confidentiality pledge; what got said in here stays here. I'll go with Letty now to find her teachers."

Because this rite of passage created a communal space in which Letty felt safe to divulge the harsh realities of living at the intersections of being Mexican, female, economically impoverished, and undocumented, this firewalk represented a profound demonstration of familial cariño. The compassionate listening and questioning from the circle fueled a conversation that not only affirmed Letty's intelligence, craft as a writer, and honesty, but also pushed her to resist the temptation to give up. Given the precarious position of undocumented youth, who are often treated as "unwanted" and "discardable" (Conchas, 2016, p. 157), it is noteworthy that Letty's firewalk ended with peers encouraging her to persevere so that the sophomore class could graduate together. Letty's peers communicated that not only was she an integral member of their school community, but that she possessed the capacity to surmount obstacles and self-advocate. This firewalk shows peers and an adult ally practicing *acompañamiento*—the act of supporting another by accompanying her, relating to her, and loving her (Sepúlveda, 2011, p. 206). Contrary to the experiences of many undocumented youth who suffer from invisibility, low expectations, and inadequate support (Gonzales et al., 2015), the familial cariño Letty experienced through the firewalk promoted her academic success and personal growth.

Two years later, during her senior firewalk, Letty shared plans to attend a community college and one day become a pediatrician. "I want to take the things that I have gone through to help others grow." Recalling sophomore year, she described herself as lacking confidence and struggling with oral presentations. "Talking in front of other people is hard." With tears rolling down her face, she admitted to still feeling overwhelmed by family responsibilities and anguished by a friend's recent suicide. When asked how she coped, she reported seeing a counselor and being motivated by her little sister. "She looks up to me. I don't want to fail her." When the moment arrived for co-advisees to stand, the entire circle rose. Then, one by one they offered praise: "You're hella smart!" "You're strong!" "Your senior defense was amazing!" "You never gave up!" Ms. Chin, her advisor, spoke last:

> I'm standing because of a number of things you said in your firewalk and the growth I've seen in you. Letty, your senior investigation and defense on sexual abuse was moving, and I know you worked extremely hard on it. To know that you've gone through that much is hard to fathom, but we all go through tough times and how we handle those times determines what kind of adult we'll become. You have shown that you believe in yourself. I admire the way you care for your siblings and how you carry the weight of others. You've also learned to take care of yourself through your passions for music, soccer, writing, and drawing. I am confident you have the tools you need to get through any struggle. Now, it's time for your cinnamon roll hug!

With this last reference, the circle stepped forward and enveloped Letty in a group hug. This embrace of smiling youth and two adults (Ms. Chin and Ms. Mahelona, an administrative assistant the students affectionately called "Mama Jasmine") exemplified familial cariño.

Through this final rite of passage, Letty demonstrated her grasp of the Habits of Life. Empathy surfaced in her grief over her friend's suicide and in her commitment to remain a role model for her sister. Courage appeared in the tenacity she exhibited by staying in school despite family obligations and personal setbacks. Integrity emerged in her honest self-appraisal.

Finally, Letty's honors distinction on her senior defense and her aspiration to pursue college and pursue medicine confirmed her curiosity and love of learning. The fact that MHS organized this ritual for every sophomore and senior each year attested to the school's commitment to nurturing students' whole selves and honoring their lived experiences. MHS's firewalk rituals enhanced familial cariño by affording opportunities for interpersonal trust and mutual respect to flourish. Immersed in this milieu, youth came to view their individual progress and survival as linked to the welfare of classmates and school community.

TENSIONS IN FAMILIAL CARIÑO

Despite its benefits, familial cariño should not be romanticized. Its provision carried nettlesome tensions. MHS adults grappled with whether it was possible to care too much, whether personalism might at times become invasive, and whether it was healthy and sustainable to care so intensively for youth.

Hand-Holding and Infantilizing

First, adults at MHS wrestled with how to ensure that familial cariño liberated rather than crippled students. Several parents and teachers as well as an alumnus noted how the intense provision of full-service support sometimes veered dangerously into hand-holding, especially in the academic arena. One parent observed, "The teachers pay a lot of attention to students. . . . They tell students over and over, 'Do your work . . . get your application in.' . . . Teachers follow students around. . . . The teachers almost hold students' hands to get them in [to colleges and internships]." Ricardo, an MHS graduate and CBSC college counselor, remarked, "There is a really strong sense of community here, but . . . teachers really do a lot in trying to help them [students]. . . . Sometimes I don't know if it's too much because we can benefit from doing stuff on our own." Mr. Behari fretted over how "Some teachers want to go to every kid's house and watch them do their homework and give them the computer, hold their hands, type their essay. We can't do that. They have to be able to fly on their own." The fiercest voice drawing attention to this tension was Ms. Clark, who criticized well-intentioned colleagues for readily extending deadlines and offering multiple chances to students who had disregarded school and failed to self-advocate:

> When you offer students multiple opportunities upon multiple opportunities and you're doing all the heavy lifting yourself as a teacher and you're paving the way for them, and they can't even take a step forward, what you're saying is, "It's OK for me to do all the work and for you to sit there." And I think that is the wrong message to send.

Summing up her position, she asserted:

> We have to empower the kids. . . . We can only get them halfway;
> they've got to get themselves the other half. I get a little bit cautious
> and afraid of liberal, bleeding-heart teachers who want to save
> and hug everybody and everything. I think that sets kids up for
> failure. . . . [In college,] no professor's going to coddle you . . . so
> how do I teach you this world of schools so that you have the skill set
> to advocate for yourself once you get to the next level?

Adding another layer, Ms. Clark emphasized her unique perspective as
a teacher of color, whose parents, a Black father and Mexican mother, had
practiced a "tough love" approach:

> I have parents of color. They parent differently. They don't parent you
> to smile and nod and everything's great, and "Oh, you tried your best,
> you're so adorable, I believe in you." Parents of color don't parent
> like that. They parent to prepare you for the world you're about to
> face. . . . I don't want my students to go out there and then be shocked
> at the way the world actually works. . . . We're going to start training
> you now for the way the world works.

Ms. Clark highlighted the danger of what some term the *pobrecito*
(poor baby) or *¡Ay bendito!* ("Oh, you poor little thing") phenomenon
whereby well-meaning educators, who unconsciously hold deficit views
of students, harm youth by lowering expectations and offering care in
ways that undermine agency (Antrop-González & De Jesús, 2006). For
Ms. Clark, enveloping youth in familial cariño meant refusing to accept
students' challenging life circumstances as excuses for academic medioc-
rity. She expressed regret that MHS had not sufficiently explored these
issues and contended that an outcome-driven approach for professional
development had sidelined topics that did not have tangible results:

> What's the outcome? I don't know what the outcome of a
> [professional development] conversation about race and equity is,
> except for maybe you'll walk into your classroom the next day and
> approach it slightly differently. But it's not quantifiable; it's not
> grounded in data. So it's really hard to push when time together as
> an adult staff feels so fleeting. It's hard to push for agendas like that,
> when instead you can talk about how there's not enough time to build
> a senior project together, or there's not enough time to come up with
> this policy that we really need right now.

These critiques from several parents, teachers, and the former student illustrate the dual challenge of enacting familial cariño from an antiracist stance and supporting educators to undertake the ongoing individual and collective introspection necessary to ensure that caring relations nurture, uplift, and heal.

Confidentiality and Privacy

Familial cariño hinges on educators gaining a deep understanding of students' lives, interests, families, and communities. With this knowledge, educators can more readily build relational trust, develop culturally responsive curriculum, and provide psychosocial support. By judiciously sharing knowledge of students among themselves, teachers at MHS sought to enhance the network of support and ensure that no child fell through the cracks. In practice, the intimacy that accompanied familial cariño meant that teachers, staff, and peers were often privy to profoundly personal details about students' lives. Attesting to this, freshman Mateo reported, "This is a small school, and teachers, they know each other. They know the students, and they *really* know you." Ms. Glass, a math teacher, put it more bluntly, "We are up in everybody's business." She credited this deep involvement with keeping the campus safe and secure, especially from gang activity.

This intense intimacy had its liabilities. Four of 29 student focus group participants expressed uneasiness with such high levels of familiarity. As Carmen, a junior, shared, "Everything that happens in the school, you cannot hide it. All the teachers know. They just email a little too much. If you get in trouble, they email each other and at your next class your teacher already knows." Jaime, a junior boy prone to breaking rules, objected to how his transgressions often became public. "The office is trying to sneak into everyone's life. They're trying to be nosy." Expressing a more nuanced position, Alma, another junior, chaffed about how "the teachers gossip about us," but confessed to appreciating teachers' interest in her well-being. "I really like how at this school, whatever happens, if I have problems at home affecting me, they [teachers] take that into account—they really talk about it because they know that everything's affecting us." These students' observations illuminate the tension of personalism and privacy.

Phillippo (2012) documented this tension in three high schools in which educators' efforts to get to know students well at times conflicted with "students' preferences and cultural norms about discussing personal matters" (p. 454). Her research demonstrated how breaches of privacy and invasive personalism can erode trust and impair student–teacher relationships. Given that MHS students disclosed a range of personal concerns (including gangs, homelessness, alcohol/drug dependency, pregnancy, sexual abuse, legal status, bullying, etc.) in confidential settings such as advisory community circles, firewalks, and informal conversations, the determination of how, when, and whether to share knowledge of students' lives with others required extreme sensitivity and ethical discernment. The weight of such responsibility was brought home by a nationally recognized school reformer who observed firewalks and came away stupefied by students' vulnerability and disclosures. She expressed concerns about the psychologically intense issues discussed, possible violations of health privacy, and legal risks. The last included worries related to the omnipresent threat of immigration raids in the surrounding community. Fortunately, teachers seeking to support suffering students could avail themselves to the network of care, which included several community partners and health providers able to intervene if necessary. Taking such steps and navigating precarious contexts, though, illustrates the complexity of cultivating supportive teacher–student relations that respect students' privacy and still engender familial cariño.

Work Overload and the Specter of Burnout

Familial cariño necessitates a considerable expansion of educator roles. For example, Mr. Keo reported being not only a math teacher, but also "a counselor, security guard, door stopper, van/bus driver, advisor, health professional, and community panelist." Speaking to these demands, Mr. Simmons described the school as a "really special place to teach, but it's a very difficult place to teach because the expectations for you are very high. . . . You have to have your game on, and sometimes that can be pretty grueling." Having "your game on" involved showing up authentically on a daily basis to nurture students as bodymindspirit beings living within particular communities, cultures, and families. To meet the hungers of these youth, teachers extended themselves beyond paid duties. They tutored students outside of instructional hours and attended sports competitions, *quinceañeras* (15th birthday celebrations), political rallies/protests, and family religious observances (communions, baptisms, and funerals). Students recognized teachers' extraordinary efforts, expressing appreciation for their availability during lunch, after school, and on the weekends. "Whatever you need, they're there for you. Anything you need, they'll get it for you."

According to Luz, the scope and intensity of this work created a professional environment in which "everybody is a workaholic." As an outsider, I marveled at the energy, intensity, and commitment MHS teachers displayed as they collaborated to advance the school's mission. MHS staff maintained a light-heartedness that made their hard work not feel like grim drudgery. Several factors contributed to this culture. First, 65% of the faculty were under 30 years old, two-thirds were single, and less than a quarter had dependent children. These demographics allowed teachers to devote substantial discretionary time to MHS. Second, the school's social justice mission encouraged teachers to value beauty, hope, and joy in the midst of struggle.

Third, the faculty and administration intentionally set out to enjoy their work together. They adhered to what they called the "Ricardo Pryor" agreement (so-named after the comedian Richard Pryor), which required them to "have fun, demand joy, and celebrate each other." In this spirit, they launched meetings with team-building activities that usually elicited much laughter and solidified their connectedness. They also had a weekly ritual for publicly acknowledging colleagues' accomplishments and gestures of support (such as covering a class, being a critical friend, assisting an advisee, etc.). In addition, MHS conducted three multiday, overnight staff retreats each year (August, January, and June). These gatherings occurred offsite in places of natural beauty and featured a balance of collaborative planning, reflection, and recreation. The sense of community forged through retreats was augmented by weekend social gatherings during which staff converged to relax and blow off steam. Together, these activities deepened friendships and generated familial cariño among staff.

Despite these supports to nurture faculty well-being, the workaholic environment still took a toll. The stress of assisting marginalized students struggling with a range of chronic and complex traumatic circumstances prompted some teachers to leave. Ms. Glass left the school midway through her 3rd year. Explaining her departure, she said:

> I've had dreams about school every night for the last week or so. It's heavy on my mind. . . . I think that I am really burned out. . . . Teaching at MHS is a lot better in some ways than your average teaching position, but it requires a lot more of you as an individual than other teaching positions. It becomes your entire life. . . . I didn't feel like I really fit in that well with the staff, many of whom have their entire social lives made up of other teachers. . . . It felt many times like it wasn't enough socially for me to just be doing my job well. If I didn't come to happy hours, to whatever, I wasn't really doing enough. And then there's just doing the job, which is huge. There's so much more that we do as a school than other schools do, and that's a lot of what makes it effective, but also what makes it really hard to sustain.

Ms. Glass's being "really burned out" is a classic example of how work overload can spawn dissatisfaction and manifest in emotional exhaustion, a reduced sense of personal accomplishment, and detachment from students (Maslach, 1999; Maslach & Leiter, 1997). Ms. Schmidt, a 10th-grade humanities teacher, departed MHS after 5 years. In an email exchange with me, she wrote:

> I know the lack of boundaries at MHS [between students and teachers *and* between school and community] was why we were successful, but I also think it is what burns out teachers and drives many to leave. . . .

> I gave sooooo much of myself to the students and that school that
> when I left (which was tremendously hard), I knew it was an end of
> an era. I won't go back to 80-hour weeks and high blood pressure
> from the stress and worry and vicarious PTSD [post-traumatic
> stress disorder] . . . so while I miss the kids and the struggle and the
> challenge, I know I needed something new.

While Ms. Schmidt's account of working double the typical U.S. 40-hour
work week made her an outlier, her peers also reported long hours. On the
faculty survey, MHS teachers indicated working on average 65 hours a
week. Clearly, caring deeply for students was a labor-intensive endeavor
involving considerable stress.

That stress sometimes manifested in what Ms. Schmidt termed "vicarious PTSD," a condition also known as secondary traumatic stress (STS).
STS occurs when "trauma transfers from students to educators, particularly
teachers who interact regularly and closely with traumatized students"
(Lawson et al., 2019, p. 429). This transfer may occur "from listening to a
student's account of a traumatic event, reading or otherwise learning about
the event(s), and being repeatedly or extremely exposed to aversive details
of the event(s)" (Lawson et al., 2019, p. 429). During my intensive data collection year, MHS lost three youth to gun violence. These tragedies shattered the community and galvanized the school to launch a Peaceful City
Campaign (elaborated in Chapter 5). The cumulative impact of these losses
surfaced in anguished listserv exchanges. Following the homicide of Ernesto,
the third victim, Ms. Barrett shared, "I am deeply saddened, pissed off, and
feeling lost." Ms. Whitmore rhetorically asked, "How do you even express
this sadness?" And Ms. Dupont fumed, "I am so frustrated and don't know
what to say. He was my advisee and a great human being. Fuck this bullshit!
I am so angry!" Contending with profound loss taxed teachers enormously,
especially since in the midst of their own grief, they had despondent students
to comfort.

In an odd paradox, however, the raw humanity and deepening familial
cariño born of tragedy seemed also to touch educators' hearts in ways that
fortified their commitment to students, the school, and the community. For
example, an impromptu memorial held in MHS's teen center on a Saturday
afternoon less than 24 hours after Ernesto's passing attracted 100 people,
including eight teachers, a host of EDP coaches, classified staff, and community partners, as well as Ernesto's family and peers. Altars with pictures,
flowers, and santos candles set the scene, and César purified the space by
burning sage. As a community, we wept, we shared remembrances, and we
promised to embody Ernesto's love in our own lives. Many tributes were
spoken solely in Spanish without translation. Before departing, we each
tied a braided bracelet around another person's wrist, looked the re-
cipient in the eyes, and said, "You are not alone." We pledged to remember

Ernesto's legacy whenever we saw that bracelet encircling someone's wrist. The human connection present in that room confirmed Anzaldúa's (1987/2012) observation that "our greatest disappointments and painful experiences—if we can make meaning out of them—can lead us toward becoming more of who we are" (p. 68).

These sentiments surfaced in César's keynote graduation address 2 weeks later:

> When I found out that Ernesto was shot and killed, I screamed so loud, I hurt my voice. . . . Through dark times we have made it together . . . in the end, we must celebrate our community to push through tough times and find creative solutions. Our relationships to family, friends, and community are way more valuable. . . . Life is to be cherished.

César's insights reveal the comfort and joy inherent in familial cariño. For educators feeling the pain of assaults on their community and the pleasures of close ties with colleagues, students, and families, familial cariño represented a double-edged sword. Familial cariño carved their hearts open to love more deeply, but also left them scarred with lingering wounds.

For some teachers, vicarious PTSD and STS proved too much and prompted exit, but a considerable number remained in the struggle. To its credit, MHS retained teachers longer than most urban schools. In a longitudinal study of teacher retention in 16 urban public school districts in seven states, Papay et al. (2017) concluded that "13% to 35% of novices left their district after one year, while 44% to 74% left within five years" (p. 435). Against this metric, MHS teachers showed staying power. Of the 17 teachers who taught at MHS when this study began in 2011, four continued to teach there as of the 2019–2020 school year, and those who moved on stayed at MHS an average of 7.3 years. The foregoing discussion illustrates how familial cariño was *both* a source of overwork, burnout, and emotional distress *and* a catalyst for joy, love, and existential meaning. This tension is endemic to authentic relations rooted in familial cariño that aim to nurture youth, especially those from marginalized communities.

CLOSING REFLECTIONS

This chapter opened with the voices of MHS community members—a parent, a community organizer, a youth development coach, a teacher, a student, and an administrator—testifying to the unity, sense of belonging, and love engendered by a school committed to ensuring that all students were not only well known but also affirmed and given opportunities to become their best selves. MHS institutionalized familial cariño by intentionally engineering a network of care that enveloped students in multiple layers of support and emphasized the Habits of Life—empathy, courage, integrity, and curiosity. The sketches offered here of students, adults, and families engrossed in reciprocal relations and partaking in activities such as pot-luck meals, town hall assemblies, firewalks, camping trips, post-sessions, and interadvisory challenges illustrate how the MHS community co-created a culture of authentic cariño that was culturally congruent and attentive to members' bodymindspirits. While the enactment of familial cariño had its complications, its presence sustained students and adults in ways that enhanced the school's ability to promote academic engagement and pursue its social justice mission. In the next chapter, I examine how MHS managed to build on the bonds of familial cariño to promote students' intellectual engagement and growth.

CHAPTER 3

Intellectual Cariño

Cultivating Engaged Pensadoras

Our bold stance is we want kids to think critically and develop Habits of Mind. We're not just educating kids, but developing adults and citizens, so we need to look at who they are as people. . . . We are all really dedicated to this charge.

—Mr. West, Principal

We're asking kids to learn how to be good thinkers, not just getting through school for the sake of getting through school. . . . [by] teaching kids to think, to analyze, to debate, to have a perspective, to take a stand . . . we're creating lifelong learners who will be more likely to transform society because they're able to think critically about the society in which they live.

—Mr. Behari, humanities teacher

Ya tengo dos hijos que ya se graduaron de aquí. . . . Lo que me gusto a mi era de que se salieron a la universidad y que la nivel de académico es alto de Molina High. (I have two kids that already graduated from here. . . . What I like was that they went to college and the academic level at Molina High is high.)

—Alejandra, mother of three MHS students

MWC: How would you describe MHS to a student considering coming here?
Javier: The teachers stay after school, take extra time to help you.
Sylvia: Yeah, all the teachers stay after school to teach you.
Valentina: And you're never, like, sitting down. You're always doing something. It's hands-on.
Sylvia: And you learn better like that, like how she said, that you're not always sitting down and bored.

—Freshmen student focus group

Critical thinking. Lifelong learning. Rigorous academics. Hands-on learning. At MHS, these phrases, which surfaced repeatedly in my conversations with educators, students, and families, were not buzz words trotted out to impress visitors, but rather compelling ideals reflecting the school's mission to "engage" and "inspire" students through "transformative learning experiences." Galvanized by a vision of students becoming active *pensadoras* (thinkers)[1] eager and ready to succeed in college and act as community change agents, MHS educators enveloped youth in intellectual cariño—a solicitous and sustained care aimed at awakening students to the power and pleasure of using their minds well.[2] Viewing learning as much more than an interior, individual activity, MHS teachers grasped the affective and social dimensions of cognition. They constructed learning opportunities that invited youth to use their brains, hearts, and hands to understand the world and construct meaning as a community of learners.

Building on the robust student–teacher relations established through familial cariño, MHS educators strove to understand students as learners and enact pedagogies responsive to their needs, interests, histories, and communities. This orientation prompted teachers to pay careful attention to how students, both individually and collectively, perceived, processed, and reacted to learning tasks and to adjust instruction in ways likely to elicit students' deep engagement. At the root of this intellectual cariño was a desire for students to become confident and capable learners—learners who relished the challenge of solving difficult problems, deciphering inscrutable texts, and persuading others through reasoned argument—learners who enjoyed exploring perplexing ideas, imagining new worlds, contemplating ethics, and creating beauty. MHS educators believed that students fortified with and disposed to use such Habits of Mind (HOM) would possess a real-world intelligence that would enable them to successfully navigate multiple settings and enjoy purposeful lives rich with meaning and service.

The prominence of intellectual cariño at MHS meant that educators prioritized engaged learning *for life* over academic achievement *for school*. This priority represented MHS's desire to break with the status quo of many U.S. high schools that have pursued academic achievement in alienating rather than engaging ways. Constrained by persistent "school grammars" such as regimented bell schedules, Carnegie units, siloed subject departments, ability tracking, textbook-driven curricula, and accountability pressures (Tyack & Cuban, 1995), conventional high schools have long struggled to serve students well.[3] Evidence of this struggle appears in empirical accounts of bored students suffering through teacher-centered instruction and dreary fragmented school tasks and eagerly awaiting the ring of a bell to release them into the real world (Flores-Gonzáles, 2002; McNeil, 1986; Page, 1998; Pierce, 2005; Powell et al., 1985). Surveys of youth add to this bleak portrait. One survey of over 42,000 students from 103 high schools across 27 states within the United States found that two-thirds of adolescents reported being bored every day in school; they cited "uninteresting material" as their leading objection and "No interaction with teacher" as another (Yazzie-Mintz & McCormick, 2012). For low-SES youth of color, facing the added obstacles of deficit perspectives and assimilationist practices, high schools have proven to be subtractive places that devalue their intellectual capacities, home cultures, and languages (Valdés, 1998; Valenzuela, 1999). Against this backdrop, this chapter seeks to expand readers' views of what is possible when committed, caring adults embody intellectual cariño and intentionally organize a school around "transformative learning experiences."

INTELLECTUAL CARIÑO: ANALYTIC, RESPONSIVE, AND RIGOROUS

Before examining how MHS institutionalized intellectual cariño and promoted engaged learning, it is important to clarify the term. At its most basic, *intellectual cariño* is a fusion of two words. "Intellectual" within these pages describes individuals, often in the company of others, who think intelligently to make sense of the world while being attuned to their bodymindspirits and steeped in reverence for humanity (Facio & Lara, 2014; Lara, 2002). Cast in this way, "intellectual" conveys how thinking and the social construction of knowledge are activities that liberate individuals to understand themselves and their surrounding contexts in ways that enhance meaning, agency, and community. In the sphere of the classroom, intellectual cariño involves teachers modeling this kind of intellectual activity and making the teaching of such thinking a central and explicit feature of instruction. Such instruction depends on teachers possessing well-developed mental models of thinking—overarching and elaborated schemas that map out thinking processes; guide "how, when, and where to promote students' thinking"; and provide "the criteria for assessing thinking" (Ritchhart, 2002, p. 183).

"Cariño," the second half of this construct, draws attention to the caring, respectful, and reciprocal relations educators cultivate with and among students to enhance learning. Recognizing that intellectual activity arises from "the motivating sphere of consciousness, a sphere that includes our inclinations and needs, our interests and impulses, and our affect and emotion" (Vygotsky, 1987, p. 282), this cariño embraces students as whole beings, not as disembodied thinkers tasked with doing school. In anticipation of the potential frustrations and vulnerabilities students encounter as they learn, teachers guided by this cariño construct welcoming spaces "not to make learning painless but to make the painful things possible, things without which no learning can occur—things like exposing ignorance, testing tentative hypotheses, challenging false or partial information, and mutual criticism of thought" (Palmer, 1983/1993, p. 74).

This cariño, then, encompasses what some scholars have termed "hard care," whereby teachers pair nurturing instrumental relationships with high academic expectations (Antrop-González & De Jesús, 2006). In this sense, intellectual cariño is not all sweetness and light; it involves teachers persistently pushing students, even in the face of resistance, to discover and express the fullness of their bodymindspirit intelligence. Ultimately, this cariño nurtures positive human relationships within learning settings in the hope of enculturating students to see themselves as intelligent agents able to navigate and transform the world.

THE FOUR PILLARS OF INTELLECTUAL CARIÑO

At MHS, intellectual cariño rested on four pillars. These pillars, which buttressed MHS's culture of learning, were not officially codified but nonetheless shaped educators' work in profound ways. They initially emerged as themes from grounded analyses of MHS schooling practices and were subsequently refined through comparative analyses with existing literature. These pillars grounded MHS's curricular endeavors, providing stability and clarifying to all members of the community "This is what we care about." Put simply, these pillars conveyed to students the message "We care that each of you learn. We care that you use your knowledge and skills to make the world better. We care that your education helps you to become a better person in your own eyes, as well as in the eyes of your community. We care that you experience intellectual joy and the pleasure of using your mind well." The remainder of this section elucidates each pillar.

Pillar 1: Advanced Learning and Thinking Are Attainable by All Students

The first pillar holds that advanced learning and thinking are essential for and attainable by all students. While the oft-spoken phrase "All children can learn" has become an almost hollow reform slogan over recent decades, MHS embraced this belief earnestly. In contrast to tracked high schools in which a minority of students enrolls in college preparatory course sequences, all students at MHS fulfilled University of California and California State University "A–G" course requirements. This policy defied the longstanding practice of excluding nondominant students from such classes and placing them instead in "ESL ghettos" (Valdés, 1998) in which "dumbed-down" materials parse learning into simplistic, decontextualized, discrete tasks and topics (e.g., vocabulary, mechanics, and language errors) and thus inhibit deep content knowledge development (Bruna et al., 2007; Oakes, 1985; Page, 1998). MHS's graduation requirements ensured that all students experienced challenging curricula. These expectations signaled to students that they were all "reachable and teachable" (Ashton et al., 1982).

MHS also refused to allow students to do the bare minimum. Knowing that low GPAs impair eligibility for 4-year universities, teachers instituted a "no D" policy that forced students to master content or face recovering credits through independent study or retaking courses. This high bar encouraged students to invest themselves in their courses and strive for mastery.

As Ms. Clark noted, "We have high expectations, but we also know that kids can meet our expectations if we set them high. . . . They know that and they perform to our standards for the most part." These high expectations emerged quite clearly in teachers' survey responses. The prompts "Teachers at this school are committed to improving student achievement" and "This school has high standards for students' academic performance" garnered mean scores of 4.9 and 4.4 respectively on a 1–5 scale with 5 representing strong agreement.

Students echoed these reports, noting high levels of academic press from teachers. Carmen, a junior, recalled how teachers supported her through an academic slump:

> [The teachers] tend to see something we don't see in each other. . . . I started slacking off in my grades starting sophomore year. I was getting lazy; I was getting stressed and I'm like, "I don't want to do this anymore, I really don't see a point in it." I really wasn't looking ahead. But next thing you know, my advisor says, "Why are you slacking off? You know you're a smart student. You have to be responsible for all these things. You can make it far. Why are you not doing it?" And I would get really irritated, "Just get off my case." But he wouldn't. . . . They pull you aside and they have a serious talk. They remind you. You just can't believe someone's really there to support you like that.

The reference to teachers nurturing academic potential even when students themselves have not yet embraced their potential illustrates how educators working within an environment of intellectual cariño championed learning and thinking and academic success as worthy enterprises to which every student could and should aspire.

Along these lines, students and teachers reported frequent after-school tutorial sessions during which teachers coached struggling students until they mastered material. Emblematic of this practice, Mr. Tran shared:

> In terms of raising Latino success, I want students to believe that they are actually capable of succeeding. . . . There have been times when I've sat with a student on a certification [assessment task] for 4 hours, just sat there and worked with them, picked at their brain. They're like, "Why are you spending so much time with me?" "I'm spending this time with you because it's going to pay off at the end." And it's been true, where it's been 3 or 4 hours with a particular student, maybe two sessions, and they pass the certification after that. So it paid off. By working and making them think really hard, asking them tough questions, they were able to build that confidence. I'm also imparting philosophical ideas on them, just to have faith in themselves.

Mr. Tran's account illustrates how MHS teachers not only embraced the attainability of advanced learning but sought to convince students, especially those with diminished academic skills and confidence, to believe this proposition as well. Ms. Schmidt underscored this point:

> In some schools, there's a philosophy among teachers that if students want to learn, they will, and if they don't, that's their problem. I don't feel like any of us have that attitude. We're all very much selling the learning. We recognize that some of our students come to us not sold on school at all, and we find it to be our job to sell it to them. We want them to leave as people who are still curious and want to learn more, and I think we take a lot of responsibility for that.

Ms. Schmidt's remarks about "selling learning" convey how teachers demonstrated intellectual cariño by taking responsibility for enticing all students, even those lacking *ganas* (desire) and *empeño* (determination), to "want to learn more."

Pillar 2: Learning and Thinking Are Empowering

The second pillar of intellectual cariño asserts that learning and thinking are empowering activities that not only enhance one's experience in the world, but also enable social transformation. In accordance with hooks's (1994) view of "education as the practice of freedom," MHS educators embraced the idea that nondominant, low-SES Latinx students, when given the opportunity to engage in "transformative learning experiences" and develop the skills, knowledge, and habits necessary to succeed in college and beyond, could become change agents interrupting patterns of injustice and inequity. Ms. Glass explained:

> We are very explicit in talking about our goal as a school. It is not just "Go to college." It's "You, as a person of color in an oppressive society, go to college, educate yourself, become a doctor to change the healthcare fields because they're inequitable." . . . So we say "Educate yourself. . . . It's especially important that you, who you are, know that you can do anything you want and that these are the ways we're going to help you navigate the dominant culture to get there."

Her comments highlight how the social justice focus of MHS's mission linked schooling to community uplift and the transformation of inequitable structures.

MHS educators communicated this empowerment message during formal ceremonies, daily rituals, and student–teacher interactions. On the first day of school, students heard Principal West invoke Malcolm X's (1964) pronouncement that "Education is an important element in the struggle for human rights. It is the means to help our children and our people rediscover their identity and thereby increase their self-respect." EDP director Luz reinforced this theme with her call-and-response chant "Reading and writing are revolutionary!" Students heard this slogan daily prior to study halls and again before heading home.

To prepare students to navigate the dominant culture and become change agents, MHS promoted the HOM model (inquiry, perspectives, evidence, logical reasoning and analysis, and reflection/metacognition), framing it as a set of skills that would allow students to analyze, argue, and advocate in ways that would enable them to participate fully and effectively in college and careers, as well as in liberation struggles. In classrooms, HOM appeared in highly visible posters, daily learning targets, and assessment rubrics. The explicit focus on particular critical thinking processes moved teachers past the abstract rhetoric of "rigor" and prompted them to engineer a "thinking curriculum" (Resnick, 2010) in which the cognitive load was high and the content elicited students' interest and metacognition. Mr. Behari highlighted a radical rationale for MHS's intensive focus on HOM:

> There is a social justice element to teaching using the Habits of Mind. When you can think critically, you're not just accepting society for the way it is. People who think critically can see the ills, can analyze the ills, can break them down, and are the ones who advocate ultimately for social change. That's part of the mission.

Grounded in this paradigm, HOM became a "constant thread" weaving intellectual cariño into and across students' learning. As such, HOM functioned schoolwide to promote rigor and consistency throughout the curriculum and reify the mind as a tool for liberation.

Pillar 3: Learning and Thinking Are Complex Processes Enmeshed in Identity

The third pillar of intellectual cariño centers on the idea that learning and thinking involve complex, social, cognitive, cultural, and emotional processes that shape identity (Faircloth, 2012). Framed in this way, teachers are identity workers because their expectations and pedagogical choices contribute to students' identity construction in and beyond the classroom (Gutiérrez, 2013; Nasir & Hand, 2008). Enacting identity work with cariño means acknowledging students' "identities as negotiated, fluid, and multiple, rather than achieved, unitary, or consistent" (Faircloth, 2012, p. 187) and helping youth maintain a sense of personal integrity as they negotiate emerging identities and venture into unfamiliar terrains as pensadoras. Principal West explained that the work of expanding students' "overall vision of where they saw themselves going" could occur only when students were able to "connect their learning to something bigger that changed the way they saw themselves." Ms. Clark echoed this point, sharing that she and her colleagues hoped that an accumulation of "transformative learning experiences" would reshape "the way that students view[ed] themselves . . . [especially their sense of] what they can achieve and accomplish." Pointing out that schools are "fundamentally Eurocentric and White," Ms. Clark acknowledged, though, that students' academic journeys were fraught with identity challenges. Adamant that students should never "have to change who they are when they walk in the classroom door," Ms. Clark reported that the MHS faculty was always asking itself, "How are we working together to make sure that students' skills are always increasing and that students feel good about themselves?"

Committed to nurturing students' identities as capable learners and designers of their own futures, MHS teachers embraced interdisciplinary, project-based learning with performance-based assessments as a core pedagogy (Curry & Athanases, 2020). Claiming this was "something we do really well," Ms. Schmidt asserted that projects were "one of the hallmarks of our school . . . a way of engaging all students . . . [because] the products that students create are more meaningful. They're thinking deeper about the issue. It becomes a memorable, real learning experience for them." Her references to "meaningful," "memorable," and "real" hint at the ways projects engaged students' whole selves and departed from superficial "doing school" activities. Ms. Clark elaborated, explaining that MHS teachers were

> not teaching from textbooks. We're teaching very real-world skills, and also engaging students in understanding the world that they live in and the world around them. A lot of times . . . school is a disconnected entity from their lives, their communities . . . but when you do things like the Power of Food project in 9th grade or when you are a political pundit in 12th grade, when you're asking students to engage in the world they actually live in and look at it with a critical lens, those are all transformative learning experiences.[4]

Students valued this project-based approach. Camila, a junior, noted that while her friends at other schools struggled with "teachers [who] don't take the time to explain to the kids. . . . [who] give kids a textbook and say, 'Read this and do this worksheet,'" she had teachers who developed "hands-on projects" to "make you think." Project-based learning, then, constituted a key way teachers enacted intellectual cariño to promote students' intellectual growth and identities as real-world pensadoras.

MHS's project-based curricula reflected what my SOLES colleagues and I termed the five C's—Connection, Challenge, Culture, Communication, and Collaboration (Athanases et al., 2016).[5] *Connection* operated as a foundation for the other C's and surfaced in bonds of familial cariño between teachers and students and among students as established through instructional interactions. These interpersonal connections generated mutual respect, making it safe for students to take risks and engage in the rigorous work demanded by interdisciplinary projects. *Challenge* was reflected in the HOM model, as well as in efforts to promote "disciplinary literacy," the capacity to read and respond to "specialized and sophisticated" texts featuring "high levels of abstraction, ambiguity, and subtlety" (Shanahan & Shanahan, 2008, p. 45; see also Moje, 2015).

Culture involved harnessing culture and context as supports for learning. As Chapter 4 elaborates, MHS teachers regularly connected students' lives to topics of academic study and built on prior knowledge by accessing cultural, linguistic, and community resources (Irizarry, 2007; Ladson-Billings, 1994, 2014; Moll et al., 1992; Paris, 2012; Paris & Alim, 2014). Through activities such as the Digital Immigration Film Project (described in Chapter 2), the *Día de los Muertos Altar y Ofrenda* (Day of the Dead Altar and Offering) project, in which students paid tribute to loved ones, and the My Voice Matters personal radio narrative, which Letty in Chapter 2 referenced in her firewalk, students had sustained opportunities to connect their lives to school. Ms. Glass stressed, "The projects that are specifically around culture make kids feel a sense of connection to their family's past, their heritage, as well as a connection to seeing their future." By constructing opportunities and spaces that affirmed youths' multifaceted selves, MHS took seriously students' yearning for *"un mundo en donde caben muchos mundos,"* a world within which many worlds can fit (see Figure 2.4). This orientation toward culturally sustaining pedagogies distinguished MHS from urban schools in which hyper-accountability and hyper-standardization pressures have eroded culture-based instruction (McNeil, 2005; Royal & Gibson, 2017; Valenzuela, 2005).

The fourth and fifth "C's"—*Communication and Collaboration*—reflected MHS's commitment to ensuring that projects immersed learners, especially emergent bilinguals (EBs), into multivocal settings requiring sustained language production (Applebee et al., 2003; Valdés et al., 2007). Through debates, Socratic seminars, fishbowl discussions, cooperative jigsaw groups, Complex Instruction, and structured academic controversies, MHS teachers facilitated substantive conversations in which students responsively built on each other's contributions and jointly explored authentic questions (Cohen, 1994; Cohen et al., 1999; Glazer, 2018; Johnson & Johnson, 1988; Nystrand, 1997). In the survey, teachers indicated that students "collaborate[d] in small groups to complete academic tasks" and had "opportunities for extended student-to-student talk on academic topics" several times a week. This emphasis on dialogic pedagogies represented a noteworthy departure from widely documented classroom discourse trends in which teachers dominate and talk follows an IRE pattern (initiate–reply–evaluate). The rarity of genuine dialogue in U.S. classrooms (Applebee et al, 2003; Nystrand & Gamoran, 1991; Nystrand et al., 2001), especially in lower tracks, marked MHS's dialogic instruction as unusual.

Importantly, MHS's emphasis on communication and collaboration featured efforts to validate home languages, advance academic language, and promote metacognition around code-switching. Camila, a junior, observed, "they don't isolate us from talking Spanish. They actually want us to show and express where we're coming from."[6] Benicio, also a junior, added that teachers stressed the message "Learn how to code-switch. Learn how to deal with situations [like when to be] professional or not." Ms. Barrett recounted how she explicitly introduced code-switching as a way for students to use different registers and languages with different audiences (employers, teachers, parents, and friends) "to get what you want and need in your life." She guided students to understand "we all have multifacets, not just this one person, this one image that people have of us. So, you're not fake [when using academic language] necessarily; you're just emphasizing other pieces of yourself." Her acknowledgment of how language and identity are intertwined provided students a way to see how the use of academic, professional language did not necessitate sacrificing one's cultural identity or assimilating into the dominant society; rather, it was a means of getting desires and goals fulfilled. In this regard, Ms. Barrett, along with her colleagues, encouraged students to develop a mestiza consciousness (Anzaldúa, 1987/2012; Delgado Bernal, 2006), an awareness that accepts contradictions and ambiguities, juggles cultures, and embraces plurality. By incorporating the five C's into its project-based curricula and attending to the ways learning could enhance students' identities, MHS enveloped youth in intellectual cariño.

Pillar 4: Learning and Thinking Are Pleasurable

The final pillar of intellectual cariño hinges on the idea that transformative learning occurs only when teachers enable learners to experience the stimulation and joy of intellectual activity. This orientation toward learning as pleasure contrasts markedly with accountability orientations that construe learning as a competitive "race to the top" requiring teachers and students to work doggedly to improve scores and meet externally imposed benchmarks.[7] Too often in such contexts, the educational enterprise becomes a chess game with "a thousand serious moves" (Hafiz, 1996, p. 124) locking those who inhabit schools into a trance of problem fixation and grimness. While MHS was not spared these accountability pressures, educators resisted them with help from administrative buffering. Principal West, acknowledging his district's accountability orientation, noted that at times he felt "a lot of pressure to go to direct instruction on everything, go down to fine-grained skills, [and] get your test scores up." He and his staff chose instead to focus on the goal of "turning students on to learning" and cultivating lifelong learners who were "engaged and excited about learning." As Mr. Tran explained, "At MHS, we try our best as a staff to make school engaging and not the same mundane thing every day." These efforts often involved novel reconfigurations of school spaces, time schedules, and teachers' roles to elicit students' academic engagement and expand learning beyond the boundaries of classrooms.

Pillar 4 manifested in curriculum and instruction designed to activate students' "cognitive emotions" (Scheffler, 1977)—those affective responses that arise when a learner desperately yearns to understand something, becomes consumed by an intellectual pursuit, feels an intimate connection to a topic of inquiry, delights in solving a problem, or understands something previously opaque. Seeking to kindle students' excitement and fuel lifelong learning, teachers cared about students enjoying their classes. Mr. Avila epitomized this stance:

> Part of my philosophy of teaching is that teaching has to be fun and learning has to be fun. . . . If you include a lot of pleasure in what you teach and what the students learn, there's humor, there's fun, and kids always leave the classroom with a smile. . . . You don't want kids to leave your classroom and say, "I hate this class. I hate this teacher. I'm not gonna do homework today 'cuz I don't get it." I'm always looking for that piece of satisfaction where kids leave my class and they want to come back, and they want to bring their homework and share their homework and say, "Look, I got it! Because yesterday was fun, and this is the outcome of fun, I am learning."

Mr. Avila's colleagues voiced similar commitments. Ms. Clark shared, "I am always trying to be relevant and engaging to students. I'm always trying to let them enjoy themselves in the learning." Mr. Behari asserted, "The teacher's job is to make the curriculum as meaningful and interesting as possible. You do everything you can to make your curriculum valuable, to sell it, to convey it as valuable . . . to make kids like learning."

This emphasis on making learning pleasurable calls to mind Noddings' claim that the means and ends of education are inseparable. If a student succeeds at learning X, but in the end hates X (and possibly also the teacher who taught X), then instruction has failed because it has fallen short of the ethical imperative to ensure that students become "better" as a result of their schooling (Noddings, 1984, p. 174). At MHS, teachers believed that students became "better"—more likely to adopt identities as active and able pensadoras equipped to navigate life—when they had cumulative opportunities to play with ideas and experience learning as a fun, embodied, and generative process. Through dynamic activities such as dissecting frogs, constructing electrical circuitry boxes, debating the addictiveness of marijuana, enacting mock trials, and sculpting their bodies into tableaus of literary scenes, MHS teachers enlivened school. As 9th graders Valentina and Sylvia attested in one of the epigraphs to this chapter, students were engaged in "hands-on" activities and "never sitting down," which helped them to "learn better."

These efforts to infuse pleasure and play into learning did not compromise rigor. Explaining how curricular-based games or the infusion of rap music into a lesson might be fun, Mr. Behari faulted such approaches for too often becoming pedagogical "gimmicks" without substance. He insisted that students' cognitive emotions sprung to life when "the ideas themselves are interesting. The ideas, the concepts, the thinking, the thought processes behind the lesson are the interesting part, not the gimmick." At MHS, teachers leveraged the pleasure-inducing dimensions of thinking about complex ideas to entice students to engage in cognitively effortful activity. In focus groups, several students described their classes as both "fun" and "hard." For instance, Camila said Mr. Avila's Spanish class was "pretty fun and pretty hard. . . . It's difficult for me . . . [but] I feel like I like his class." Similarly, Alma effused, "I *love* Mr. Behari's class. He jokes about everything, but he can be really serious and gives us hard work." These students' positive regard for their learning matters because positive emotional engagement "focuses [learners'] attention on the task; promotes relational processing of information; induces intrinsic motivation; and facilitates use of flexible learning strategies and self-regulation" (Pekrun & Linnenbrink-Garcia, 2012, p. 269). Hence, student enjoyment has profound implications for students' learning, engagement, and academic performance. Intellectual cariño, therefore, involves teachers igniting students' passion through intellectually rewarding and emotionally gratifying learning activities.

Through adherence to these four pillars, MHS educators constructed a culture of engaged learning that allowed students to experience schooling as additive rather than subtractive. Table 3.1 summarizes these pillars and identifies ways they manifested in MHS's organizational practices.

INSTITUTIONALIZING INTELLECTUAL CARIÑO

Having gone some distance toward mapping the contours of intellectual cariño, I turn next to examining how MHS enacted intellectual cariño schoolwide. I highlight two key organizational structures that facilitated intellectual cariño and contributed to MHS's culture of engaged learning. First, I discuss how the staff's intensive collaboration as a professional community yielded internal accountability. Second, I elucidate how the school engineered an expansive learning ecology to optimize students' educacíon. Following this presentation, I bring readers inside five activity settings within this ecology to illustrate intellectual cariño's enactment in daily instruction,

Table 3.1. Four Pillars of Intellectual Cariño and MHS's Associated Practices/ Structures

Pillar	Practices/Structures
1. Advanced learning/ thinking is attainable by and essential for all	• Mandatory college preparatory course enrollment (A–G) for all • Robust academic press • Individualized academic support and guidance • No "D" policy • Block schedule to permit deep, sustained inquiry
2. Learning/thinking is empowering	• Mission statement reifying "transformative learning" as a path toward dismantling injustice and inequity • Habits of Mind • Emphasis on college, career, and community readiness
3. Learning/thinking involves complex processes enmeshed in identity	• Interdisciplinary, project-based learning • Culturally sustaining pedagogies • Teacher persistence in the face of student resistance • Encouragement to use home language
4. Learning/thinking is pleasurable	• Hands-on, meaningful, real-world learning activities • Innovative, dynamic assessments • Expanded learning beyond classrooms

academic rites of passage, internships, town halls, and post-session. I conclude with a discussion of some of the tensions MHS encountered as it institutionalized intellectual cariño.

Internal Accountability Through Robust Professional Community

The four pillars of intellectual cariño did not materialize out of thin air, but rather emerged from concerted effort and long hours of dialogue among educators and community members. Inspired by the reforms championed at Central Park East High School in New York (Meier, 1995), the Coalition of Essential Schools (Sizer, 1984, 1992), and Outward Bound's expeditionary learning model (Cousins, 1998; Farrell, 2000), MHS crafted a mission that reified "transformative learning experiences" as a means to interrupt injustice and inequity. Mission statements are often pro forma declarations cobbled together to appease external accreditation agencies and bolster a school's legitimacy in the eyes of others. MHS's mission, however, resonated deeply with teachers, inspiring them to work hard, innovate, and remain laser focused on transformative learning as an overarching goal. Their unity around this mission cohered them into a learning-centered professional community exhibiting high levels of internal accountability. MHS educators individually and collectively accepted responsibility for designing, implementing, and maintaining cohesive organizational structures to support students' deep learning (Abelmann et al., 1999; Newmann et al., 1997).

This internal accountability involved teachers identifying clear student performance standards, collecting data to monitor student performance, participating in sustained professional learning communities, and continually refining structures (formal and informal) to optimize learning.

At MHS, educators' collective commitment to the mission laid the foundation for a culture of learning suffused with intellectual cariño. Principal West noted, "We are definitely a mission- and vision-driven school" and as such, when "trying to hire staff and bring in teachers, the first question will always have to be, 'Is this person a powerful educator aligned with the school's mission and vision?'" MHS's success at assembling a faculty aligned with the mission was evident in teachers' visible enthusiasm for it. They announced the mission at the start of weekly meetings and posted it on every agenda. They invoked it as they developed and implemented curriculum and recited it spontaneously in interviews. A schoolwide survey highlighted their strong endorsement. On Likert statements (scaled 1–5, 5=strongly agree), MHS teachers agreed that "This school has a clearly stated goal" (4.8 mean); "The school is doing a good job in reaching its stated goal" (4.4 mean); "Faculty support the school's stated goal" (4.5 mean); and "Teachers at this school are committed to improving student achievement" (4.9 mean).

Their consensus served as a touchstone binding them together with moral purpose and fostering intensive investments of time and energy. As Ms. Whitmore observed, "I think teachers are very passionate about what they teach. They spend a lot of their time thinking about how to teach well." Echoing her, Mr. Avila expressed pride in being part of "a tremendous team of dedicated people that believe in interrupting the injustices of education." He credited this team with spurring him to work harder toward fulfilling the mission. His admiration suggests how the staff's professionalism and strong work ethic generated peer pressure to teach with excellence.

To fulfill its mission, MHS adopted a distributed leadership model in which educators shared responsibility for making students and the school successful. Mr. Simmons emphasized this aspect of the professional culture during the August staff retreat. Offering a historical perspective, he shared:

> When we founded the school, we wanted to make sure that all decisions were made as a group. The principal was not the person leading this group. . . . I find this to be a central strength and foundation of this school. I agree that first-year teachers have different priorities, but they need to understand that they will grow out of that, and they do need to participate in the decision-making. They must grow into becoming a leader. It's an expectation in this school that we will become leaders.

Mr. Simmons characterized teacher leadership as an expression of intellectual cariño and socialized newcomers to understand their obligation to care about and contribute to school operations in order to ensure students' optimal learning.

Teachers exhibited leadership in myriad ways. An instructional leadership team (ILT), comprising the principal, Luz (the EDP director), and two teachers (one from humanities and the other from science/math, each with one release period), coordinated the school's academic program. A professional development (PD) committee composed of the principal and four teachers organized 2.5-hour faculty collaboration sessions held weekly on Wednesdays, as well as annual staff retreats. Principal West expressed pride in the PD committee's work, highlighting how its "staff-led, well-thought-out, well-designed professional development . . . create[d] a community of learners where people are always in the growth mindset and they're constantly trying to get better at their work."[8] Teachers also expressed satisfaction with PD. Ms. Howard, recalling a retreat, reported, "I personally really enjoyed it because it changed my thinking. . . . We're allowed to be intellectuals, talking through issues in an academic and structured way." Mr. Tran concurred, describing PD as "very helpful" because it allowed faculty to "use theory." He explained, "We're using data to drive instruction. . . . We talk about good teaching practices; what does it mean to create a group-worthy task?[9] . . . to differentiate? . . . What does that look like in our classrooms?"[10] The marriage of theory and practice within PD provided sustained opportunities for instructors to discuss, model, and rehearse a range of best instructional practices such as Complex Instruction, recasting student language into academic language, and structured academic controversy. Given Sarason's (1990) astute observation that "it is virtually impossible to create and sustain over time conditions for productive learning for students when they do not exist for teachers" (p. 145), the robust internal accountability MHS teachers displayed in regard to their own professional learning fortified the school's culture of engaged learning and its expression of intellectual cariño.

Because teachers' professional development profoundly shaped instruction and students' learning, it is important to understand in broad strokes its substance. During my intensive data collection year, the PD committee identified three priority foci—assessment of student learning, student engagement, and instructional differentiation to accommodate students' varied academic needs, especially the needs of EBs and special education designees. Teachers launched the year with protocol-guided conversations in which they unveiled and vetted year-long course assessment plans. Orchestrated as teacher "firewalks," these sessions involved collegial critique aimed at refining assessments to ensure that they incorporated HOM, reflected high standards, and aligned with department frameworks for vertical articulation across the grades (see Appendix D). In one firewalk, humanities teachers validated Ms. Howard's decision to assess students' peer reviews of analytic writing but pressed her to reformulate the assessment so that it would include "real-world authentic audiences" and thereby make students appreciate "writing as a revolutionary tool." Conversations such as these not only deprivatized teachers' practice but allowed teachers to develop a comprehensive view of what students were learning across classes and grades in ways that inclined them toward caring about students' overall learning.

This orientation surfaced also in inquiry projects undertaken by the entire faculty to examine why some students failed culminating assessments. Explaining the philosophy undergirding this inquiry, Principal West said, "I never feel comfortable with failing a kid. That means it's a failure of us as an institution, that we're failing as well." To overcome such institutional failures, pairs of teachers, proceeding on the belief that systematic attention to students' thinking and learning would yield insights likely to improve instruction and student outcomes, investigated student perspectives by interviewing two students who had failed an assessment in their colleague's course. The pair then discussed students' responses, brainstormed remedies, and in some instances observed each other's classrooms to deepen feedback. Representative insights from these conversations included the need to cultivate stronger personal relations, differentiate tasks, and fine-tune scaffolds. Refusing to explain away student failure and locate deficits within students, these teachers instead scrutinized their own practices and built their capacity to reach and teach all students, thereby displaying intellectual cariño.

A final noteworthy element of MHS's PD centered on teachers' efforts to implement and debrief the senior investigative project. Intent on constructing a capstone "transformative learning experience" that would ensure students' readiness for postsecondary studies, career opportunities, and civic participation, teachers iteratively redesigned the project from year to year, tweaking features to improve it. They devoted several hours to rubric negotiation and collaborative review of student work samples leading up to students' final products and defenses. During the initial implementation years, Mr. Avila reported teachers being dismayed by "pretty bad" student performances and asking themselves "Why is that happening?" Realizing that students needed better preparation, the school decided to "challenge the students more" and instituted an interdisciplinary sophomore defense to better scaffold students toward masterful senior projects. According to Principal West, this shift reflected the understanding that "the consequence of rigor, if it's not scaffolded well and supported, is that kids fail out of the system and it just becomes a hurdle." Again, the staff's desire to promote student learning and prevent failure underscored how educators, committed to intellectual cariño, reconfigured learning opportunities to enhance intellectual growth.

Through these varied PD experiences and collaborative learning opportunities, MHS teachers strengthened their professional community and internal accountability. As Little (2006) argues, such learning-centered collegial work enables schools to make headway toward achieving goals in part by bolstering teachers' capacity to teach to high standards. By being well organized for professional learning and grounded in intellectual cariño, MHS positioned itself to "reap the benefits of demonstrable student gains and enduring teacher commitment" (p. 3).

Rich, Expansive Ecology of Learning Settings

Perhaps the most important outgrowth of MHS educators' collaborative work was the creation of a rich, expansive ecology of learning settings organized to support students' holistic growth as active pensadoras. These settings, many of which were introduced in Chapter 2's discussion of the "network of care," included classrooms, advisory, internships, EDP, town halls, post-sessions, and rites of passage such as firewalks and defenses. MHS educators worked strategically to coordinate these settings so that students' movements from classroom to classroom, from school to home, from peer activity settings to other community sites cumulatively enhanced learning and engagement. This ecology mirrors Gutiérrez and Larson's (2007) ideal of an expansive, interconnected range of activity settings "saturated with tools, forms and networks of support, and a variety of ways of organizing learning" (p. 73).

Figure 3.1 displays the key features of the school's ecology laid against the backdrop of the broader communities of family, neighborhood, city,

Figure 3.1. MHS's Ecology of Learning Settings

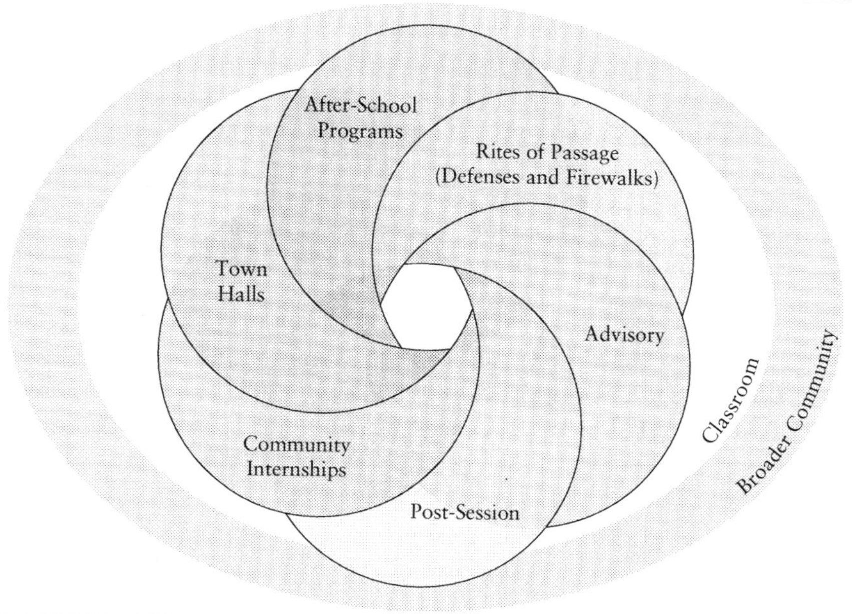

state, nation, and world. Of note in this graphic is the way in which various settings overlap to convey both how participants traversing from one setting into another carried some residue of prior settings and how the purposive overlap of settings afforded opportunities to intensify participants' learning. The overlapping areas also convey the complex, layered nature of learning and social identity since participants absorb a range of diversified resources, funds of knowledge, Discourses,[11] and dispositions as a consequence of inhabiting these multiple settings. To illuminate the affordances of MHS's various activity settings, I turn next to finer grained portrayals of student learning to illustrate intellectual cariño.

Intellectual Cariño in Classroom Settings

"Our instructional time is sacred." This phrase, a rebuff from Ms. Clark to a newly assigned district literacy coach who had proposed administering reading tests during core academic classes, illustrates the extent to which MHS educators valued and protected instructional time. Ms. Clark's stance corresponds with views that classrooms and the arrangements therein—instructional routines, teacher roles, materials, and student activity—are the "technical core" of schools, largely responsible for determining the success or failure of educational organizations (Meyer & Rowan, 1977, 1978; Rowan, 1990; Scott, 1997). Given the "sacred" role of instruction, classrooms occupy a central position in Figure 3.1's representation of MHS's learning ecology. Historically, the technical core of U.S. schools has been marked by enduring continuities such as the "persistence of whole group instruction, teacher talk outdistancing student talk, question/answer format drawn largely from textbooks, and little student movement in academic classes" (Cuban, 1982, p. 117). My colleagues and I entered MHS interested in how novel configurations of the technical core might account for the school's success as evidenced in metrics such as college-going rates, college preparatory course completion rates, and standardized achievement scores (see Table 1.1). To investigate this proposition and understand how and to what extent teachers' instruction elicited Latinx students' engagement in academically challenging work, we examined six focal classrooms (three humanities, one Spanish, two math). The quotidian quality of observed lessons initially perplexed us. Ms. Barrett, a seasoned educator responsible for coaching novice teachers, conjectured that beyond highly engaging project-based activities, much instruction was conventional. "I definitely don't think we're doing state-of-the-art instruction or brand-new techniques." Despite first impressions and Ms. Barrett's assessment, as we mined the data further, we came to appreciate how students benefited from solid day-to-day instruction delivered by culturally attuned, capable teachers. While some readers may express the view that such instruction was "just good teaching," Gloria Ladson-Billings (1995) reminds us that pedagogical excellence has often been lacking in classrooms populated by Brown and Black youth. Overall, the instruction we observed reflected intellectual cariño and provided a firm foundation for a culture of engaged learning, which found its fullest expression in interdisciplinary projects and settings beyond the classroom. Before examining those expanded settings, I wish to give readers a window into daily "routine" instruction to demonstrate why Ms. Clark and her colleagues viewed what transpired in classrooms as "sacred."

The classroom instruction findings presented here draw on videotaped observations of six lessons per focal teacher (39 hours total with an average of 6.5 hours per class) as well as several informal, spontaneous observations of focal classes conducted when focal teachers invited researchers to observe particular activities. Additional data include three 1.75-hour-long semi-structured interviews with focal teachers, focus group interviews with focal students representing a range of academic performance and English language proficiency, and finally, an archive of instructional material and student work associated with each observed lesson. Analysis of these data involved qualitative and quantitative procedures. Holistic reviews focused on dynamics such as student–teacher dialogic interaction, quality of student engagement, and knowledge construction.

Quantitatively, we used the CLASS-S protocol (Pianta et al., 2006, 2012) and two elements from the Center for Research on Education, Diversity, and Excellence's Standards Performance Continuum (CREDE/SPC) (Hilberg et al., 2003) to assess a range of teacher–student instructional interactions associated with enhanced student motivation and learning (Allen et al., 2011; Doherty & Hilberg, 2007; Doherty et al., 2003). CLASS-S assesses 11 dimensions—negative climate, positive climate, teacher sensitivity, behavior management, content understanding, analysis and problem solving, productivity, regard for adolescent perspectives, quality of feedback, instructional learning formats, and student engagement—along a 7-point scale with low levels scored 1–2, mid-levels 3–5, and high levels 6–7. In order to boost the "fit" between the CLASS-S instrument and our research focus on nondominant learners' academic growth and engagement, we included two additional measures from the CREDE/SPC instrument—language/literacy development and contextualization/connections to student life. We adjusted the 4-point CREDE/SPC scale to align with the 7-point CLASS-S scale. We clustered these 13 constructs by the five C's (connection, challenge, culture, communication, and collaboration) (see Appendix E for a summary of instructional dimensions[12]). To contextualize focal teachers' instruction, I also compared MHS's aggregate ratings against samples from two research studies. Table 3.2 shows that MHS scores were consistently in the mid to high range and exceeded comparison samples by an average of 1.2 points. These results suggest that instruction at MHS was accomplished and effective. In what follows, I present classroom findings organized by the five C's.

Table 3.2. Descriptive Statistics (M & SD) of CLASS-S® & CREDE/SPC Dimensions Across Three Studies

5 Cs			MHS	MET	MTP
	Teachers (n)		6	698	78
	Grade levels		9–12	7–9	7–12
	% of Latinx students		82	31	5
	% of students eligible for free/reduced lunch		93	56	31
Connection (Familial cariño in the classroom)	Absence of a negative climate (NC)	M	7	6.4	6.6
		SD	(.0)	(.51)	(.44)
	Positive climate (PC)	M	6.2	3.9	4.2
		SD	(.49)	(.69)	(.74)
	Teacher sensitivity (TS)	M	5.9	3.9	4.4
		SD	(.61)	(.64)	(.68)
	Behavior management (BM)	M	5.7	5.5	5.3
		SD	(.88)	(.69)	(.74)
Challenge (High rigor and expectations)	Content understanding (CU)	M	5.1	3.5	3.7
		SD	(.98)	(.67)	(.61)
	Analysis and problem solving (APS)	M	4	2.3	3.0
		SD	(1.07)	(.62)	(.63)
	Productivity (P)	M	5.4	5.5	5.1
		SD	(.92)	(.69)	(.64)
Culture (Lived contexts)	Regard for adolescent perspective (RAP)	M	4.7	2.8	3.5
		SD	(1.06)	(.72)	(.66)
	Contextualization/connections to student life[a] (CNTX)	M	3.9	–	–
		SD	(1.79)		
Communication and Collaboration (Language-rich activity)	Quality of feedback (QF)	M	4.8	3.1	3.9
		SD	(.77)	(.66)	(.75)
	Language and literacy development[b] (LLD)	M	4.2	2.8	–
		SD	(1.54)	(.67)	
	Instructional learning formats (ILF)	M	5.5	3.8	4.2
		SD	(.64)	(.67)	(.65)
	Student engagement (SE)	M	4.8	4.3	4.6
		SD	(.89)	(.63)	(.75)

1	2	3	4	5	6	7
	Low			Mid		High

a. This dimension was added from the CREDE/SPC instrument and therefore has no comparisons.

b. Because of considerable overlap between the more recently added CLASS-S dimension of instructional dialogue (ID) and the LLD dimension of CREDE/SPC, I included the ID score from the MET results as a comparison.

Note: This table displays 11 CLASS-S and two supplemental CREDE/SPC dimensions (CNTX and LLD) clustered by the five C's of connection, challenge, culture, communication, and collaboration. MHS instruction exhibited mid to high levels of accomplished performance (scores over 4.5 shaded in gray), surpassing comparisons. The Measures of Effective Teaching (MET) study (Kane & Staiger, 2012) involved a random national sample of math and ELA teachers from six states who were observed four to eight times. The MyTeachingPartner (MTP) Study (Allen et al., 2011) involved Virginia teachers from 12 schools who were observed six times. MET and MTP statistical data were extracted from Pianta et al. (2012, p. 118).

Connection. The first trend we observed across focal classes was the presence of interpersonal connection among teachers and students. Teachers established safe, orderly, and affirming learning environments (absence of negative climate, presence of positive climate, and effective behavior management), garnering a high mean rating of 6.3 on the CLASS-S scale. These features, which overlap with familial cariño, reflected teachers' desire to nurture students' sense of belonging and have been linked to Latinx students' academic engagement (Cooper, 2013). Scorers' written notes contain repeated references to classrooms in which teachers and students exhibited mutual respect and camaraderie through playful joking, personal storytelling, laughing, handshakes, and fist bumps. Students in focus groups expressed affection and gratitude to their teachers. The comments summarized in Table 3.3 underscore how teachers' cariño manifested in efforts to connect to students as people, support students during academic struggles, offer encouragement, listen, and generally treat students with kindness. Students' positive regard for and rapport with focal teachers appeared to bolster students' willingness to undertake challenging academic work.

Challenge. Instructional interactions within focal classrooms received high mid-level scores related to challenge and rigor (content understanding, analysis and problem solving, and productivity). MHS's composite mean score of 4.8 situated focal classrooms above comparisons (3.7 in MET and 3.9 in MTP). Mid-level CLASS-S performance is associated with occasional (yet uneven) opportunities to (a) explore content in meaningful ways with attention to broad, organizing concepts; (b) participate in challenging tasks involving complex problem solving; and (c) engage in focused tasks without unnecessary distractions or waiting periods. Scorer notes related to challenge referenced instances in which students made connections between literary themes, character development, and figurative language to formulate arguments; engaged in higher order critical thinking as they elaborated

Table 3.3. Students' Characterization of Focal Teachers

Teacher (Focal Class)	Student Comments from Focus Groups
Mr. Avila (Spanish 3 for heritage speakers)	• He makes it fun. . . . If you don't get a certain topic, he stays after school. . . . He actually does care about us. . . . He knows our strengths and weaknesses and where we're reaching to . . . I feel like he motivates you. (Camila) • He's like a father. (Demetrio)
Ms. Barrett (9th-grade English)	• She is nice. . . . She is there to help you. She is always trying to help. (Javier) • She always helps anybody. She takes the time to help each person. (Renata) • She writes notes, just to say, "Keep your head up," that she was gonna be there for me. . . . She encourages me to do better. (Yasmin)
Mr. Behari (11th-grade humanities)	• He's really nice. He's fun. I don't get bored at all. He has his way to teach the class, and you have entertainment with him. He's fun. (Jaime) • He's just a good teacher. (Hector) • I really think he's committed to his job. (Alma)
Ms. Clark (9th-grade reading)	• She helps us. . . . She is open to who we are. . . . She supports us and helps us out. (Claudia)
Mr. Keo (9th-grade math)	• He's a good listener. And now and then during class sessions he gives me a little advice and tries to help me out. He's my second therapist. (Julio) • He doesn't judge you. He helps you no matter what. (Sylvia)
Mr. Tran (11th-grade geometry)	• He's a good teacher. . . . He's never in a bad mood. He's always nice. (Juliana) • He's willing to stay after school and help you. (Marisol)

geometry concepts while responding to a series of probing teacher queries; hypothesized possible correlations between fast-food restaurant location/density with population demographics; and discussed confusing text passages in pairs to unpack meaning. Because these interactions demanded that students employ HOM and disciplinary literacy (Shanahan & Shanahan, 2008), they reflected MHS's embrace of intellectual cariño, especially Pillar 1 (challenging academic work for all). Hector, a junior, confirming this view, expressed gratitude for how Mr. Behari challenged him to use his mind well. "Mr. B teaches well. He changes our way of thinking a lot, but he also pushes me a lot because he expects a lot from me."

On occasion, we also observed lessons that lacked challenge. Less successful interactions included activities in which students summarized passages in a novel but refrained from meaningful exploration of the text; decorated two sentences on index cards rather than undertaking extended writing, analysis, or metacognition related to the ideas referenced in the sentences; and practiced basic literacy skills by looking up words in dictionaries. Overall, challenge appeared to be present fairly regularly in MHS classrooms, but it was not consistently sustained across activities.

Culture. MHS's composite-mean score for culture as measured by the dimensions of regard for adolescent perspectives, teacher sensitivity, and contextualization/connections to student life yielded a composite score of 4.8. While this indicator lacks a full comparison because we added the CREDE/SPC contextualization indicator to acknowledge the importance of home and community connections for culturally, linguistically, and economically diverse students, the respective MET and MTP composite scores were 3.4 and 4.0. Once again, MHS scores fell in the high mid-range and reflected instructional interactions in which (a) students sometimes shared ideas/opinions and exercised choice in topics of study and (b) teachers sometimes connected content to life experiences and expressed interest in students' concerns, questions, and problems. Evidence of MHS teachers tapping cultural and linguistic resources surfaced in content related to the experiences of youth of color and urban living (e.g., Guatemalan war, poverty, violence, food deserts, immigration, graffiti, and racism). In several observed interactions, students explored topics closely linked to their personal lives, sometimes peppering their oral participation with Spanish. For example, in one class, students recounted and explained their elders' disdain for rap music and narco-corridos (Mexican ballads glorifying the drug trade). In another observation, students discussing Anna Deveare Smith's book *Twilight Los Angeles* referenced a gang-related fight that had occurred in their neighborhood the day before. In a math class, students analyzed census statistics from neighborhoods within their city.

Not surprisingly, culture was especially honored in the Spanish class. We observed students frequently sharing personal stories drawing from prior knowledge to examine an array of topics, including the injustices suffered by day laborers, the dangers posed by vigilante groups patrolling immigrant crossing routes into the United States, and heritage traditions. This last item was more than a "foods and faces" cursory treatment and involved students undertaking substantive research on subjects such as the Aztec calendar, *La Lucha Libre* (Mexican wrestling), *La Llorna* (the weeping woman), and *el molcajete and tejolote* (indigenous stone tools for grinding food).

In these ways, MHS teachers, in accordance with Pillar 3 of intellectual cariño, incorporated students' lived realities into the classroom and affirmed home cultures and communities, communicating to students that they did not need to sacrifice identities and community connections in order to participate successfully in school. While the culturally sustaining interactions described demonstrate how MHS teachers managed to incorporate cultural resources on a fairly regular basis, their scores also indicate room to weave these resources even more deeply into instruction.

Communication and Collaboration. Dimensions related to communication (quality feedback, language and literacy development, instructional learning formats, and student engagement) earned a composite mean score of 4.8, while the respective comparative scores for MET and MTP were 3.5 and 4.3. Again, scores in the 3 to 5 range constitute mid-level performance and reflect interactions in which (a) learning objectives are identified, (b) teachers sometimes facilitate student participation through questioning and encouragement in ways that generate feedback loops and extend understanding, and (c) students occasionally engage in sustained language expression (10 minutes) with teacher guidance and modeling in small groups. One example of a higher scoring lesson featured small groups of students discussing and analyzing the descriptive imagery and evocative dialogue in Amy Tan's novel *The Joy Luck Club* in a fishbowl arrangement. To prepare for this discussion, Mr. Behari invited colleagues who had prep periods during his 11th-grade humanities class to join him to model what a book club discussion among adults looked and sounded like. Congruent with Pillar 4's accent on learning as pleasure, he prefaced this activity with the hope that students would become lifelong readers who enjoyed reading. "I want you guys to sit around a table when you're older and talk about books, just because it's fun. . . . It expands your brain. . . . It makes you think about the world in a new way." Through *The Joy Luck Club* discussion, students engaged in sustained, 35-minute, student-led dialogue in which participants conversed organically, referencing text from the novel to support and refute positions, chaining exchanges to collaboratively construct meaning, and exploring themes of bicultural identities and healthy communication in relationships. Jaime, the student facilitator, who incidentally was classified as a special education resource student, shared his main takeaway: "You cannot know yourself without knowing your roots." His remark highlights the ways in which student-centered, dialogic learning promoted healthy, ethnoracial identity development and, as such, reflected intellectual cariño's attention to the complex, social, cognitive, cultural, and emotional processes involved in learning (Pillar 3).

Another notable series of language-rich dialogic interactions occurred in geometry when students involved in a Complex Instruction activity (Cohen, 1994) grappled with a group-worthy problem related to the height/base ratios of triangles. At the outset, Mr. Tran explicitly underscored the importance of students solving the problem through dialogue and provided models of the kinds of talk he expected. (See Figure 3. 2 for his PowerPoint guidance.)

Figure 3.2. Geometry Group Work Expectations

Today's Group Work Themes

Everyone Contributes

- No one person can solve this problem alone—everyone must be involved.
- Ask "What do you think?" "How do you see it?" "What do you want to try?"

Repeat Back What You Heard

- Make sure you understand your teammates' ideas by saying what you understood.
- "So you're saying we need to. . ." "Do you mean that we should. . .?" "What do you mean by. . .?" "I get where you said. . . , but I'm not sure I get. . ."

During students' collaboration, Mr. Tran periodically interfaced with student groups to probe and push understanding, asking questions such as "So what did you notice? And what does that mean to you? How can you tell that?" These instructional moves functioned as contingent interactional scaffolds creating productive feedback loops that extended students' thinking, disciplinary knowledge, and HOM (Athanases & de Oliveira, 2014). Focal students indicated feeling some level of frustration when Mr. Tran refused to supply answers, but they understood that "he wants us to figure it out as a team and not just ask help from the teacher." One representative student indicated that the groups were "helpful at times, 'cause I get to ask my teammates if they know how to do it and they help me." This kind of student-to-student talk and peer assistance has proven especially helpful in assisting EBs develop competence (Cohen et al., 1999).

Of course, not every observed interaction afforded opportunities for substantive, multivocal dialogue. Interactions receiving lower scores included segments in which students had no sustained time for reading, writing, or speaking, or when students were placed in cooperative arrangements, but opted to work side-by-side independently rather than talk. In general, though, observations confirmed Mr. Trung's view that MHS teachers functioned as literacy teachers regardless of their disciplines and, consequently, organized instruction to support students' acquisition of the academic English and literacy skills needed to engage productively in higher order cognitive tasks.

Overall, the solid day-to-day classroom instruction we observed in focal classrooms reflected intellectual cariño because students were engaged in activities that affirmed their intelligence, challenged them to use their minds well, and expanded their identities as pensadoras able to inhabit the worlds of school and home. That said, the learning in classroom settings seemed fairly conventional and, as such, did not fully realize the mission's ideal of engaging "transformative learning." Pondering this, Ms. Barrett credited learning settings beyond the classroom as making MHS "more of a transformative place. . . . It's the whole experience here, the personalized attention, the other pieces that we offer that make MHS more transformative." I turn next to the transformative "other pieces" that unfolded in other settings within MHS's learning ecology.

Intellectual Cariño Beyond Classrooms

We observed numerous occasions in which learning transpired in stimulating and transformative ways outside classrooms. In these settings, intellectual cariño surfaced in activities designed to strengthen students' healthy identity development and generate pleasurable learning experiences. Such activities expanded "the object of learning to include the relationships between traditional school text, the context of discovery, and the context of practical application, thus transforming the activity of school learning itself from within" (Engström, 1991, p. 256). Expanded learning transpired in performance-based assessments engineered as rites of passage, workplace internships, student-led town halls, and post-sessions. The following section offers descriptive snapshots of these four spheres to underscore their dynamic, multifaceted nature.

Senior Investigative Projects and Defenses as Rites of Passage. When asked about MHS's core learning activities, Principal West underscored how "transformative learning experiences" were accomplished through a set of annual "high-leverage," "high stakes" interdisciplinary projects that engaged students in performance-based assessments of increasing rigor over the course of their high school career. He shared:

> I would say project-based learning is at the heart [of realizing our mission]. . . . The idea of defense, that students have to defend their arguments publicly, to panels, at various checkpoints. . . . there's this value of everybody having some say in who you are as an individual, whether it be your 10th grade classmates, whether it be advisors that are watching your defense, members of the community, staff that taught you the 9th grade to the 12th grade, they all have a say in whether or not you ultimately get to graduate. So there is that value that you're not just performing for me in my class, you're performing for the whole community.

His choice of the word "heart" conveys how culminating assessments and especially defenses were not only central features of MHS's learning culture but also important institutional rituals that pumped vitality into the school community. The metaphor of "heart" also captures how these assessments were expressions of intellectual cariño in that administrators cared enough about them to structure calendars, bell schedules, and courses around them and channel considerable resources toward their maintenance (not to mention defend them to district authorities as better assessments than district-wide benchmark exams).

The pinnacle of project-based learning at MHS was the year-long senior investigative project, which required students to demonstrate mastery of HOM prior to graduation. These projects involved researching self-selected, health-based topics usually related to internships, but sometimes chosen because of personal connections or curiosity. This thesis-driven project asked students to apply the scientific method; locate, read, and distill relevant articles; and interview an expert. Seniors synthesized inquiry results into research papers and PowerPoint presentations containing literature reviews, methods, findings, discussions, conclusions, and MLA citations. Students' advisors played a central role by approving research questions and proposals early in the year, helping revise final papers, and chairing defense panels. The dialogic process of preparing the paper with an advisor's guidance and then defending it also reflected the C's of communication and collaboration since students had to display HOM by effectively articulating their reasoning and knowledge to members of the community.

Senior defenses were climactic, intense rites of passage involving the entire MHS community. Students' advisory cohorts contributed to the experience by acting as dress rehearsal audiences, providing encouragement, and attending defenses. As Mr. Tran noted, "There's this culture of sophomore defense and senior defense, where everyone's pushing each other, the advisory's pushing the sophomores to pass, the seniors are getting encouragement." All the swirling and building attention culminated during 3 days in May when a special bell schedule permitted the entire school, as well as dozens of community members and internship mentors, to participate in defense panels. Although each defense was expected to last 45 minutes (5 minutes introductions, 15 minutes presentation, 10 minutes question and answer, 10 minutes for evaluations, and 5 minutes transitions), many sessions lasted over an hour with question and answer periods extended to more than 30 minutes. Seniors shared projects on a range of topics, including home birth, marijuana addiction, Planned Parenthood, asthma, the Affordable Care Act, miscarriages, bone marrow transplants, kleptomania, and waterborne diseases in Nicaragua. On presentation days, we observed students rehearsing their speeches in hallways before small groups of peers and offering reassurance to one another, panelists posing challenging questions and pressing students to elaborate evidence and arguments, parents publicly (and sometimes tearfully and in Spanish) expressing admiration for their children's accomplishments, and students shrieking and hugging each other in the aftermath of successful performances.

Rafael, for example, presented his project on Internet addiction (IA) to an audience that included two intern mentors from a local Internet company, a city employee who mentored him his junior year, students, his mother, a university professor, a reporter, his advisor, and another MHS teacher. Poised and prepared, Rafael advanced his slides seamlessly, making eye contact with his audience as he explained parallels between IA and gambling addiction. He detailed the student survey he conducted to assess his peers' Internet usage. Arguing that current treatment models for IA were inadequate, he concluded with recommendations for new approaches. During the question and answer period, Rafael fielded challenging questions and disclosed his own IA and recovery journey. This personal disclosure highlighted the ways in which seniors often predicated their research on compelling, personal concerns and used their investigations as a means to make sense of lived experiences.

Following his presentation, Rafael exited the room and the audience began its evaluation. Eleventh graders filled out reflection forms indicating successful elements of the performance while the scoring team (advisor, teacher, and professor) used a rubric to guide public deliberation. The scorers lauded Rafael's professionalism and synthesis of content knowledge but expressed concern about the absence of interview data that would have qualified as meeting the assignment guideline regarding evidence. They weighed this omission against Rafael's metacognitive self-critique regarding this choice and his use of survey data. In the end, they penalized him for not following the guidelines and not sufficiently analyzing survey results. This latter concern demonstrated scorers' desire to hold Rafael accountable for knowledge (Michaels et al., 2007) and ensure that the evidence underpinning his conclusions was accurate and persuasive.

When Rafael reentered the room, the audience took turns sharing the strengths of his presentation. At this point, his mother offered a long tribute in Spanish, choking up as she expressed pride in seeing her eldest child present so well. Then, the long-awaited moment arrived when scorers revealed their final assessment. Upon hearing the verdict of pass with honors (a point away from distinction), Rafael bowed his head, put his hands over his glasses, and sobbed. Moved by his emotion, his mother went up and embraced him. They wept together in a long hug while the audience absorbed the poignancy of the moment and the magnitude of Rafael's accomplishment. Clearly, his project and defense entailed both intellectual and affective processes that held significant identity-shaping possibilities.

This snapshot of Rafael illustrates how these annual rituals came to assume symbolic importance at MHS. The principal explained that the involvement of younger students as evaluators and audience members was a conscious design choice to seed images of the future in students' minds. Given the range of performance levels (33% of Rafael's class passed with honors or distinction, another 33% passed, and 34% did not pass on the first round and had to re-present their research and/or revise research papers in order to graduate), student observers were in essence apprenticed toward understanding what mastery of HOM looked and sounded like in practice. This wide participation set the tone for students' entire school experience and made transparent MHS's high expectations for critical thinking and transformative learning.

The presence of community members added authenticity and further amplified the impact of students' research. Reflecting on the value of the senior project/defense, Linda, a senior, shared:

> You obviously are gonna use all the skills that you learned because in college and just in life in general you're gonna have to advocate for yourself. Advocating for yourself is a really big skill that they teach you here, and presentation skills as well—how you present yourself and when you do a presentation, how well can you speak to an audience. They obviously prepare you really well for that because in sophomore defenses, senior defenses, and other projects, you have to talk in front of people.

Linda's remarks demonstrate how the senior defense (and other projects) expanded learning beyond "doing school" and became a vehicle to promote confidence and competence. Linda's recognition that rites of passage such as the senior defense prepared students "really well" for college and "life in general" also underscores how these assessments became meaningful activities deserving of youth's time and energy. Because students understood that the designers and facilitators of such rites of passage cared deeply about their preparation for college and life, these assessments were important vehicles through which MHS expressed intellectual cariño.

Internships as Windows into the World of Work. As part of its social justice mission to diversify health professions and improve community health, MHS required all juniors and seniors to participate in year-long internships. Typically, students spent two afternoons each week interacting with adult mentors from health-based or community-based organizations. This setting within MHS's learning ecology reflected intellectual cariño because it enabled students to connect school knowledge to real-world problems and phenomena and forge affirming relationships with adults embedded within institutions of power. Stanton-Salazar (2001) emphasizes the importance of such experiences, arguing that healthy development and social mobility depend on students' access to and participation in institutional settings that generate social capital. Through mentor relationships, youth receive "vital resources and institutional support that enable young people to become effective participants within mainstream institutional spheres" (p. 20).

Dolores, a Latina community-based partner and MHS founder, extolled the benefits of internships:

> What a gift for those kids. They're not only prepared academically when they leave the school, but they are prepared for life in some sense. They know what it's like to be responsible, going to work, dressing in a professional way, behaving in a professional way, leaving behind the little kid behavior.

Dolores's remarks suggest how internship settings heightened students' capacity to navigate multiple worlds and thereby "prepared them for life." Camilla, a junior, concurred, sharing "Internships open your mind to the future. You're like, 'Damn, I want to see myself like that [mentor].'"

Although observations of internships proved nearly impossible because of medical privacy regulations, I gained insight into this setting through listserv postings and an internship exposition. In one posting, Ms. Whitmore mused:

> As an internship coordinator, I sometimes take for granted that nearly all 120 of our juniors and seniors are out in the community working twice a week. They're coming back with incredible stories that I think advisors, teachers, and mentors should be tuned in to. It adds a whole additional level of engagement to explore with our kids. Briefly, here are a few snapshots from some incredible experiences this week. Some are sad, and some are ridiculously impressive.
>
> • Rafael Flores [the student whose senior project was chronicled earlier] was invited to speak at an Internet media summit. Among notary corporate guests, Rafael presented to Google and Facebook reps. He was there to represent why student internships are so important.
> • Alonso Garcia had a patient he was working with pass away this past week. He seemed a little shaken, but his supervisor helped him work through the processing. Please check in with him and give him some extra love if you're close with him.
> • Carmen Torrez and Guillermo Valdez built an architectural model of a hospital waiting room. They're learning from actual architects.

Ms. Whitmore's suggestion that teachers "should be tuned in to" internships and "explore" these opportunities with students to enhance school engagement reflected MHS norms that encouraged educators to care about students' learning beyond the purview of academics and to tap lived experiences as valuable resources. Her report also highlights the range of skills students developed as they navigated the world of work.

Evidence of those skills surfaced powerfully during a spring exposition in which juniors displayed tri-fold posters showcasing their internships and provisional research questions for senior projects. Clad in medical scrubs, laboratory jackets, and other professional outfits, juniors shared tales of their internships with underclassmen, who attended the event in order to begin identifying internship choices. Lonzo reported enjoying a bio-engineering assignment at a children's hospital and learning to fix machines such as medical TV monitors. He shared his appreciation for the one-on-one connections he had with medical professionals and how conversations with these professionals prompted him to clean up his language and comport himself more professionally. Jaime enthused about the emergency room of the county public hospital, remarking on how this locale made him acutely aware of differences in health access between privately insured people and those reliant on government-backed options. He reported switching his career aspiration from auto-mechanic to nurse based on his hospital rotation and focusing his senior project on the 2010 Affordable Care Act as a way to deepen his understanding of public health policies. Alma, placed at the same hospital, described rotations in physical therapy, pediatrics, pharmacy, and medical interpretation. This last setting made her realize the value of being bilingual and the importance of patients truly understanding doctors' diagnoses and treatments. In a focus group, she elaborated:

> Because we are in a medical hospital environment, they always remind us . . . [that] people in general, adults, they don't see teenagers as responsible. They don't trust us doing the stuff that we are doing, but at my internship they really believe in us. They let us rotate in the hospital. I think that's very—that's something that not all schools do, and I really like it because in the future I see myself in a hospital environment, so I'm already taking a step ahead.

The testimonies of these youth illustrate how internships intensified intellectual cariño by providing opportunities for students to explore the professional world of adults, make connections between school learning and the real world, and consider how they might contribute to community health.

Town Halls as Platforms for Organizing, Informing, and Persuading. Town hall assemblies were another setting in which students engaged in expanded learning and benefited from intellectual cariño. Town halls occurred roughly half a dozen times a year to celebrate special occasions such as the start of school or an ethnic heritage month. Reflecting MHS's commitment to empower students, town halls were generally student-led and almost always coupled with an anticipatory group reflection activity in advisory. The planning of these gatherings with assistance from adult coaches required youth to grapple with big ideas and apply HOM authentically. Preparation entailed 1–2 months of planning during which students read texts (history, song lyrics, websites, etc.), debated themes, crafted activities or presentations (PowerPoints, skits, spoken word performances, etc.), designed agendas and multimedia supports, and coordinated schedules and logistics with school personnel and guest speakers. Because these tasks offered multiple entry points for participation, event production allowed students to recognize and value different ways of being smart. Moreover, the high visibility of student organizers on stage during town halls functioned as a kind of status treatment (Cohen, 1994) in which the positive, intellectual contributions of students, especially those who struggled academically, were acknowledged and celebrated.

The 2012 Women's History Town Hall organized by FISTT (Fearless, Intelligent Sisters Thriving Together), MHS's young women's empowerment group, offers a representative example of these hybrid learning settings. During March, the 20 or so youth in FISTT, who met after school weekly with coaches, Ms. Howard and Ms. Mahelona, planned a 40-minute advisory activity and a 50-minute schoolwide program. For advisory, a FISTT member facilitated a student-developed lesson whose objectives were to "(a) reflect on important women in our lives, (b) prepare for the Women's History Town Hall event, and (c) promote awareness about issues that impact women in our community." During the advisory session, students watched and discussed a video of Maya Angelou reciting her poem "Phenomenal Woman," shared in a community circle about women they admired, and collaboratively created a poster honoring those women. Many students nominated mothers, sisters, and girlfriends as admirable, but Rosa Parks, Mother Theresa, Jane Fonda, Selena Quintanilla-Pérez, and Luz (the EDP director) were among others mentioned. The lesson closed with students receiving hot pink women's awareness ribbons to affix to clothing or backpacks.

The town hall was an upbeat affair. Students entered the auditorium to Beyoncé's "Run the World (Girls)." Advisory posters festooned with pictures of famous women and students' loved ones adorned panels lining the stage. Surrounding walls showcased giant hand-painted black-and-white poster portraits of famous women—Le Ly Haslip, Harriet Tubman, Frida Kahlo, Fanny Lou Hammer, Dolores Huerta—with quote bubbles floating from their mouths. FISTT youth wore matching black T-shirts emblazoned with a pink woman symbol and a fist raised in protest.

Their program opened with an audience participation activity which invited students to stand if a statement applied to them. The auditorium rumbled as students stood following prompts such as "Please stand if you, or someone you know, has been called a 'bitch,' 'slut,' or 'skank' in any language" or "Please stand if you, or someone you know, has been raped, sexually assaulted, or sexually harassed." Facilitators encouraged the audience to look around and notice how widespread these problems were. Afterward, several students accompanied by Mr. Keo on guitar sang TLC's "Unpretty." The lyrics urged women to overcome feelings of physical inadequacy. During the song, a PowerPoint scrolled images of famous women and female MHS students and staff. Next, students performed skits depicting relationships and sought audience input on which portrayed a healthy dynamic. A PowerPoint about healthy dating followed. For the penultimate segment, a student shared an original poem entitled "To my daughter" that touched on immigration reform, college access, and reproductive rights. The poet envisioned her future daughter "speak[ing] Spanish like the women before us" and "learn[ing] about strength and tradition." The finale featured the African American mother and older sister of a FISTT member. The mother shared about being a medical social worker working with abused women, and the sister recounted being assaulted by a boyfriend. The event concluded with all students standing and shouting the names of women who had made a difference in their lives, and then Beyoncé boomed through the speakers again and students filed out. In the aftermath, FISTT students converged on stage for a group hug and celebratory photo.

This event wove multiple voices and contexts into a unified program that displayed FISTT students' craftsmanship, imagination, and critical thinking. While the town hall and accompanying advisory lesson addressed serious issues, they unfolded in ways that felt affirming and even joyful. As such, this town hall (and others) reflected intellectual cariño by affording an empowering opportunity for youth to explore their shared identities through creative, intellectual collaboration.

Post-Session as a Path Toward Self-Knowledge and Socratic Sensibility. As chronicled in Chapter 2, the school year at MHS culminated with a special 13-day period known as post-session in which students and teachers joined in playful, creative activities aimed at fulfilling art and physical education course requirements. MHS's tradition of post-session promoted student–teacher and student–student bonding while also underscoring the boundless and pleasurable nature of learning. Sophomores camped in Yosemite. Some students biked through California redwoods and along the coast. Others learned to surf. Some explored their city's artistic gems such as museums and street murals, while still others engaged in community service projects. The disruption of normal school routines coupled with socioemotional and/or physical challenges (in both urban and wilderness environments) opened up spaces for students to reflect individually and communally about their most intimate realities. These contemplations strengthened students' "Socratic sensibility." According to Duncan-Andrade (2009), this sensibility entails a capacity and willingness to engage in metacognitive and existential reflection motivated by Socrates's assertion that "the unexamined life is not worth living."

The generative power of post-session emerged in students' written reflections following a 500-mile bike trip. The 18 students, two teachers, and three volunteers who participated in this adventure camped in tents and spent evenings fireside sharing stories and bonding. Three days into the trek, the group received the news that Ernesto, their beloved classmate, had been murdered (see Chapter 2). The group deliberated about whether to cancel the ride and return home for memorial services or push onward. They decided that Ernesto would want them to continue and agreed to dedicate their ride to him and use the trip as a way to process their grief. Ten days later, a screaming crowd waving banners greeted the exhausted yet triumphant riders as they rolled onto MHS's quad. Students' written reflections following the trip include

> This trip opened my eyes to new things, [sic] never in my life would I have thought that I could do 500 miles in 13 days, but I did and I feel I really accomplished something. Now, I feel like I am able to do anything. It was fun spending a lot of time with my classmates and building a stronger relationship with them.

> This is a tour I will never forget, [sic] just being on the open road was like a mental massage and I did a lot of self-reflection. The reason I joined this trip was to try something new and I don't regret it whatsoever. I'm planning to pass this beautiful experience on to others, [sic] it's like cascading leadership. I was exposed to something new, was given the tools, [sic] now it's up to me to pass it on to my people.

These comments suggest how the biking post-session nurtured students' bodymindspirits, strengthened their Socratic sensibility, and provided an outlet for students to process grief in ways that left them empowered. The confidence students expressed with regard to trying new things and persisting through difficulty positioned them to approach future tasks—academic and otherwise—with assurance and determination.

Another resonant example of how post-session promoted students' self-reflection surfaced during a debrief of the Yosemite "river challenge" activity. This Outward Bound–inspired activity segregated students into two groups by sex and asked them to construct a "bridge" from two wooden 2-by-6 planks and two pallets. The same-sex configuration provided an opportunity for students to collaborate without the pressure of performing under the gaze of another sex and also to bond with members of their own sex. Unable to follow each group to separate locales, I observed the young men as they attempted to usher all group members across the bridge without falling into the "river." They erupted victoriously when they thought they had accomplished the challenge, but Mr. Avila, the boys' facilitator, informed them that one board had faltered, leading the final crosser to touch the ground. After much bickering, the young men successfully reconstructed the bridge and got everyone across. Thrilled, they jumped atop one another in a mosh pile, hooting with delight.

Afterward, as darkness enveloped the meadow and stars glimmered, Mr. Avila led the young men in a discussion as they lounged in the grass. He opened with words of praise for their success and complimented them for using a pinecone as a totem to authorize speakers. Next, he invited students to share what frustrated them during the experience. Students expressed exasperation over "everyone arguing," "no one listening," "only one person wanting to take charge," and "people not wanting to take risks." Mr. Avila then inquired about possible connections between these observations and classroom interactions. The following exchange ensued:

Student A: You know how we're learning something? Someone asks for help and then everybody says, "You're stupid" or //
Student B: //What! That never happens!
Student C: I never heard that!

Many voices clamor to deny Student A's account.

Mr. Avila: You're talking too much, please! Shhhhh!
Student A: In math class, several people want to ask for help, but they're just scared because there's a small group of people that keeps like making hella noise because they already know the material, but not everybody knows it.
Mr. Avila: Can you guys see the connection he's making right now?
Unidentified Student: Yeah.
Mr. Avila: So what do you guys need to do for the next 2 years?
Unidentified Student: Cooperate.
Unidentified Student: Listen!
Mr. Avila: How?
Student D: We need to work with each other and listen.
Unidentified Student: Understanding people's feelings.
Mr. Avila: Understanding people's perceptions and feelings. That's excellent. What else?
Unidentified Student: Not thinking about yourself.
Mr. Avila: Not just thinking about yourself.
Student D: No sophomore left behind!
Students: A lot of patience!
Mr. Avila: That's good. The next 2 years are, believe it or not, going to be connected to what you did here tonight.

This conversation illustrates the ways in which a post-session activity catalyzed reflection that enhanced students' Socratic sensibility and likely spilled over to enrich school learning. Student A's risk-taking to identify a problematic classroom dynamic, as well as Mr. Avila's extended series of queries, prompted participants to ponder their behavior and coalesce around the shared goal of having all sophomores graduate. The fact that this activity and debrief were purposely conducted to elicit analysis, problem solving, and metacognition also shows how MHS educators cultivated students' HOM in a range of settings and understood how play conjoined with intimate moments of interpersonal learning could enhance students' overall schooling experience and identity formation.

In sum, these four settings—demanding project-based assessments, workplace internships, student-led town hall assemblies, and post-sessions—altered the social organization of school and enriched the learning ecology of MHS. Movement across and performance within these settings extended students' repertoires of practice by immersing them in meaningful activities that engaged and affirmed their bodymindspirits. In this manner, participation in these settings enabled students to reconceive their identities and embrace new futures for themselves and their communities. Additionally, these four settings heightened the power and pleasure of learning for students by connecting and extending classroom academics into expanded real-world settings. For teachers, these settings afforded sustained and cumulative opportunities to develop deeper knowledge of students, which in turn enhanced their capacity and willingness to nurture students' learning in holistic ways. Ultimately, the purposeful design of this robust ecology constituted an institutional expression of intellectual cariño driven by a desire to promote students' access to transformative and empowering learning opportunities.

TENSIONS IN INTELLECTUAL CARIÑO

While MHS's rich ecology of educative settings saturated with intellectual cariño marked it as an exemplary school, it was not a utopia. Part of the beautiful struggle involved educators through internal accountability deliberating difficult trade-offs related to sustaining the school's social justice and equity-driven mission. Curricular tracking emerged as a salient controversy. The founders of MHS embraced a philosophy of detracked, heterogeneous classes believing that this approach would best foster all students' academic development. According to Mr. Keo, MHS's faculty was "always trying to figure out how we can make the higher achieving students as well as the lower achieving students successful. Our goal is to keep them together as long as possible." Principal West expressed pride in the school's policy of having every student take the A–G requirements necessary to enter the CSU/UC system. He explained, "There's no tracking at all throughout the program. Kids are required to take the exact same classes. They don't have any electives. . . . They take what the school offers, and that's it."

Beyond MHS's core academic program, however, there were important exceptions to the detracking stance that profoundly impacted students' course-taking sequences and perceptions of themselves as more or less capable pensadoras. These exceptions included (a) a reading intervention elective that placed 9th- and 10th-grade students with low Scholastic Reading Inventory (SRI) scores (under 750) in a scripted literacy program entitled Read 180, pulling them away from the electives of life skills (grade 9) and advanced biology (grade 10); (b) an optional zero period geometry class for 9th- and 10th-grade students seeking to take calculus in 12th grade; (c) a 10th-grade repeat algebra 1 class; and (d) a senior elective course that placed students likely to attend 4-year colleges in a college writing class and the remainder in a medical assistant certification course. The master schedule was also skewed by a cohort of students selected for a prestigious hospital internship that required its interns to leave campus early. Several teachers complained that this internship "pull[ed] the cream of the crop from us" and left their afternoon classes without higher performing students twice weekly. All of these exceptions to detracking arose from efforts to support the needs of MHS's diverse learners—those who were EBs struggling to read and those seeking admission to selective colleges, who clamored for more AP offerings and futures as doctors and nurses.

Support for Emergent Bilinguals

With regard to EBs, the Read 180 class proved especially problematic.[13] On the surface, this course represented an effort to differentiate care and provide support to EBs, allowing them to close skill gaps and catch up. MHS leaders claimed Read 180 served this purpose. In an accreditation self-study report, MHS boasted (without substantiating data) that "most students show significant growth in the program, from 300–500 Lexile points in the course of a year."[14] The same report referenced numerous district awards for improving EBs' academic achievement. Despite these success indicators, our observations in Ms. Clark's 9th-grade reading class raised questions about the efficacy of the Read 180 intervention. Across observations, students appeared procedurally cooperative in a "doing school" kind of way, but overall, the instructional interactions we witnessed—even when Ms. Clark, a respected pedagogue and beginning teacher coach, "went rogue" and aborted her script and pacing guide—lacked vibrancy and engagement. The class also suffered from inadequate resources. Ms. DuPont, another reading intervention instructor, objected to the conditions of the

Read 180 classroom. "The computers in there don't work. There are old books in there, so there's a lack of resources for reading intervention." Ms. Clark, who was teaching the class for the first time, registered grave concerns:

> I'm just going to throw this out there: I *hate* tracking. I absolutely think, for all the transformational visioning learning kind of stance that we try to take, when you have a master schedule that supports tracking, you are absolutely a hypocrite. . . . I was actually really excited to teach a class like this, because I've never taught one. . . . The problem with an intervention class is that they [students] know—they know, and you can't get rid of the fact that they are the lowest of the low and they feel it and they know it, and the expectations that they set for themselves are low because of that. . . . It's really hard to be the one voice in the room saying, "You can do it; you can do it," and then because the curriculum is scripted and comes from somewhere else, it's very worksheet-y. . . . I understand sentence starters and frames and all that kind of stuff, but they're not being asked to do a lot of thinking at any point.

Ms. Clark objected to how the Read 180 class stigmatized students and how the curriculum dishonored students' interests and intellects because it came "from somewhere else" and did not ask students "to do a lot of thinking." Low–mid-range observational scores on CLASS-S and CREDE/SPC dimensions corroborated Ms. Clark's negative views.[15]

Given the warnings of literacy scholars who caution against instruction that neglects disciplinary literacy and concentrates instead on decontextualized tasks, basics, vocabulary, mechanics, and language errors (Bartolomé, 2008; Bruna et al., 2007; Mohan & Slater, 2006; Valdés et al., 2007), Ms. Clark's criticisms coupled with observational data suggest that EBs were not sufficiently supported by the Read 180 program to extend their literacy practices and become prepared for challenging academic work.[16] While MHS did engage these students in the settings previously described and exerted considerable effort toward ensuring that all teachers were literacy teachers (Athanases & Curry, 2018), the existence of the Read 180 program ran counter to the school's espoused goal of interrupting patterns of inequity because it perpetuated deficit views of EBs and amounted to a "scholastic quarantine" imposed on youth to remedy deficiencies (Rose, 1985, p. 352). As such, the Read 180 program failed to uphold the four pillars of intellectual cariño because it lacked academic challenge, overlooked the revolutionary possibilities of literacy, undercut the formation of positive learner identities, and resulted in dull, plodding instruction devoid of pleasure. In this regard, the Read 180 program as implemented mirrored other documented remedial courses for nondominant students that socialize students toward developing "unproductive and weak strategies for literacy learning" (Gutiérrez et al., 2009, p. 225). Thus, this intervention constituted a lost opportunity for MHS to optimize support for EBs.

College Preparation or Vocational Training

Read 180 was not the only departure from the school's detracking philosophy. Several teachers expressed deep concern about the introduction of a medical assisting class during the second semester of the 2011–2012 school year that arose from a district-led Regional Opportunity Program (ROP) initiative. Mr. Behari and Ms. Wang voiced frustration about how the newly devised class "sacrificed academic college readiness for professional job skill-building." Mr. Behari spoke bluntly:

> The medical assisting class . . . takes half of our seniors out of college writing and puts them into a professional course, which to me messages the idea that half of you are going to college, and the other half of you will get a job because you can't hack it. I don't think that was the intention, but I think that's the message it sends. This was a decision made by the ILT and the administration. It was never discussed amongst anybody.

Principal West defended the class as a pragmatic response to economic realities:

> There's been a lot of debate around the medical assisting class. Why are we offering medical assisting? One of the reasons why is because, you know, honestly? About 80% of our kids that go to the community college don't follow through with the community college. They're not transferring to 4-year colleges. . . . The rate is just abysmal. . . . they're hitting all these barriers along the way, then they ultimately give up. And one of the huge barriers is financial aid. . . . Maybe if we teach these kids a skill and they get into the community college and they're also doing medical assisting, there's a natural progression. If they're in that [medical] setting and they see the nurses and the dental hygienists who make $80,000 a year, maybe that's going to be the thing to motivate them to continue on that path. . . . also secondarily, it gives them a revenue stream that's not working in McDonald's or fast food.

Framed in this way, the medical assisting class was about supporting students to overcome the financial barriers impeding college access and improving students' upward economic mobility.

The controversies related to the medical assistance class and Read 180 demonstrate the challenges of enacting intellectual cariño in the face of hard choices, as well the *choques* (collisions) that sometimes occurred as MHS educators grappled with dilemmas. MHS's detracking commitments seemed to be under threat of erosion. Ultimately, this tension highlights the grueling and continuous work necessary to maintain an educational program that truly reflects intellectual cariño and is responsive to students' needs.

CLOSING REFLECTIONS

The robust presence of intellectual cariño evident in MHS classrooms, culminating assessments, internships, town halls, and post-session spawned a culture of engaged learning in which students embraced intellectual activity as personally gratifying. As they traversed the multiple, overlapping settings of MHS's learning ecology, students exhibited interest, experienced engrossment, and derived meaning from their schooling. Importantly, intellectual cariño at MHS was not focused exclusively on getting youth to do school well, garner higher test scores on achievement tests, or gain admission to college. Instead, teachers channeled their intellectual cariño toward enabling youth to "become agents of change in their own lives and community." This focus meant that students and teachers harnessed HOM to collectively and deeply examine complex problems and issues in authentic ways. Ultimately, the engagement that resulted transformed schooling away from the gloomy, emotionally flat scenes depicted so often in the literature on U.S. secondary schools and prepared students to be both college and community ready. Given the impoverished instruction and learning that most Latinx students usually endure, MHS's enactment of intellectual cariño was impressive.

CHAPTER 4

Critical Cariño

Nurturing Strong Sociocultural Identities, Political Awareness, and Civic Engagement

I want students to realize that there's a struggle. There's *la lucha* . . . the struggle is that I've got to break all these walls and overcome all these obstacles. . . . I've got to make a difference not just for me, but also for my family and my community. I want students to respect themselves, their Latino heritage, to learn their roots because I want them to know where they came from, where their parents came from, and where they're supposed to be going. I want them to have a level of honor and respect of their roots and make a difference.

—Mr. Avila, Spanish teacher

In our students' communities, the ability to think critically about social and political issues is particularly important and valuable, especially in this city where the social structure is constantly oppressing and minimizing students' opportunities. Our students need to have the knowledge and ability to think critically about the social structures that oppress them; that capacity empowers them more than anything else does.

—Mr. Behari, humanities teacher

It's good to have a school that is actually focused on you and your neighborhood . . . because I've had friends who have died in violence in this city. It's good that our school cares and wants to change things like that around.

—Esperanza, MHS junior

At MHS, there is a sense of community and responsibility, the sense of ownership that the problems not just of the school but of [our city] are for them to solve. The kids feel that they have an active role to solve them. They are really hopeful.

—Luz, extended day program director and CBO partner

The act of educating students of color is sort of an act of revolution, something that is done with an eye towards increasing equity in an inequitable world.

—Ms. Glass, math teacher

La lucha por la felicidad y la libertad (the struggle for happiness and freedom) compelled MHS educators to cultivate critical cariño, authentic cariño's final component. This cariño communicated two messages to students. First, their worlds beyond the school walls mattered. Second, school learning should prepare them to confront and transform the structural inequities built into White supremacist, capitalist society. By centering themes of social justice and nurturing students' sociocultural and political identities, MHS educators extended themselves beyond efforts to promote socioemotional and intellectual growth and demonstrated a deep commitment to supporting students' collective well-being outside of school.

While prior chapters foreshadowed critical cariño by examining familial cariño's emphasis on educación, cultural affirmation, collective upliftment, and radical healing, as well as by elucidating intellectual cariño's empowering possibilities, this chapter explores how MHS educators enacted critical cariño through pedagogies of liberation aimed at helping students to understand themselves, their communities, and the world within sociohistorical contexts. The chapter launches with a theoretical overview of critical cariño. Next, I examine four core instructional strategies that exemplified MHS's enactment of critical cariño, followed by a discussion of three organizational structures—the mission, curricular autonomy, and community partnerships—that enabled these practices. The penultimate section delves into three tensions that complicated critical cariño. The first tension related to incongruities between the school's social justice mission and neoliberal reforms. The second revolved around supporting non-Latinx students in a Latinx majority school. The third arose from educators' varying levels of political consciousness and resultant disputes over how best to empower youth and enact "transformational" learning. The chapter's conclusion considers the outcomes and benefits of infusing a school with critical cariño. Specifically, I argue that MHS's robust critical cariño promoted students' democratic agency and fortified their capacity to transform and transcend oppressive structures. In doing so, MHS educators advanced the school's mission to interrupt injustice and inequity and equip graduates to be "community ready"—prepared and willing to do their part to tackle and solve the problems of their city and nation (Middaugh & Kahne, 2013).

CRITICAL CARIÑO: POLITICAL, LIBERATORY, AND HUMANIZING

Critical cariño builds on critical care theory (Antrop-González & De Jesús, 2006; DeNicolo et al., 2017; Ginwright, 2016; Rolón-Dow, 2005) and involves educators providing opportunities for nondominant students to interrogate social oppression and collectively confront institutional structures that have historically marginalized them. Seeking to fortify students' sociocultural identities and political clarity, this cariño pays explicit attention to students' lived experiences as raced, cultured, gendered, and classed members of particular communities situated within broader historical contexts. Such identity development sometimes entails deeply personal (and painful) soul-work (Carmen et al., 2015) to interrupt internalized racism (shame and hatred of ethnic/racial identities) as well as victim consciousness. Grounded in this paradigm, MHS teachers strove to cultivate safe spaces conducive to such soul-work. Speaking to this effort, Mr. Tran explained, "One of the norms here is having a caring environment. It's not every man or woman for themselves. It's about making sure that everyone is successful so we can help each other." This communal ethic (spotlighted in Chapter 2's focus on familial cariño) meant that teachers expressed critical cariño by helping students overcome barriers and heal wounds hampering their growth, success, and agency.

Critical cariño involves humanizing pedagogies. Figure 4.1 illustrates the enactment of critical cariño by displaying educators' justice and pedagogical stances arranged along intersecting axes.[1] The horizontal justice axis highlights how curriculum content can span a continuum from acritical to critical. The far-left end features content that endorses the status quo, while content on the far-right end emphasizes themes of social oppression and the urgency of social change. The vertical axis draws from Freire's (1970/2005) criticism of traditional "banking education" that positions teachers as authorities dispensing decontextualized, discrete knowledge to passive

Figure 4.1. The Enactment of Critical Cariño

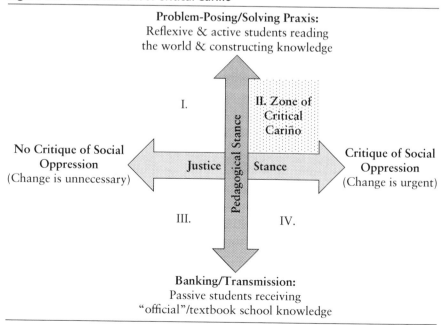

Problem-Posing/Solving Praxis:
Reflexive & active students reading
the world & constructing knowledge

I.   II. Zone of Critical Cariño

No Critique of Social Oppression (Change is unnecessary)   Justice   Pedagogical Stance   Stance   Critique of Social Oppression (Change is urgent)

III.   IV.

Banking/Transmission:
Passive students receiving
"official"/textbook school knowledge

students. This transmission model conceives curriculum and instruction as apolitical and culturally neutral when in fact the monological, top–down delivery of "official" knowledge reflects the hegemony of the dominant society and perpetuates the status quo. In contrast, Freire advocated for emancipatory pedagogies that engage students in joint reflection on and action within the contexts of their daily lives—what Freire termed "praxis."

The zone of critical cariño (quadrant II) encompasses learning experiences in which teachers guide students to simultaneously grapple with social oppression and actively investigate and interact with the world. This zone differs from quadrant I because the problems students take up in that sphere are of a more conformist nature and lack attention to injustice and inequity (e.g., How do we raise school spirit? How do frogs' bodies function? How can littering be prevented?). The zone of critical cariño contrasts most dramatically with quadrant III, in which teaching is conventional, textbook-driven, and apolitical. Finally, quadrant IV instructors differ from those in the zone of critical cariño because they act as indoctrinating authorities rather than co-investigators and coaches.

At MHS, the enactment of critical cariño meant that students examined real-world issues and problems seeking to understand their root causes and then envisioning and implementing remedies. MHS's project-based learning (described in Chapter 3) connects to the vertical axis. Speaking to how teachers enlivened learning by encouraging students' active participation in real-world problem solving, Ms. Wang observed, "Engagement is ramped up pretty immediately. . . . It's like the ultimate student ownership. Ideally, students get to display what they can do with the information that they've learned." Her comments echo Luz's view that the school encouraged youth agency by inviting students to take "ownership" and "responsibility" for solving "the problems of the school and their city." Suggesting the interplay between the two axes, Mr. West explained that MHS teachers wanted students to understand how "they can make a difference, that they can change reality if they don't like the things they see on the ground." The pursuit of such change meant that teachers, through their instruction, facilitated students' "access to all the power structures" and cultivated students' understanding of "the systems" and "how to negotiate them." Critical cariño, then, involved pedagogies that engaged students as active readers and agents in the real world.

Fueled by MHS's explicit social justice mission, the curriculum centered themes of social oppression aligned with the right end of Figure 4.1's horizontal axis. This justice stance manifested itself in youth and teachers collaboratively examining the ways in which structural inequities borne of capitalism, racism, and colonialism shaped and harmed students' lives and society. Mr. Behari explained that "talking about race and equity in your curriculum is highly valued here, particularly in the humanities." Emblematic of this focus was Mr. Avila, who reported "push[ing] the immigration piece . . . [so]

students themselves can analyze the obstacles . . . of poverty, language, racism, prejudice, discrimination, legalization, [and] human rights." Issues such as food deserts, police misconduct, environmental degradation, and gun violence were taken up as legitimate topics deserving of inquiry and as intractable problems demanding students' creative solutions. According to Principal West, one of the jobs of MHS teachers was to heighten students' "aware[ness] of the grander system that is actually working against them and how they have to be conscious about it if they're going to defeat it and ultimately succeed."

MHS's justice stance also involved culturally sustaining and revitalizing pedagogies (McCarty & Lee, 2014; Paris & Alim, 2014) that tapped the cultural and linguistic funds of knowledge embedded within students' homes and communities (Moll et al., 1992). Rather than viewing students and their families as broken, deviant, or deficient, MHS educators recognized the inherent value and strength residing within students' ethnoracial communities and cultural heritages. Oriented in this manner, they worked diligently to connect youth to the cultural wealth present within their communities. Ms. Clark noted that MHS's community–school orientation meant that "we are constantly trying to increase communication between ourselves as a school and the home. . . . We look for opportunities to have kids use their home life in the classroom. That is transformative." Yosso (2005) explains that students' homes and communities hold vast storehouses of community cultural wealth, including (a) aspirational capital—the capacity to sustain hope and dream about better futures regardless of present suffering or barriers; (b) linguistic capital—the capacity to communicate in more than one language; (c) familial capital—the material and psychic supports offered by extended kin (biological and fictive) who nurture community memory, cultural intuition, and ethics of collective upliftment (Delgado Bernal, 1998, 2006); (d) social capital—the connections to people and social networks that can unlock resources and provide guidance to surmount obstacles; (e) navigational capital—the micropolitical literacy to steer oneself effectively through dominant institutions in order to achieve goals and/or initiate progressive change within those institutions; and (f) resistant capital—the knowledge and skill to challenge societal inequities and oppressive power relations.

MHS educators recognized that these cultural assets unfolded within multicultural environments in which participants regularly exchanged and absorbed the traditions, arts, music, languages, fashions, discourses, and so on of multiethnic others. This awareness moved MHS beyond simplistic, essentialized notions of culture and led educators to embrace a complex, hybridized, cultural pluralism as a vital part of their justice stance (Paris & Alim, 2014). Through this pluralism, MHS planted seeds of solidarity and coalitional politics.

Because oppression, racism, and colonialism have generated intergenerational trauma, social toxins, and soul wounds, MHS's critical cariño pedagogies opened up humanizing spaces for students to face the spirit-murdering impacts of discrimination and inequity (Williams, 1987). Students had opportunities to acknowledge and release their collective inner pain and discover internal resources offering "knowledge, strength, and energy to persist and be resilient" (Anzaldúa, 2002/2013, p. 571). The school's investment in this healing work surfaced in annual firewalk rituals (see Chapter 2) and classroom invitations to mine personal experiences for existential meaning. In an end-of-the-year listserv post Luz alluded to the depth of such work:

> I am honored to walk with you in the journey of hope as well as pain. . . . Even though the system is a monster . . . MHS is a center of hope and opportunity. Our school is not afraid to challenge any monster and we have changed our world by changing each youth, family, teacher, staff, partner and community member that walks through our doors.

Her reflections hint at the ways MHS nurtured healing-centered engagement (Ginwright, 2016) and fostered critical hope (Duncan-Andrade, 2009) and "freedom dreaming" (Kelley, 2002)—all creative processes that supported youth to imagine and build communities able to persist and prevail against the "monster" in *la lucha por la felicidad y la libertad*.

THE RELATION BETWEEN CRITICAL CARIÑO AND CRITICAL PEDAGOGY

Although critical cariño shares affinity with critical pedagogy, especially the latter's insistence that teaching for liberation is fundamentally "an act of love opposing the lovelessness which lies at the heart of the oppressors' violence" (Freire, 1970/2005, p. 45), these two approaches are not synonymous. Somewhat surprisingly, I encountered the phrase "critical pedagogy" at MHS only once, and its source, Ms. Grace, was a teacher on special assignment who taught for less than a year at the school. Given that critical pedagogy was not part of MHS's discourse, situating their work within this tradition seemed problematic.

Another complexity was that MHS's enactment of critical cariño departed from empirical accounts of highschool–level critical pedagogy. These accounts often document standalone courses in which youth receive explicit instruction in sociological theories a lá Freire, Gramsci, Fanon, and Bourdieu and gain familiarity with concepts such as hegemony, counter-hegemony, habitus, and social reproduction. In these courses, youth investigate problems within their communities and engage in civic activism (Camangian, 2015; Hidalgo & Duncan-Andrade, 2009; Oakes & Rogers, 2006). Often students determine which topics and problems to investigate.

At MHS, though, state and district mandates and content standards obligated teachers to channel their curriculum and instruction along particular paths. As such, they had to creatively weave critical cariño into the fabric of college preparatory courses.

MHS's STEM (science, technology, engineering, and math) focus coupled with its career academy elements also implicated the school in neoliberal agendas promoting evidenced-based scientism as the optimal way to reap prestige and resources and solve complex problems.[2] Critical pedagogues regard STEM with suspicion, viewing it as "a counterrevolutionary move" that "narrows our understanding of the world and how we seek solutions to human suffering . . . [while] trapping us in a bankrupt ideology that leaves the underlying roots of oppression untouched" (Darder, 2020, p. 11). Given MHS's choice to embrace STEM as means to achieve its social justice goal of preparing bilingual, bicultural health professionals capable of diversifying and transforming health care institutions, the school occupied a curious and contested political space that still reflected critical cariño. Virtually absent in this space were the kinds of explicit Marxian critiques of political economy and class struggle associated with the theoretical scholarship on critical pedagogy (McLaren & Jaramillo, 2014). MHS educators preferred instead to use the language of social justice. Given that some critical pedagogy advocates view social justice rhetoric as an "equity discourse" that has "tamed explicit liberation agendas" (Camangian, 2015, p. 428) and tacitly legitimized capitalism by accepting its "brute intractability" (McLaren & Jaramillo, 2014, p. 70), MHS's embrace of critical cariño departed from radical/classic iterations of critical pedagogy.

Another disjuncture between what I am calling radical/classic critical pedagogy and the critical cariño I observed at MHS was that the school, through its promotion of HOM, avoided the imposition of dogmatic liberatory ideologies. In keeping with Ellsworth's (1989) observation that the "key assumptions, goals, and pedagogical practices fundamental to the literature on critical pedagogy—namely, 'empowerment,' 'student voice,' 'dialogue,' and even the term 'critical'—are repressive myths that perpetuate relations of domination" (p. 298), MHS educators shunned authoritative, indoctrinating instructional approaches. The critical cariño I witnessed at MHS did not wrap itself up in "repressive myths," but rather attempted to keep learning "real" through efforts to ensure that school knowledge was connected and relevant to students' daily lives and community contexts, as well as focused on critical literacy. As Ms. Howard explained, "To make revolutionary change, you have to know how to read and write. . . . That's how you're going to change how the world works." Critical cariño as enacted at MHS, then, focused mostly on nurturing students' capacity to read the world and the word as a path toward social change. It was not confined to any one class, but rather infused schoolwide into settings across the learning ecology.

An additional distinguishing feature of critical cariño as practiced at MHS was how educators approached the "beautiful struggle" not as a battle to be waged against evil, dominant powers, but rather as an urgent quest to unveil new transformative futures that have not yet been imagined. In this regard, critical cariño can be viewed as a "pedagogy of invitation" (Keating, 2013) that strives to move beyond antagonistic, oppositional, dichotomous paradigms. Critical cariño promotes instead an inclusionary, post-oppositional, and "realistic politics of hope" (p. 5) that asserts radical inter-relatedness and "the possibility of planetary citizenship" (p. 46). As Keating suggests, this shift from struggling *against* to struggling *toward* and *with* is important because oppositional politics trap us in "conflicts that often subtly reinforce the very systems against which we struggle. This oppositionality saturates us and limits our imaginations . . . [leaving us] locked in an embattled, us-against-them status quo" (p. 3). Keating elaborates the debilitating effects of such combat:

> We can't turn off the negative energies once we remove ourselves from the battlefield. We take these energies with us, into our work, our homes, our minds, our bodies, our souls. They eat away at us, devouring us as we direct this oppositional thinking at one another and ourselves. We fragment. We crumble. We deteriorate from within and then we regroup. We begin again and onto the next corrosive battle. (p. 9)

Recognizing that certain forms of resistance may compound suffering, MHS educators attempted to carve out new spaces, alliances, and practices that would enable youth to unearth and connect to their inner strengths and creative powers. These educators worked to construct transformative experiences aimed at allowing youth to taste the pleasure of *felicidad y libertad* in the course of their present schooling and refrained from pitching school as something to be endured in order to reach a distant but better tomorrow. These educators understood that active, critical pensadoras were more likely to become social change agents if they had opportunities to understand multiple perspectives, act boldly, dream audaciously, forge authentic relationships with diverse others, and know themselves well. Mr. Behari intimated that these kinds of expansive opportunities were necessary because "students should care about humanity, not just their own people."

In summary, critical cariño as practiced at MHS shared critical pedagogy's interest in liberation, but pursued this end in unorthodox ways. The school combined a praxis-based pedagogical stance with a social justice and STEM orientation to create humanizing opportunities for students to investigate and respond to their lived realities as raced, classed, and gendered individuals enmeshed within particular communities with particular histories. At its core, critical cariño builds on the sense of belonging and solidarity borne of familial cariño and the critical thinking cultivated by intellectual cariño to nurture students' critical literacy and passion for justice. It aims to fuel students' desire and capacity to upend the structures and ideologies that oppress them.

CRITICAL CARIÑO ENACTED

This section highlights four curricular practices that exemplify critical cariño. The first advances narrative as a vehicle to promote students' healthy ethnoracial identity development. The second entails the use of compelling social issues to catalyze students' political interest and democratic engagement. The third involves tapping the community as a resource to enrich student learning. The fourth (and most aligned with classic critical pedagogy) features students conducting impact projects to address community concerns. Through these practices, which responded to students' sociohistorical realities and supported youth to collectively confront social inequity, MHS pursued its social justice mission and displayed its commitment to the beautiful struggle.

Narratives as Vehicles for Reflection and Resistance

The stories we hear and tell each other powerfully influence how we perceive ourselves as individuals, community members, and citizens. Cervantes-Soon (2012) reminds us of the indivisibility of narrative and agency. "As the narrator tells her story, she breaks the silence, negotiates contradictions, and recreates new identities beyond the fragmentation, shame, and betrayal brought about by oppression, colonization, and patriarchy" (p. 374). Unfortunately, the canonical stories promulgated in U.S. schools have often erased the existence of historically marginalized youth by elevating White narrators and characters, encouraging amnesia about our nation's troubled past, and glorifying myths of American exceptionalism, equality, and individualism. Fine (1987) explains that such erasure "obscure[s] the very social, economic, and therefore experiential conditions of students' daily lives" and also "diverts critique away from the economic, social, and educational institutions which organize class, race, and gender hierarchies" (pp. 157–158). Loath to perpetuate such subtractive curricula, MHS teachers exhibited critical cariño by carefully choosing which published stories entered their classrooms and by inviting youth to author and publicly share their own narratives. MHS centered the stories of people of color in ways that validated students' existence, celebrated their strengths, explored their complex identities, and attended to sociopolitical realities.

Over the course of their 4 years of humanities, MHS students read a range of literature written by authors of color, including *Twilight Los Angeles* by Anna Deveare Smith, *Our America: Life and Death on the South*

Side of Chicago by LeAlan Jones and Lloyd Newman, *The Absolutely True Diary of a Part-Time Indian* by Sherman Alexie, *Macho* by Victor Villasenor, *The Circuit* by Francisco Jimenez, *In the Time of Butterflies* by Julia Alvarez, *The Autobiography of Malcolm X*, *Kindred* by Octavia Butler, *Native Son* by Richard Wright, and *The Joy Luck Club* by Amy Tan. Mr. Behari explained that "It's just expected as a person teaching in this community that you teach authors of color; if you don't, people will notice." MHS educators taught inclusionary literature featuring characters who faced struggles similar to those confronted by students, as well as themes likely to foster awareness of social oppression.

The grade 9 and 10 humanities teachers taught several traditional texts, such as *To Kill a Mockingbird, Romeo and Juliet, Animal Farm, Lord of the Flies, Night, and Slaughterhouse Five*. This choice also reflected critical cariño as it was an effort to ensure that students became "global citizens" who had familiarity with the dominant culture's canon and the "culture of power" contained therein (Delpit, 1988). Emblematic of this stance, Ms. Barrett explained that Shakespeare was "a gatekeeper" and argued that "if my students are going to go to college, they're going to do Shakespeare. They need to know who he is. Nobody else in this school teaches Shakespeare." She reported students' enthusiasm for *Romeo and Juliet*. "They love it, and I think that's because it feels off-limits to them. . . . They thought, 'We weren't ever going to know who this guy was.'" She conjectured that *Romeo and Juliet* allowed students to see themselves as part of the "academic intellectual world." MHS's literacy coach echoed this stance and noted that MHS teachers taught a range of interesting texts. "I've worked at other bilingual schools where they think everything has to be about Latino culture. Students get tired of that. They also need to know about other things." She scoffed at teachers unnecessarily narrowing the curriculum and thinking "'You're Latino, so we're going to teach you about your culture'—a bunch of White teachers! At MHS it's more real. Students just want to know about the world." The inclusion of some canonical texts ensured that students developed multicultural capital—a blend of resources from dominant and nondominant cultural communities. This rich exposure enabled youth to navigate diverse cultural contexts (Achinstein et al., 2015).

Across the humanities, literary discussions explored how texts mirrored (or not) students' lived experiences, how U.S. society treats marginalized others, and how social phenomena—concentrated urban poverty, Indian reservations, migrant labor, imperialism, racism, and immigration—have historical roots and lasting consequences. As an example, Ms. Barrett used *The Absolutely True Diary of a Part-Time Indian* with freshmen at the beginning of the year to explore questions such as. "How do you see yourself as a student? Do you see yourself as a student? What identities do you claim? Do you want to be seen as smart? Does being smart mean going to college?" The ensuing conversations and written personal narratives not only prompted students to reflect on how their academic identities intersected with their sociocultural locations, but also helped them build a connected classroom community.

In Ms. Shmidt's 10th-grade classroom, the *In the Time of Butterflies* unit culminated with students writing essays in response to prompts such as the following:

- What role does education play for resistance to oppression and inequality? How do revolutionaries use literacy in their resistance? Use at least three examples from the text to defend your opinion.
- Why do some people stand up and resist injustice and oppression? What makes people courageous enough to do this? Choose a character from the novel and use textual evidence to prove why this character exhibits courage.
- Choose three Mirabal sisters and compare and contrast their views of gender and feminism. How do these different views affect their lives and roles?

Through assignments such as this, MHS students regularly wrestled with meaty, sociopolitical themes, sharpened their historical understandings, and engaged in critical conversations about oppressive cultural norms and institutions. Literature served as a rich resource for students to contemplate their lives and consider paths to resist oppression and pursue justice.

Beyond the literature of published authors, MHS students regularly authored their own stories. Principal West described these narratives as a key vehicle for the school to affirm Latinx culture and connect students to their families' heritage traditions. After rattling off an illustrative list of written and spoken narrative projects, Mr. West summed up his point. "Students' personal narratives are definitely something that we totally value. It's one of those unstated things. It's not written on a document, but the students' personal narrative is *huge* for us." He reported telling students that "one of the things that each one of you has is a tremendous story, a story of resiliency, a story that you need to craft and write. . . . where you come from means something, and it [your story] will change society."

Chapter 2 provided a glimpse of one such narrative assignment in its portrayal of the 11th graders' digital immigration stories. On the Academy Award showcase night for these films, students, staff, and families listened with rapt attention to narratives documenting escapes from political repression, desert journeys, employment and language difficulties in *el Norté*, the pursuit of the American Dream, and the symphony of satisfaction and sorrow arising from *una vida nueva* (a new life) in the United States. Although these narratives concentrated on the experiences of Mexicans and Central Americans, tales of Senegalese and Vietnamese immigrants were also featured. Importantly, students' digital stories did not get bogged down in "pain narratives" (Tuck & Yang, 2014), but rather conveyed students' nuanced admiration for the strength, perseverance, ingenuity, humanity, and desires of immigrants. Reminiscent of the syncretic *testimonios* documented by Gutiérrez (2008), these hybrid texts brought global and historical contexts to life and allowed both authors and audience members to expand their understandings of themselves and their broader community.

Another powerful example of MHS's emphasis on narrative surfaced in Ms. Schmidt's sophomore My Voice Matters project. This assignment involved writing and recording a personal essay for radio that would allow listeners to understand something important about each author. One student who succeeded in having his essay aired on the radio said the experience was like "getting to share a piece of your soul with the outside world." To hook students into the assignment, Ms. Schmidt posed questions such as "What makes you unique?" "What do you want others to know about being you (what's it like to be your age, your race, your gender, from your city, attending your school, etc.)?" "What makes you mad? What makes you happy?" "Who inspires you?" Students wrote autoethnographic narratives covering a range of subjects, such as parent–adolescent relationships, embarrassment, bullying, immigration, violence, and politics. Every year, several essays appeared on public radio. Ms. Schmidt also organized an exhibition for students and staff to listen to the final recordings as a community. At this celebratory event, students cheered enthusiastically and made nominations for best performance awards.

To give readers a flavor, I spotlight three narratives that aired on public radio. Renata recounted her father's detainment by ICE (the U.S.'s Immigration and Customs Enforcement agency). She reported how agents handcuffed her father in the family's apartment, allowing him to only briefly bid his children farewell with a kiss on their foreheads and a few *consejos* (pieces of advice). "*Ayudenle a su mama y portense bien, hechenle ganas a la escuela y pronto vamos a estar juntos otra vez. Las quiero mucho.*" (Help your mother and behave yourselves well, work hard in school and soon we will be together again. I love you very much.) Placing this experience in a broader context, Renata explained:

> Here, our family grew, adapted to the U.S. but kept our Latino roots alive by speaking Spanish and following our parents' traditions. We support each other to achieve our goals and live our days working hard and trying to fit in as best as we can, scared of unexpectedly being stopped by police and seeing our dreams vanish by being sent away. We are simply hard-working immigrants that come for the American Dream to succeed and overcome any obstacles in life as long as we are united.

Renata's narrative informed others of her existence and humanized the immigrant experience. Her testimonio reframed deportation, casting it not as a distant, necessary government policy, but as one that had caused her pain, generated fear, and fueled her desire to succeed. Renata conveyed the complexity of wanting to maintain her "Latino roots," while also striving to "fit in" to U.S. society and chase the American Dream.

Renata's classmate, Badeeah, created a narrative focused on her hybrid identity as a Mexican Palestinian American. She explained: "I live three lives in one. I live as an American that desires my independence. I live as a Palestinian that holds onto my religion. And I live as a Latina who values family and togetherness." Her essay explored how these cultures clashed and yet how each enriched her. Through her testimony, Badeeah positioned herself beyond essentialized racial/ethnic identities and challenged monolithic readings of the marginalized Brown "other." Badeeah forced her audience to "re-examine their own desires for fixed labels and static categories of identity" (Keating, 2013, pp. 78–79). Her references to observing Ramadan, listening to Arabic music in Spanish at *la playa* (the beach) en México, and shopping for "fresh new swag" so she can have a new look, suggested how her transcultural selves made her a "unique, open-minded person." Through her narrative, she claimed a world within which many worlds could fit.

The third narrative, authored by Luis, was a tribute to his Guatemalan mother, who, along with her 10 siblings, "lived in severe poverty for most of her childhood—no shoes, no toys, no clothes," often enduring hunger and existing on "a single tortilla for dinner." Luis detailed his parents' move to the United States and how their first years in el Norté were "the exact opposite of the American Dream." Over years of hard work cleaning homes, his mom climbed upward and attended night school. Eventually, she secured a job as a medical clerk and Luis's family obtained financial stability. Admiring her rise "from deep poverty and struggle to the comfortable life she is able to live now," Luis declared, "My mother is the strongest, most perseverant [*sic*] person I know. So whenever I need something to inspire me, I don't turn on the TV or read a magazine. I simply look to my mom." His narrative contested status-quo stories of poor, urban parents being too disadvantaged and encumbered by socioeconomic pressures to concern themselves with education. His listeners heard how Luis's profound respect for his mother and family history had fortified his strong sense of self.

Renata's, Badeeah's, and Luis's tales demonstrate how MHS educators tapped personal narratives to affirm students' ethnoracial identities and extend their sociopolitical awareness. These radio essays underscored how personal narratives "are more than stories. They are an important site of resistance. . . . [partly because] they invent, reform and refashion personal and collective identity" (Montoya, 1994, p. 27). By nurturing such narratives, MHS teachers joined other critical educators who have employed autoethnography to envelop youth in critical cariño (Camangian, 2010; Cariaga, 2019; Cruz, 2012; DeNicolo et al., 2015; Fuentes & Pérez, 2016; Jimenez,

2020; Rodriguez, 2018). This work enabled dispossessed, immigrant, and undocumented youth to become knowledge producers, crafting truth-telling counter-narratives that talked back to a society that demonized them. The public dissemination of these narratives to broader, authentic audiences represented a refusal to be erased and silenced. The self-reflection prompted by these narratives strengthened students' connections to community cultural wealth, offered a therapeutic outlet to release trauma, and validated their existence.

These narratives allowed teachers to know students more deeply and better tailor instruction to meet students' needs. Alluding to this benefit, Ms. Schmidt noted:

> There is a lot of talk lately about "culturally relevant pedagogy" and I think more important than learning the general culture of a group of students is learning the specific DETAILS of your individual students' lives. This requires more work and will change year to year, but it is SO much more authentic than simply implementing curriculum that is somehow related to a group of students' race, religion, ethnicity, etc.

Ms. Schmidt's commitment to learning the unique aspects of students' cultural identities represented an expression of critical cariño.

Another noteworthy element of Ms. Schmidt's My Voice Matters unit was how it extended an open-ended invitation to share whatever perspectives students desired. This choice reflected critical cariño because it gave students the option to withhold stories they wished to keep private. Tuck and Yang (2014) warn against pedagogies that overemphasize and glorify pain narratives. They reference well-meaning ESL teachers, who, in the name of developing students' "authentic voices," repeatedly encourage students to write pieces following "a rarefied pattern of refugee-as-victim" (p. 251). They contend that White liberal teachers who solicit such stories may unwittingly reinforce limiting stereotypes that condemn youth to seeing themselves primarily as wounded victims and doomed members of the underclass (p. 252). By keeping her assignment open, Ms. Schmidt allowed students to exercise agency and reveal/explore what they wanted.

Because they shared their stories with each other in the classroom, all students had opportunities to consider, reflect, and draw inspiration and wisdom from the compelling narratives presented by their peers. On one occasion, I saw another teacher during a life skill's class on substance abuse play a My Voice Matters recording in which the narrator describes growing up with an alcoholic parent. This centering of a student-composed text to enrich learning further demonstrates the high regard MHS teachers had for narrative and how these recordings traveled beyond Ms. Schmidt's classroom to impact multiple audiences. Critical cariño flourished in these classrooms because students' lived experiences occupied centerstage and kept learning "real." Together, these accounts demonstrate how MHS teachers harnessed narratives (both published and personal) to attend to marginalized students' unique ontological needs and sociocultural identities.

Controversy as a Vehicle to Arouse Curiosity, Passion, and Agency

If the prominence of narratives at MHS underscored teachers' roles as identity workers, their penchant for organizing instruction around controversy, argument, and debate highlighted their role as "democracy workers" (Hess, 2009, p. 25). Explaining that debate was "a philosophy of the school," the school's literacy coach indicated that controversy was "a great way to get kids more involved, engaged, and interested." Undergirding this expression of critical cariño was the belief that participation in substantive dialogue and argument prepared students to become informed, active, and efficacious citizens able and ready to challenge injustice. Mr. Behari pitched debate as a transformative pedagogy and steered PD toward expanding his colleagues' debate facilitation skills. "You're creating a student who can think and who can analyze and who's excited about digging out truth and fighting for it."

Across the disciplines and grades, MHS students encountered regular opportunities to investigate, analyze, and debate contested issues such as the n-word,[3] sweatshop labor, genetics testing, climate change remedies, military aggression, unauthorized (im)migration, and electoral politics. Structured Academic Controversies (Johnson & Johnson, 1988) were a common cooperative learning strategy to elicit deliberative dialogue. Students even found themselves debating tricky questions in math. Mr. Tran reported that during Complex Instruction cooperative group time, his favorite moments occurred when students sparred:

> There would be profanity hurled back and forth between two students because they firmly believed their solutions were correct. They tried to defend their solutions. . . . Having students debate about mathematics demonstrates their engagement level and also that they're really concerned about their stance on the particular problems.

His recollection of mathematical disputes brimming with profanity and unleashing "a crazy uproar" echoed students' accounts of debate in other classrooms.

Mr. Behari's students cited debates as the best part of his class. They highlighted a "war room" on military aggression in which they acted as either hawks or doves trying to influence the U.S. president. "We debated back and forth. Some people got mad. . . . they were all screaming at each other and they got up and they were hitting the table." These glimpses into classrooms suggest the ways in which students and teachers at MHS were habituated to impassioned, embodied debate as normative classroom discourse. While references to profanity-laced talk and table pounding may suggest vitriol and a lack of civility, Mr. Behari was quick to remind colleagues and students that the point was not competition, but the intellectual thrill of "a back-and-forth of ideas" that allows participants to understand "the ideas better than before." According to him, the magic happens when "kids are trying to go into ideas and see weaknesses and strengths in arguments, pulling from different sources and trying to figure out what happened. The inquiry process is inherently interesting for students—that's where kids get excited."

This pro-debate/deliberative dialogue orientation distinguished schooling at MHS from that experienced by other U.S. youth. In a study of 2,366 California high school students, Kahne and Middaugh (2008) discovered that sizable numbers of adolescents reported limited exposure to activities such as discussions of current events and social problems, open classroom climates, simulations of civic processes, and opportunities to practice civic skills. Disturbingly, these scholars also identified access to these high-quality learning opportunities as dependent on students' race and class. While students identifying as White reported having numerous opportunities to voice opinions and engage in civic learning, Latinx and Black youth had fewer opportunities. Based on these findings, these scholars argue that schools exacerbate inequality by failing to offer historically marginalized populations adequate opportunities to support their development as conscientious and effective citizens. This supposition appears to have some validity given research demonstrating that across demographic groups, Latinx youth are "by far the most 'civically alienated' and the least likely to be 'broadly engaged'" (Sullivan & Godsay, 2014, p. 2). Against this backdrop, MHS's efforts to promote debate for its predominantly poor, Latinx student body represented an important expression of critical cariño because it fostered students' capacity to engage in democratic processes and close what some have deemed a "civic empowerment gap" (Levinson, 2010).

MHS teachers inducted students into debate early. In their life skills class, freshmen were introduced to the story of Wiley College's African American debate team that defeated the reigning (all White) national champions during the Jim Crow era (Scherman, 1997). After watching a clip from *The Great Debaters*, a fictionalized movie of the team, students discussed how the Wiley debaters' incisive arguments and rhetorical agility allowed them to challenge segregation. Debriefing the scene, students admired the debaters' dramatic oral delivery ("I liked how she raised her voice and repeated words for emphasis"), logical argumentation ("She used her opponent's argument against him"), and deep knowledge ("They had stats and facts. Evidence"). Lessons such as this socialized students into seeing debate and argumentation as avenues to fight for worthy causes.

Some debates took on legendary status. One much anticipated "classic" was the senior government class's annual simulation of the Supreme Court's

1966 landmark *Miranda v. Arizona* case that led to the requirement that police read defendants the Miranda warning. Anticipating that students would
relate to the Latino immigrant defendant, Mr. Behari organized this moot
court in conjunction with a Know Your Rights unit that plunged students
into studying the U.S. Constitution's Bill of Rights alongside six notable
Supreme Court precedent cases.[4] He launched the unit with an activity designed to incite interest. Directing students to "switch into lawyer mode,"
he asked them to view a video of himself desecrating the American flag
and decide whether he should go to jail. Students credited this lesson with
provoking their interest in the unit's essential question "How can government most effectively protect citizens' rights?" Over the course of the unit,
students gained awareness of a host of controversial issues: voting access via
ballots in multiple languages, gay marriage, and racial profiling of Arabs at
airports.

For the Miranda trial, Mr. Behari assigned groups of five students
to argue for either Arizona or Miranda. To prepare, students read and
discussed the Bill of Rights as well as accessible summaries of precedents.
They hashed out hypothetical scenarios set within their own city that
required them to evaluate the constitutional validity of government actions. One scenario asked students to determine if police had violated the
rights of four young Latino men clad in gang colors whose car was pulled
over and searched. The search uncovered concealed, loaded weapons.
Wrestling with these circumstances, students considered the principle of
unlawful search and seizure and weighed the importance of due process.
Recalling this discussion, one senior, Anna, shared, "It pushed my thinking. . . . One, 'cause it's violating their rights after they said, 'No, don't
check the car.' But two, the illegal guns cause suffering. . . . I was in the
middle at first. . . . but I decided it's a violation of their rights." Anna's
internal debate about this scenario demonstrates how Mr. Behari not only
connected the Constitution to students' lives in thought-provoking ways,
but how he sharpened students' critical analysis of the Constitution. These
activities deepened comprehension of both the law and the Miranda case's
key controversies.

Other preparations included deconstructing and imitating debate
rhetoric. Students practiced posing analogy questions, proffering alternate
explanations, identifying omitted facts, challenging a source's legitimacy,
summing up evidence succinctly, and infusing passion into oral delivery.
They wrote essays analyzing the case and worked with their team to develop opening and closing statements as well as arguments elucidating how
the fifth, sixth, and 14th Amendments either confirmed or disproved that
Miranda's rights had been violated.

The culminating assessment occurred after school in the stately library,
where vaulted arched ceilings and wood-paneled wainscoting provided an
air of formality.[5] In an email soliciting participation, Mr. Behari coaxed his

colleagues to volunteer to roleplay Supreme Court justices. Promising them excitement and a complimentary alcoholic beverage at the next MHS faculty gathering, Mr. Behari wrote:

> It's that time of year again! The seniors will be arguing the case of Ernesto Miranda and will debate whether or not the police violated his constitutional rights. The debates are set to be memorable. The battles fierce. All they need are willing adults to serve as Supreme Court Justices to try the case. Don't worry, you will not have to be approved by any Republicans in the Senate. Just email me, and I'll put you on the list of esteemed justices. Here are the job requirements:
>
> 1. Approximately an hour and a half commitment after school.
> 2. A dedication to pushing students on their thinking but supporting them when they struggle.
> 3. A willingness to wear a black robe and be honored like the ministers of justice that you are.

Mr. Behari's irreverent invitation netted enthusiastic replies. Principal West jumped in first, announcing "I love the Miranda trials!" and offering to serve twice. In all, close to a dozen staff stepped up annually to be justices. This widespread participation was an expression of institutional critical cariño, conveying to students teachers' desire for them to grow into thoughtful, informed citizens—citizens who not only understood the wheels of justice, but who might also one day make those wheels spin. The lightheartedness with which Mr. Behari framed the activity speaks to the way in which MHS infused a refreshing dose of levity and playfulness into serious academic work and social issue controversies.[6] This balance added a special emotional charge to the court proceedings with students and justices arriving professionally dressed and pumped with anticipation.

On the big day, student legal teams arranged themselves around conference tables, spreading out documents, notecards, and bottles of water. Justices seated themselves along a long table, and the session commenced with the pounding of a gavel. Lead-off speakers approached the bench and exhibited decorum.

> May it please the Court, I would like to submit Arizona's opening statement. Ladies and gentlemen, we are here to discuss the truths that lie behind a case and expose the unlawful act committed by Ernesto Miranda against Patty McGee, who was raped and robbed of innocence. . . . In Miranda's case, his 5th, 6th, and 14th amendments rights were not violated. . . . Our case will prove that felons like Ernesto Miranda should be held accountable.

In the exchanges that followed, students and justices delved into whether Miranda had been compelled to confess, whether a lawyer should have been present during interrogation, and whether Miranda had enjoyed the benefit of "equal protection of the laws." Grappling with justices' pointed questions, teams huddled and whispered to brainstorm rebuttals and responses. The proceedings unfolded with seriousness and engagement, ending with the justices conferring and announcing a decision.

Mr. Behari considered the moot court a "good authentic assessment" to evaluate students' capacity to develop and defend arguments. Reflecting on students' performances, he shared:

> It was really rewarding to see kids stand up to complex questioning and complex argumentation and stand behind the points they're trying to make. I'm envisioning my kids at UCLA on Bruin Walk in the face of a Bruin Republican, who's trying to take down their cause, and they're able to stand up and assert themselves in an effective intellectual way. That's my vision of what I'm preparing them to do.

Mr. Behari's delight in his students' argumentation skills and his image of them being equipped to assert themselves in the face of challenge highlight the connection MHS educators made between argumentation and democratic deliberation. Mr. Behari sought to build students' confidence and ability to hold their ground "in an effective intellectual way" when confronted by those with opposing views. Some scholars argue that such cross-cutting political talk, although rare in the U.S.'s currently hyper-partisan political climate, is the cornerstone to a healthy deliberative democracy (Hess, 2009). By supporting students to not only think critically, but to converse cogently and persuasively, MHS's emphasis on debate represented an expression of critical cariño because it paved the way for students to participate fully in democracy.

To promote students' effective political cross-talk and self-advocacy, Mr. Behari and his colleagues stressed the importance of viewing controversies from multiple perspectives. Indeed, understanding different perspectives was enshrined as one of the five HOM. Mr. Behari's students noted how his instruction stretched them to consider multiple points of view. Hector observed how Mr. Behari "puts out a new topic. . . . [And] we all come in there with one mentality about that topic, but yet he gives us evidence and other points of views that contradict it." One focus group discussed this facet of the government class and Miranda trial in particular:

> *Linda:* In Mr. B's class, he makes you think about both sides. When he tells us one side, we're always complaining, "Oh, we know what you're gonna do already. You're gonna make us think about the other side." It's like vice versa. But I get what he's trying to do, because at the end of the day—

Jesús: He kind of gets us to think more.

Linda: —it really does make you think about both sides. It's kind of—I don't know, it's just—

MWC: Why would thinking about both sides matter? You guys have your side; why does it matter to understand the other side?

Anna: There's people in the world who choose sides because they're biased, like, one perspective, so they're like, "OK, I'm staying with it." And they only hear one perspective. He's trying to tell us both perspectives so we won't be biased and we could see both of them. To me, at first it was confusing. I'm like, "Oh, my God, am I gonna help a rapist [Miranda]?" And then I thought about it, and I thought, "But his rights were violated." It's kind of neat. . . . The Miranda case got me frustrated because it made me feel that people trust in the police and the police give them lies. They pushed him [Miranda] to the wall, not literally, but they pushed him to the wall so he could confess—so then that made me think and I was just mad.

Linda: And that's the thing. There are multiple stories, multiple sides to each story, and it's up to you to choose carefully and trustfully what side you want to believe in. You don't want to believe in stupid facts.

These students understood how seeing issues from multiple sides allowed them to be more informed, detect bias, weigh evidence, and resist "stupid facts." Kuhn (1999) characterizes such thinking as evidence of an "evaluative epistemology" wherein individuals recognize that "all opinions are not equal and knowing is understood as a process that entails judgment, evaluation, and argument" (p. 22). Fortified with the capacity to know how they know and decide what to believe and revise beliefs as warranted, students can achieve advanced metacognition. Kuhn contends that such cognition is "arguably the most important way in which people both individually and collectively take control of their lives" (p. 23). Nurturing this kind of critical thinking exemplifies critical cariño praxis. It equips youth to deconstruct contested issues, defend their rights, and participate in democratic processes.

Mr. Behari's students came away from the Know Your Rights unit and Miranda trial invested in their constitutional rights. Linda said the unit made her realize that "it's really important to know your rights because most people just know freedom of speech . . . but there is so much more that you need to know." She added, "I also learned that it's important to pay attention to the outside world" and that "the justice system is really unfair." Her classmate Anna indicated that the unit had inspired her to "come back to my community as a lawyer" in order to defend "people of color who are criminals who are being treated unjustly." These outcomes suggest the ways that opportunities to debate and argue controversial issues enabled students to "read" and navigate the world and imagine themselves as democratic agents.

Community as a Resource to Enrich Learning

The third critical cariño pedagogy involved educators and students venturing beyond school walls and using the local community as a classroom. In some instances, these community extensions linked students to their biological families. In others, community connections occurred through activities undertaken with businesses, nonprofits, museums, neighborhoods, and government agencies. These opportunities enriched schooling by fortifying students' community cultural wealth, enhancing curricular relevance, and heightening awareness of social oppression.

At times this pedagogy overlapped with MHS's emphasis on narratives. For example, the narratives students documented through interviews with community members for their digital immigration stories helped them bring Mr. Behari's essential question "Can all immigrants achieve the American Dream?" to life. Rather than simply reading published biographical stories, students had the opportunity to dialogue with someone in the community directly affected by immigration, making the issues close and real. Mr. Avila also had his Spanish students interview an immigrant and compose poems based on those conversations. Recalling this assignment as powerful and as an example of why Mr. Avila's class was "awesome," Camila shared:

> It made me think and made me cry too, it was a poem. . . . We had to interview someone, *un inmigrante que nos inspira* (an immigrant who inspires us). I picked my dad. I really didn't know. I had never got [sic] the chance to really sit down with my dad and ask him about his childhood, and ask him *por qúe tiene carácter así* (why he has a personality like that). And when I did that poem and he gave me all that information, it made me think, "Wow, I know where you're coming from. I know where all that happiness and that sadness is coming from." I would be like, "You're always mad," but I would never ask him, "Why? What's wrong? Are you OK? Do you need anything?" So that class makes us value the things that we have because Mr. Avila makes us reflect.

By tapping into the assets residing in students' homes and neighborhoods, these assignments strengthened students' understanding of themselves as immigrants and of the United States as a country of immigrants. For Camila, the conversation with her father deepened her understanding of his *lucha por la felicidad y la libertad*. Her emergent awareness of his struggle, pain, and wounds made her cry, but also amplified her aspirational capital, familial capital, and resistant capital (Yosso, 2005). Such connections between students' lived contexts—their heritage cultures, their personal histories, and their neighborhoods—added relevance to their academic learning, which boosted engagement.

One noteworthy expression of this critical cariño pedagogy emerged in Ms. Barrett's annual Our City project that culminated a 3-month long City Dreams and Dilemmas unit. Preparatory work included reading Anna Deveare Smith's *Twilight Los Angeles*, a one-woman play focused on the 1991 Los Angeles riots. Smith conducted several hundred interviews to understand the varied perspectives of Angelinos, including witnesses, victims, and instigators of violence, as well as police, firefighters, politicians, and a juror. Ms. Barrett engaged students in analysis of these perspectives, and the riots' root causes (racism, poverty, or interethnic conflict). Most student essays argued that "the most significant cause of the L.A. riots was the long history of African Americans being oppressed by Whites in the United States," but some students argued that poverty was the main culprit because it prompted people to "fight for a better economic future." Following *Twilight*, the class shifted into reading *Our America: Life and Death on the South Side of Chicago*, by LeAlan Jones and Lloyd Newman, two teenagers growing up in poverty who chronicled their neighborhood with assistance from an NPR reporter. Ms. Barrett used this text to impress on students the power of photojournalism, firsthand reporting, and local discourses.

Guided by these texts, students set out to document their own city by surveying strangers at four separate locales, interviewing community members, photographing their surroundings, and crafting documentary poems that incorporated the ideas, language, and dialect of interviewees. Prefacing the assignment, Ms. Barrett told students, "You have a voice. If there are things you don't like in our city, let's write about it. Let's get it out there. Let's tell people about it." Elaborating her intentions, Ms. Barrett indicated that she wanted students "to feel like they have a voice in what's going on in their own community, that they're not powerless." With her guidance students peer edited, curated, and assembled a book entitled *Welcome to Our City* that they presented to the local public library. The final product featured a slang dictionary; over 20 photos of urban scenes documenting gang graffiti tags, illegally dumped garbage, vandalized buildings, deserted shopping carts, security fencing, police patrols, and liquor stores; 22 documentary poems telling the stories of a *llantero* (tire worker), a fast-food employee, a waitress, a construction worker, an ex-gang member, and many students and mothers; and five essays addressing gangs, violence, and poverty. Ms. Barrett related that her students didn't believe their book would be published, so "it was priceless to see the look of delight and satisfaction on their faces when they held their professionally bound copy for the first time." She added that, in 2010, the book was purchased by the city public library and placed in the history room of the main branch, "pushing the reach of student voices even further."

Jaime, who exhibited extra initiative for the project by visiting a Home Depot parking lot on a Saturday morning to interview day workers for hire, wrote in his essay:

> Something has to be done to stop the poverty in our city, so unemployed workers that are known as *jornaleros* will actually have a chance here. This city is full of hope. Sure statistics show the city is in deep poverty, but there is still hope for everyone because there can be a change. Our city is unique in many different ways but overall it is a beautiful place. It shouldn't be known as the poorest or "ghetto-est" place ever. It deserves to be a place of opportunities not poverty.

Jaime's essay and his peers' contributions to this book reveal how local contexts were converted into vibrant classrooms enabling students to make sense of their communities, grapple with vexing problems, and participate in efforts to increase awareness and catalyze change. Although the book concentrated on disturbing themes, it also incubated hope. For example, the waitress poem expressed "high hopes," emphasized "the potential of the city," and predicted that "the city will get better because the generation that is entering high school is both intelligent and conscious." The Our City project exemplified critical cariño by tapping into community resources, examining social issues, and prompting reflection about solving community problems.

MHS also drew heavily on community resources during annual post-sessions when students ventured out en masse to experience expeditionary learning in municipal and national parks, museums, nonprofit organizations, and businesses. Some post-sessions were framed around political themes. One year, there was a post-session entitled Take Back the City designed to contest gentrification. Promotional materials for this session provocatively asked, "Bruh, why there so many White people here? Where these hipsters come from? Ever feel like the city is being taken over by outside invaders and spectators? Join this post-session and take back the city!" Students in this session toured civil rights landmarks and met with low-rider car owners to understand this facet of Chicano culture. They also produced art in an effort to document and explore "the many ways local communities resist gentrification and create their own transformation for a life worth living."

Another year, there was a post-session entitled Culture as Weapon that asked students to ponder the essential question "How can we/artists use art/culture to fight oppression?" In a reflection essay about this course, Ms. Grace indicated that the instructors "wished to engage a class of predominantly Latino/a youth in exploring cultural symbolism through a lens of empowerment. We wanted to teach students how art can be peaceful liberation and how culture might protect them from dominant forces like hegemony." To achieve these objectives, students took a walking tour of their city to examine murals, mosaics, and graffiti art. They took public transport to visit an art gallery, a museum, a community center, and a regional park known for its art installations fabricated from recycled and natural materials. At each place, students conversed with docents to learn about the artists' inspirations, histories, techniques, and aims.

This post-session culminated with students exhibiting their own art (see Figure 4.2). Their installations demonstrate how opportunities to explore surrounding environments and the people and culture within them became springboards for students to voice concerns. The composition featured in Figure 4.2A broadcasts the voices of students resisting low academic expectations and dropout pressures, asserting instead their desire to succeed, graduate, and prove naysayers wrong. The installation displayed in Figure 4.2B drew attention to gun violence and envisioned how, with communication, education, and time, the community could build peace. By giving students the opportunity to draw inspiration and knowledge from their communities, MHS educators affirmed students' lives, roots, and dreams.

While post-sessions constituted a unique activity exemplifying critical cariño, teachers also wove community outreach into the regular school year. Field trips enriched learning. Ms. Howard, the journalism teacher, organized a field trip to a news agency, where students had the chance to observe reporters and managers discuss stories and plan the weekend edition. She reported that students came away better understanding "how writing can impact the world." Sophomores attended medical conferences where they learned from professionals such as emergency medical technicians, county health representatives, surgeons, and epidemiologists. In one conference session, students analyzed health and disease data by the zipcodes in their city and discussed health inequities. While studying Elie Wiesel's memoir *Night*, Ms. Schmidt took students to a college to meet a holocaust survivor. Other teachers organized trips to universities for ethnic studies conferences, to fast-food restaurants to interview workers, and to a stream to test water contamination. In these myriad ways, MHS educators enveloped youth in critical cariño by expanding awareness of social issues and supporting students to give back to their communities and creatively express their truths in empowering ways.

Community Impact Projects

The fourth critical cariño pedagogy moved students beyond telling stories, marshaling arguments, and understanding their surroundings into the world

Figure 4.2. Student Art Displayed at "Culture as Weapon" Post-Session Exhibit

A.

The urban art installation that we did was about high school dropouts. The teenage boy represents a student who wants to graduate. He is imagining himself getting a diploma and graduating from high school. He is a really good artist. People judge him and think "You will not graduate." But he wants to prove that they are wrong. We decided to make this art installation because it represents the teenagers who drop out of school today.

B.

This urban art installation is about stopping violence. Each symbol represents the importance of what needs to be done in order for us to build peace in the community. The telephone represents the lack of communication. Instead of people using weapons to deal with their problems they should find other ways to communicate. The book represents how some people can be ignorant toward the community. They don't know how violence can make a big impact on families and friends such as the drive-by shooting. So in order to stop violence we need to educate the community. The timer shows how it can take a long time to build peace in the community. Even if it takes a long time, we are willing to make it happen.

Note: Paint on rock states "Educate the community."

of action to implement projects to meet community needs. Community impact projects (CIPs) were the backbone of EDP and were occasionally woven into academic courses. Diego, EDP's co-director, described CIPs as youth-led opportunities for students to apply school knowledge and skills and exercise leadership to generate "real actions that can make a real impact in their immediate lives." Through CIPs, Diego and his team sought to instill the value of meaningful action, lifelong learning, youth–adult partnerships, and co-creation. Guided by a participatory action research framework (Cammarota & Fine, 2010; Fox et al., 2010; Torre, 2009), students conducted community assessment scans, collected data, and identified stakeholders. After analyzing findings, students developed strategic action plans to positively impact their community. They presented proposals to teachers and community members who pressed them to consider potential obstacles and refine plans. Next, students implemented, publicized, and evaluated their CIPs. This outward action enabled youth to channel their emergent political consciousness into co-creative endeavors designed to transform oppressive structures. Such collective action is essential to overcome woundedness and victimization and thereby recover wholeness and full agency (hooks, 1989). Examples of three CIPs illustrate their power and variety.

The Real Dreamers. The Real Dreamers were a dozen youth who advocated for the Dream Act, a legislative proposal at federal and state levels granting undocumented youth access to public universities and student loans and offering the promise of resident status upon completion of 2 years of college. MHS's Real Dreamers initiated a letter-writing campaign through advisories, enlisting their peers to sway elected officials. Several Real Dreamers attended a statewide political networking conference. Recalling this experience, one student bragged how he had asked a state congressman a question during a public forum, received praise for asking a good question, and obtained the congressman's business card to follow up. Two Real Dreamers joined a national bus tour to Washington, DC, risking arrest and deportation to take their cause into the chambers of the U.S. Congress. Dolores Reyes, the faith-based community partner from City Community Organization, who chaperoned that trip, recalled how a Midwest reporter pulled her aside after a press conference to compliment a student's testimony. The reporter told her, "In my whole career, this was the most moving and strong message I ever heard from a young—from a person, period. Not a politician, not even a really well-educated person, will be not only so accurate, but articulate." The Real Dreamers demonstrated the power of MHS youth to galvanize political support. When Governor Jerry Brown signed the California act in 2011, these students had the satisfaction of knowing that their hard work had made a difference.

The Futbolistas. The 30 members of MHS's soccer club divided their time between playing the game and community organizing. One Saturday, they held a street soccer tournament during which participants spent half-time engaged in one of two student-led workshops focused on the Dream Act or capitalism. The tournament's stated goal was "to empower members of our community against institutional violence," but players also used the event to highlight the absence of safe places to play soccer in their neighborhood. This concern prompted them to design a CIP focused on acquiring a soccer field for MHS. With guidance from their charismatic coach, Desireé Campos (a former professional soccer player), club members collected data about the number of soccer fields per capita across city districts. These investigations exposed inequitable resource allocations and helped them formulate a data-based argument asserting the inadequacy of a single field for 30,000 residents. They bolstered their case with research documenting the benefits of sports on health, high school and college graduation rates, and community well-being. Drawing on this research, they applied for and received a $100,000 grant. This win came with strings requiring students to lobby their school district for matching funds. Sharing the impetus for their CIP to the school board, Guillermo, a junior explained:

> The school looked like a prison out there, so we wanted to change that idea and give it to the future for the community around us, just to make it more safer [sic] and for people to come by and play. So we decided to make this vision to get a field for us and for all our fellow students in the school.

The soccer club's successful campaign transformed the MHS campus, converting a once bleak stretch of cracked asphalt into a state-of-the-art, brilliant green turf. Its presence further enhanced MHS prominence as a vibrant community hub. The political process of mobilizing for the field strengthened students' organizing skills, thereby increasing their navigational and resistant capital and proving to them that a small group of determined youth can accomplish great things.

Free College Campaign. While the Real Dreamers and Futbolistas pursued CIPs during EDP, another CIP arose from Mr. Behari's senior government class and Mr. Simmons's advanced math class. Upset about rising tuition at California universities, Mr. Simmons approached Mr. Behari to see if they might appeal to students to tackle this issue. Seizing affordable postsecondary education as the perfect cause to galvanize students' democratic interests, Mr. Behari agreed. He developed a series of lessons to help seniors understand the 1960 California Master Plan for Higher Education, which embraced tuition-free education and the ballot

Table 4.1. MHS's Critical Cariño Pedagogies

Strategy:	Purposes:	Selected examples by grade level:
Published and personal narratives	• Foster ethnocultural and racial identity development • Enhance sociopolitical awareness • Promote ontological healing • Affirm and magnify community cultural wealth • Share counter-stories with authentic audiences • Build classroom community	• My two voices (poems on complex identity) (9) • *Time of Butterflies* essays (10) • My Voice Matters radio essays (10) • Digital immigration stories (11) • "This I Believe" essays (12) • "I am" poems (9–12, post-session) • Firewalk testimonies (10 and 12)
Controversial issues	• Spark interest in real world • Develop skills of critical thinking, deliberation, advocacy, and debate • Expand knowledge of sociohistorical issues	• N-word fishbowl discussion (9) • SAC[a] on marijuana (9) • SAC on sweatshop labor (10) • SAC on ethics of genetic testing (10) • Debate/discussion on illegal immigration (11) • Model UN on climate change (10) • Debate/"war room" on military aggression (11) • Miranda moot court (12) • Political pundit election debate (12)
Community as resource	• Promote curricular relevance • Connect youth to local assets • Validate local knowledge and contexts • Spur empathy and civic engagement • Amplify community cultural wealth	• Our City project (9) • Power of Food visit to Kentucky Fried Chicken (9) • Interviews with immigrants (11) • Medical conferences (10) • Community members on defense panels (10 and 12) • Internships (11–12) • Museum, gallery, and neighborhood tours (9–12, post-session)
Community impact projects	• Address/meet community needs • Promote civic agency and efficacy • Develop navigational capital • Foster leadership skills	• Real Dreamers campaign (9–12) • Soccer field campaign (9–12) • Free college ballot initiative (12) • Safe sex campaign (9–12) • Peaceful city campaign (9–12)

a. SAC refers to structured academic controversy (Johnson & Johnson, 1988), which is a structured dialogue process that entails students orally discussing and rehearsing information, advocating positions, exchanging knowledge with peers, critically evaluating issues, and eventually arriving initiative system. The latter examined how initiatives, although touted as a populist process, have become dominated by industry and millionaire-backed, paid signature campaigns mainly serving the interests of corporate elites. Intent on building a grassroots movement, students partnered with peers at another high school to develop and debate what policy voters might approve. They crafted a proposal with precise legal language outlining eligibility requirements as well as fiscal costs and impacts. Their draft constitutional amendment proposed making state universities tuition-free for full-time, in-state students achieving 2.7 GPAs or performing 70 hours of community service each year. Californians earning more than $250,000 a year in taxable income would shoulder the cost in increased taxes. Students submitted their plan to the California secretary of state for certification and once approved began the grueling work of gathering 807,615 qualifying signatures. As part of this effort, they designed bumper stickers and created a Facebook page to gain visibility. Armed with clipboards and signature forms, they canvassed college campuses and other highly trafficked locales. Although their efforts fell short, students gained invaluable exposure to democratic processes and once again sharpened their organizing skills. Ultimately, these students generated public awareness around an important issue and defied negative portrayals of nondominant urban youth as alienated, apathetic, broken, and "at risk."

Through CIPs such as these, MHS students exercised agency to transform their communities and improve their education prospects. For immigrant-origin youth, many of whom endure the disquieting uncertainty of "liminal legality" (Gonzales et al., 2012; Menjívar, 2006; Turner & Mangual Figueroa, 2019), such collective political action represented an important foray toward claiming citizenship rights within a participatory democracy. As such, CIPs proved to be an invaluable critical cariño pedagogy, nurturing Latinx students' organizing skills, hope, and confidence.

Table 4.1 provides a summary overview of MHS's four critical cariño pedagogies. This table underscores how critical cariño suffused multiple settings within the school and extended well beyond episodic interpersonal enactments within particular courses or programs. This institutionalization of critical cariño was made possible by three organizational structures. I address those structures next.

INSTITUTIONALIZING CRITICAL CARIÑO

The institutionalization of critical cariño refers to the establishment of schoolwide policies and norms to nurture students' sociocultural/political identities, critical social analysis skills, and participation in social justice struggles. Such efforts seek to ensure that youth collectively experience critical cariño as a coherent, constant message across various sites of learning. This continuity elevates the intensity of critical cariño and amplifies its impact. At MHS, the school's mission, commitment to professional autonomy, and community partnerships facilitated the institutionalization of critical cariño.

A Compelling, Widely Embraced Social Justice Mission

From its inception, the families, educators, and community organizers who founded MHS infused critical cariño into the school's mission, vision, and full-service community school design. Operating within a social justice paradigm, MHS's founders converged around the goal of interrupting injustice and inequity. This mission imbued their work with moral–ethical purpose and constituted the most important organizational structure fueling critical cariño. The mission's reification of "transformative learning experiences" (discussed in Chapter 3) paved the way for the curricular focus on narratives, controversy, community, and action detailed in this chapter.

As previously noted, MHS was a "mission- and vision-driven" school where staff exhibited considerable unity and enthusiasm as they invested themselves into the *lucha* for freedom and happiness. Speaking to the mission's primacy, Principal West explained, "I make decisions based on whether or not it fits into the context of the mission." This laser focus allowed the school to be strategic as it pursued its vision to "become a national model for urban education." Summing up the mission's importance, Ms. Glass shared:

> MHS is really committed to being very explicit that we're teaching students of color how to be successful in a world that has the deck stacked against them and to be successful specifically to change the healthcare field. . . . MHS tries to build really strong scholars with a sense of mission and purpose and a knowledge that they need to work harder than White kids on the other side of town because things are stacked against them. I think we're really honest with kids about that, trying to teach them the skills to be successful in that way. It's hard for me not to think of the mission and restate, "MHS seeks to dramatically interrupt patterns of injustice and poverty." I do think that's what we're doing.

Ms. Glass's remarks make clear the strong commitment to justice held by MHS educators. The mission prompted teachers to embrace a critical cariño praxis reflecting a color(ful), sociohistorical understanding of Latinx students' lived realities (Rolón-Dow, 2005). Guided by the mission, MHS educators strove to expose students to the ways oppressive systems have "stacked the deck" against them and impart the knowledge, skills, and "sense of mission and purpose" necessary to transform social, political, and economic circumstances. This quest to nurture students' cultural and political growth and passion while also promoting their academic success was indicative of institutionalized critical cariño.

Professional Autonomy, Curricular Freedom, and Relational Trust

The vibrancy of critical cariño at MHS was strengthened also by the organization's treatment of teachers as autonomous professionals capable of exercising discretion, intelligence, and creativity to design original curricula likely to advance the mission. Focal teachers repeatedly stressed how curricular freedom enabled them to serve students well and engineer transformational learning experiences. Mr. Behari, for example, waxed appreciatively:

> Our principal trusts us. He'll never come in and question anything that we're doing. It's really a nice place to be for me. My big thing is, "Just trust me. I got this. Let me figure this out." I think that there's no pressure on me to do anything other than just do the job that I think is the best for the kids. It's nice.

Echoing Mr. Behari, Mr. Tran shared:

> One of the things I really enjoy about MHS is that I'm given a lot of freedom. There's a lot of trust on the teachers that they're teaching the content, but they also have freedom in terms of what they get to teach. I feel that if I had to follow a textbook or was restricted and had to achieve these benchmarks and so forth, it would make me less stimulated. It would stunt my creativity.

Unbeholden to district textbooks and benchmarks, MHS teachers exercised creative license to meet Common Core State Standards (CCSS) and design innovative curricula such as the Miranda trial, the City Dreams and Dilemmas unit, and the free college ballot proposal. This creativity enhanced the psychic rewards of their work. These arrangements, in turn, enabled students to benefit from civically engaging and culturally sustaining instruction.

High levels of relational trust underpinned this curricular freedom and professional autonomy. Through a dynamic combination of "respect, competence, personal regard for others, and integrity" (Bryk & Schneider, 2002, p. 23), MHS forged a "community of commitment" (Ancess, 2003) within which professionals espoused a shared mission and dedicated themselves to helping each other achieve that mission. Evidence of this relational trust emerged in Principal West's faith in his staff.

> They really care deeply about changing kids' lives. They're really passionate about it, and they want to be successful. They don't want to fail at it. The thing is that way too often, we blame people for failing at something that is incredibly difficult, and we don't give them the support mechanisms that they need to become successful. . . . I believe that if you get those people together . . . and you give them the opportunity to speak and share their experiences, if you have good people, they will come up with answers that work.

Principal West's admiration for MHS's teachers' passion, deep care for youth, and desire to succeed translated into a willingness to trust them to "come up with answers that work." Convinced that the school's mission would best be served by nurturing teachers' commitment and capacity to teach well rather than by regulating and micromanaging their work, he adopted a leadership philosophy favoring commitment over control (Rowan, 1990). This orientation, which has been associated with positive impacts on an organization's overall ethos and culture,[7] mirrored and reinforced the school's problem-posing/solving pedagogical stance with youth. Teachers too were granted permission to read the world of their classrooms and communities and determine which instructional interventions would engage youth in the kinds of transformative learning experiences necessary to catalyze positive social change. For these reasons, the triad of professional autonomy, curricular freedom, and relational trust enhanced the school's enactment of critical cariño.

Community Partnerships

The final organizational structure contributing to critical cariño's pervasiveness at MHS was the school's substantial community partnerships. As noted in Chapter 2's discussion of the network of care, MHS organized itself as a full-service community school and collaborated with an array of CBOs to ensure the health, well-being, and success of students and their families. Through wide-ranging services, including medical, dental, and vision services, psychotherapy, college counseling, academic tutoring, social enrichment, and leadership training, CBOs injected vital resources into MHS students' schooling. These school–community ties amplified critical cariño by expanding the pool of resources available to students and MHS. The chief resource offered by CBOs was access to transformational role models and mentors. Solorzano and Delgado Bernal (2001) explain that these individuals are "members of one's own racial/ethnic and/or gender group who actively demonstrate a commitment to social justice" and who inspire and/or guide youth development (p. 322). At MHS, these individuals practiced what Weiston-Serdan (2017) calls "critical mentorship." Distinct from traditional, paternalistic mentor–mentee relationships that position mentees as lacking and emphasize acculturation to dominant White, middle-class standards and norms, MHS's transformational mentors espoused a philosophy of culturally revitalizing, co-creative, and youth-centered mentorship. The resulting relationships amplified students' access to community cultural wealth (Yosso, 2005).

EDP attracted a talented pool of mentors. César, the prime mover behind the Culture as Weapon post-session, regularly imparted lessons and values gleaned from his Chicano parents, both of whom were leaders within the United Farm Workers (UFW) Union. He also shared his gifts as a rap and visual artist, spearheaded BEST (Brothers Excelling and Striving Together—a young men's empowerment circle), and coached both the Rapid Fire Spoken Word Poetry club and the Town Visionaries (the youth who created the Latinx Heritage posters featured in Figure 2.4). Bringing an equally rich background, Diego, Luz's successor and coach of the Real Dreamers, was a first-generation college graduate and an Argentinian immigrant with experience teaching in the shantytowns of Buenos Aires. Desireé, the Futbolistas' coach, was another talented mentor. Her parents entered the United States as Chilean political refugees in the mid-1970s and impressed upon her the value of her immigrant roots. Her enthusiasm, athletic prowess, and beliefs about sports as a path for liberation and healing enthralled her players. Because each of these mentors approached their work with high levels of political clarity and ardor, they enveloped their protégées in critical cariño. Their daily visibility on campus and their participation in staff retreats meant that the entire MHS community benefited from their wisdom.

These mentors drew on considerable social capital to link youth to other community resources. They acted as "multicultural navigators" (Carter, 2005) who "demonstrate[d] how to possess both dominant and nondominant cultural capital and how to be adept at movement through various sociocultural settings, where cultural codes and rules differ" (p. 137). César, for example, arranged to have a local muralist join students on their Culture as Weapon neighborhood walking tour. Through his ties to a Mexican American nonprofit music academy in a nearby city, he was able to arrange a day-long retreat for youth with an accomplished singer and dancer. One year, he coordinated with a local art museum to present an exhibition of student work celebrating Día de los Muertos. These connections expanded MHS's learning ecology in ways that enhanced critical cariño.

Through these three structures—the social justice mission, curricular freedom, and community partnerships—MHS organized itself to ensure that students inhabited a school in which their political and cultural lives were acknowledged, examined, affirmed, and enriched.

TENSIONS IN CRITICAL CARIÑO

Although the findings presented thus far highlight the salutary aspects of MHS's critical cariño, this work was complicated. Three tensions involved reconciling the social justice mission with neoliberal reform logics, supporting healthy ethnic identity development for non-Latinx youth, and negotiating empowering practices for youth when educators possessed different levels of political consciousness.

Navigating Social Justice and Neoliberalism

MHS inhabited a fraught political space. First, the school functioned within a district, state, and federal public school policy landscape increasingly under the sway of neoliberalism's emphasis on the "efficiency" of competitive markets, the privatization of government services, and the primacy of individual self-interest. For Principal West this reality meant contending with "district pacing guides and benchmark exams, [and] accountability systems," which he characterized as an anathema. "All those things really go against MHS's philosophy." And yet, he understood that "the coinage of the day is absolutely your API and CST scores." He acknowledged too that "everybody knows that the freedoms we're allowed academically [at MHS] are because we have outperformed the district and our similar schools. We are doing well and you get left alone when you're doing well." Ultimately, MHS conformed to accountability regimes in order to carve out spaces to pursue the school's social justice mission and envelop students in critical cariño. Ironically, teachers had to bow to neoliberal metrics of academic achievement in order to deliver on their liberatory vision of schooling.

This tension also surfaced in the school's STEM emphasis and goal to have graduates pursue medical careers. While Mr. West emphasized the prestige and economic benefits enjoyed by health care professionals (and thereby played into neoliberal logics), he also nodded toward social justice by telling students that their higher salaries would generate "a lot of money that can go into your community." This reference to a politics of economic redistribution was coupled with the message that diversifying the health care workforce would help remedy health disparities in urban communities. Walking this tightrope between neoliberal and critical ideologies involved nimble maneuvers. In order to garner funds to expand students' opportunities, West marshaled standardized test scores, student demographic statistics, and other data-based evidence to secure grants from biotechnical corporations and healthcare entities. Because these funders were enmeshed in larger systems of power and inequality, these fund-raising efforts and the mentoring, career exposure, and leadership development made possible by these grants implicated MHS in systems that perpetuated health inequities.

This contradictory space raised questions about the school's theory of action for social change. With regard to STEM, I heard very little discussion at MHS about fundamentally reimagining health care or reforming laws and political institutions to effect macrolevel changes within the health field. For the most part, MHS seemed content with grooming students for medical careers within the existing system. Given the underrepresentation of people of color within the upper echelons of health care management and delivery, the school's press to develop medical professionals reflected a path of "conformist resistance," whereby educators guided students to "strive toward social justice within the existing social systems and social conventions" (Solorzano & Delgado Bernal, 2001, p. 318). Beyond the school's STEM commitments, however, the critical cariño pedagogies described earlier in this chapter seemed intent on nurturing students' political consciousness and "transformational resistance" to interrupt social inequality. Mr. West maintained that these two impulses did not "have to be necessarily opposed to each other." Rejecting an "all or nothing" stance, he advocated for a post-oppositional middle road that welcomed pragmatism and creative compromise. Consequently, the school charted a precarious course as it attempted to navigate social justice and neoliberalism.

Balancing Love for Brown and Black Youth

Although SOLES's research concentrated on Latinx students' success, my interest in non-Latinx students' experiences within a majority "minority" school was piqued one day when I overheard two Black students grumbling after a Día de los Muertos town hall. As they lamented the absence of celebrations for Blacks, I sensed hurt and anger. Given their small numbers on campus (13 students or 5% of the student body during the intensive data collection year), Black youth represented a very small minority. While I did not have the opportunity to examine their experiences in depth, evidence of Black youth being marginalized by the school's intensive attention to Latinx culture surfaced on multiple occasions and in teacher interviews. Ms. Clark (biracially Black and Latina) noted how Black students complained to her about "not being represented in any way." Ms. Barrett expressed concerns too.

> We do a better job with our Latino students than with any of our other students. . . . Because they [Latinx youth] are the dominant culture here, they're easier to address. I don't think we do a good job at all with our Black students. Not that we do a bad job with them, but as far as building that cultural capital . . . I don't know that we do anything.

Echoing her colleagues' sentiments, Ms. Whitmore remarked:

> I know that sometimes a lot of our Black students don't feel as
> supported. We don't attract as much of a Black community because we
> have this reputation of being a Latino school. That's something I've
> heard staff members talk about—how do we outreach specifically to
> more Black students and involve more Black families?

These concerns highlight staff awareness of students' differential and racial-ized school experiences, as well as the dilemma of how to nurture non-Latinx youth on an institutional level when their numbers were so low.

Although the humanities curricula featured a considerable number of texts addressing the experiences of African Americans[8] and the campus showcased murals of Harriet Tubman, Barack Obama, Rosa Parks, and Martin Luther King, Black students still felt alienated. Efforts to support Black youth to produce their own town hall often faltered. As one teacher noted, "Student leadership around Black History Month (BHM) in February is always a bit difficult." The 2012 BHM town hall had to be rescheduled to March because of students' organizational difficulties. That event featured a student-made video in which Black students answered the question "What is it like to be Black at MHS?" Despite poor audio quality, the message that Blacks felt like outsiders came through loud and clear. Following the screening, Luz asked the audience to reflect.

> We have a very rare thing here. A minority group, which is Latinos,
> are the majority. We are not just in numbers the majority, but there is
> a very powerful cultural norm here. We make a big deal about Cinco
> de Mayo and Mexican Independence, right? We fly the Mexican flag.
> We do a big deal about soccer and Día de los Muertos. There are three
> groups that sometimes feel alienated. The Black community, the Asian
> community, and the mixed community, Whites and Native Americans.
> It's our job as Latinos to not replicate what the system does to us to
> others. Do you understand that? We as Latinos know what the system
> does to us; we shouldn't do the same in this school to our brothers and
> sisters. So I am not Black by no [sic] measure. I am Latina, but I
> choose to support the Black History Month and the Black youth
> because this is their school too.

With these remarks, Luz affirmed Black students and invited Latinx students to reflect on their own dominant status in the school, as well as on the mar-ginalization of people of color within broader society. Although she stopped short of explicitly exposing the ways in which ethnoracial divisions have been historically exploited to maintain hegemony, her appeal to cross-racial solidarity was well received as evidenced by the audience's loud clapping.

Unfortunately, this was a fleeting moment deserving further exploration. As Shange's (2019) ethnography of another progressive California high school suggests, the multiracial, coalitional logics espoused by Luz can "cannibalize Black suffering" (p. 3) and "perpetuate antiblack racism even as they seek to eliminate it" (p. 14). These snapshots of Black youth's experiences demonstrate the challenge of establishing antiracist structures that communicate critical cariño to all students.

Competing Conceptions of Critical Cariño Among MHS Educators

A third tension that MHS encountered as it pursued social justice centered on the faculty's divergent views about how to enact critical cariño. Given differing levels of political consciousness and varied experiences living within our racialized society, staff at times debated how to empower youth. Veteran staff reported that explicit attention to race and equity had ebbed since the school's initial years and attributed this shift to an influx of White teachers and Principal West's intensive instructional focus. Signs of this tension surfaced previously in Chapter 2's mention of the *pobrecito* (poor baby) leanings of several staff and in Chapter 3's treatment of tracking debates. Here, I offer glimpses of two critical incidents in which staff struggled to negotiate how best to fulfill MHS's mission.

The first critical incident transpired during a September PD session when staff debated publishing students' class ranks on progress reports, report cards, and classroom grade notifications. Over the span of 12 minutes, 11 staff vocalized pro and con positions on public ranking. Several science teachers argued that because colleges care about class rank when determining admission, students should know that "it's important and pertinent as they plan their futures." Several humanities teachers pushed back. Ms. Clark shared her concerns. "It just feels to me like if we are trying to preach collaboration and cooperation that ranking preaches competition. It's an individual thing. It's not like your group is ranked; it's you yourself." Ms. Barrett expressed her worry that ranks could "mess with students' psychology" and damage students' academic self-perceptions. Principal West argued both sides but raised concerns about the negative consequences of labeling students. "I definitely don't want to internalize in the kids that you're in the back of the class and that's where you're always going to stay." As the debate grew more lively, several teachers pressed for a compromise. Emblematic of this group, Ms. Schmidt volunteered, "I don't personally mind if anyone else wants to rank. . . . I just won't do it." In the closing minutes of the conversation, Luz weighed in:

> As a person of color who went with people who are from this country to college, don't lower the bar for me. I need to figure out what's my ranking in order to compete. I use my community to get my ranking

up. I appreciate Eliza [Ms. Whitmore] and Anand's [Mr. Behari's]
points, but you are middle class. You are White people. You have
privilege. You have a pass. I don't, so I need to know where I rank. I
want my kids to know where they rank; that way, they have a fair
chance to compete and then we as a community collaborate to get the
ranking up. It's just a reality check for people. Not everybody has the
opportunity to just say, "Oh, I don't need to be ranked." Some people
need to be ranked in order to be competitive.

By drawing attention to the racial politics embedded in the debate, Luz
complexified the issue. Unfortunately, the press of time curtailed discussion.
Ultimately, MHS staff compromised, granting teachers discretion to rank or
not. Before the agenda shifted, Principal West squeezed in some last words
and stressed his view that ranks, if used, must "respect kids and not put
them down."

This exchange highlighted the difficulty teachers faced balancing a com-
munitarian, collectivist view of social uplift with the impulse to prepare
youth for the individualistic, competitive demands of prevailing world or-
ders. Some teachers, such as Ms. Howard, rejected the dualism, claiming
that competition and collaboration were not "mutually exclusive." However,
others remained dismayed about the meeting's process and outcome. They
would have preferred reaching a consensus and presenting a united front to
students. Recalling the conversation months later, Mr. Behari said he was
loath to put Luz "on blast" because "she's a wonderful person and she's
fantastic for our school. . . . [and] she's done way more good than she could
ever do harm to our school." And yet he confessed that he deemed her move
in this particular meeting as "unhealthy" and "off-putting rather than productive." He observed that she.

> shut off the conversation and made people upset. It didn't cause a
> fight, but there was a bunch of grumbling afterwards, to me especially,
> because I'm a person of color and I was included in that comment
> [about White middle-class people]. I had a moment of White solidarity
> with a few people, which I've never had before. [*Laughs.*]

Mr. Behari's recollections hint at the dangers that exist when discussions
stumble into contested political territory but are hastily concluded and not
revisited. His reference to "a bunch of grumbling afterwards" speaks to the
micropolitical dynamics embedded in such discourse and the vigilance
needed to ensure healthy, productive conflict. This critical incident demonstrated the precarious and emotionally charged nature of professional dialogue when issues of race, class, and privilege surface within an organization
dedicated to interrupting inequity and injustice. Although participants
shared a common mission, they held different views about how best to

realize that mission, and these differences had consequences for establishing policy and figuring out how best to embody critical cariño with and for students.

The second critical incident involved a staff listserv discussion addressing how to support struggling students. Ms. Schmidt solicited input regarding seven struggling students (three Blacks and four Latinx), who were poised to fail the semester. The students had failed a test and then not completed a study guide that was to serve as an entry ticket to retake the test. Ms. Schmidt noted that 90% of the sophomore class had passed the test with a C or better and listed the names of students who had failed with brief observations about their attendance and performance prior to the test. She wondered if she had supported students sufficiently and if she should offer another retake. Her solicitation spawned a chain of 13 emails involving seven core academic teachers, two EDP staff (Luz and César), Principal West, and the literacy coach. Three camps emerged. Principal West and Luz raised equity concerns, noting "a high percentage of African American and RSP [special ed]" students, as well as a few thoroughly disengaged students with dismally low GPAs in need of "serious intervention." This pair proposed involving students' parents, investigating the root causes of students' failure, and providing a retake. Another group, comprising the special education teacher, the literacy coach, and a few others, offered instructional feedback and focused on the learning styles and needs of particular students.

The last camp (four teachers and César) advocated for "holding the line" and "sticking to your word," arguing that offering additional chances to "save students from potential failure does not empower or inspire them to make good decisions on their own." Speaking from this position, Ms. Clark later confided to me,

> My problem with that whole exchange, especially from administration, was, "Bleeding heart sob stories, the world is so rough, let's be transformational and remember that these kids live in the *ghetto*!" OK, that's cool, I understand that, but you know what everybody has? Everybody has an ability to communicate. They can do it in written form, they can talk to you during class, after class, they could text message you, they could send you an email. I don't care how you do it. You know the skill I want you to learn here is self-advocacy.

Ms. Clark's remarks revealed frustration with well-intentioned colleagues who unwittingly adopted deficit framings of youth in their desire to promote academic success. Disheartened, Ms. Clark shared, "For me, it's very emotional. You're educating my community, not your community. *My community*. So be careful the way you do it." For her, this matter was also troublesome because communication transpired electronically and not face-to-face. She lamented, "Everybody's going to hide behind the fact that we really don't have time to talk about that." Several other teachers echoed her wish for more dialogue, but this conversation never transpired, at least not in public.

Despite the tensions evident in both incidents, these educators clearly had built a professional community with sufficient trust to expose and problematize dilemmas of practice and actively engage each other in reflection and dialogue. By "acknowledging, surfacing, and owning conflicts by critically reflecting on their differences of belief and practice," MHS staff displayed an "embracing stance" toward conflict (Achinstein, 2002, p. 101). This accomplishment was no small feat. Because such conversations entailed the interrogation of personal subjectivities in relation to systems of oppression, such exchanges themselves can also be considered acts of critical cariño. In the end, these critical incidents illuminate the thorny and ongoing complexity of educators' work as they seek to enact critical cariño and ensure that all students reap its benefits.

CLOSING REFLECTIONS

This chapter has chronicled the ways in which MHS educators enacted critical cariño to support students' healthy ethnoracial identity development, political awareness, and democratic agency. By fostering youth's reflection and action (praxis) within the context of their particular lived realities and also centering critiques of social oppression, MHS teachers expressed critical cariño—care that deepened students' understanding of their sociohistorical identities, strengthened their connections to community cultural wealth, and fueled their motivation to transform their communities. The power of critical cariño emerged in the stories of students such as Renata, Badeeah, and Luis, who crafted and broadcast narratives on public radio declaring their unique perspectives, self-worth, and humanity as Latinx immigrants. Similarly, the portrait of Linda, Jesús, Anna, and others stepping into "lawyer mode" to develop and defend arguments premised on the U.S. Constitution demonstrated how critical cariño pedagogies emboldened students to fight for their rights, attend to current events, and demand equal justice for all. Meanwhile, the 9th graders, who documented their neighborhoods and published *Welcome to Our City*, a book featuring a local slang dictionary, photos, documentary poems, and essays, illustrated how critical cariño supported students to investigate the multiple perspectives of city residents and envision hopeful futures. Finally, portraits of youth activism around the Dream Act, soccer field, and affordable college tuition highlighted how critical cariño fused reflection and action to generate legislative and material achievements that fundamentally improved students' postsecondary opportunities and access to healthy and safe play areas. These endeavors were made possible by MHS's organizational commitments to social justice, teacher autonomy, and community partnerships. Taken together, these activities and structures reflected MHS's embrace of critical cariño.

By extending cariño beyond socioemotional and academic spheres into the realm of sociopolitics, MHS sought to ensure that graduates departed "community ready" with the skills, knowledge, and desire to participate in civic actions to strengthen local communities and optimize democracy. Armed with self-knowledge, political clarity, and critical thinking strategies, MHS graduates entered adulthood with firsthand experience reflecting on the meaning of their lives, analyzing controversial social issues, collaborating with others to mobilize political action, and imagining ways to make their world more just and equitable. Critical cariño, then, proved itself an essential pedagogy to advance MHS's social justice mission.

CHAPTER 5

Authentic Cariño

Braiding Together Familial, Intellectual, and Critical Care

The trenza bring[s] together strands of hair and weaves them in such a way that the strands come together to create something new, something that cannot exist without each of its parts. The trenza is something that is whole and complete, and yet, it is something that can only exist if the separate parts are woven together.

—Dolores Delgado Bernal, 2008, p. 135

Having examined familial cariño, intellectual cariño, and critical cariño separately in prior chapters, we turn next to exploring how their co-occurrence yielded authentic cariño—a holistic care that nurtured students' bodymind-spirits in ways that supported them to hone their intellects and pursue lives of meaning. To advance this argument, I rely on the metaphor of a *trenza* (a braid). As Dolores Delgado Bernal's epigraph explains, a trenza weaves separate strands of hair into a united whole. By interlacing three separate strands of cariño (familial, intellectual, and critical), MHS added strength, beauty, and resonance to its learning ecology, thereby enriching students' educacíon.

Numerous mujerista scholars (Delgado Bernal, 2006; Godinez, 2006; Gonzalez, 1998; Montoya, 1994; Quiñones, 2016) have highlighted how the trenza is a metaphor "encoded with cultural meaning" (Delgado Bernal, 2008, p. 135). Montoya (1994) and Quiñones (2016) describe intimate, bonding moments at home when maternal elders imparted wisdom and values while plaiting their hair. From her mother's careful attention to fashioning her trenzas, Montoya intuited a "deeper message: be prepared, because you will be judged by your skin color, your names, your accents. They will see you as ugly, lazy, dumb and dirty" (p. 4). By presenting her daughter as "well-cared-for at home" (p. 4) Montoya's mother hoped to defend Montoya against racism and ensure her ability to "get along in school and society" (p. 7). This account parallels how MHS educators through their generous provision of authentic cariño groomed their culturally and linguistically diverse students to navigate and thrive in a world rife with racism and xenophobia.

Unlike Montoya's mother, who encouraged her children's assimilation to the dominant society by stressing the importance of "presenting an acceptable face, speaking without a Spanish accent, hiding what we really felt—masking our inner selves" (p. 6), MHS wove a trenza that communicated to students the value of integrating and affirming all their parts, all their worlds, all their identities in order to live lives of *felicidad y libertad* (happiness and freedom). This commitment to nurturing students' cultural integrity represented a fundamental shift from the "impersonal, irrelevant, and lifeless" schooling experienced by many Latinx youth (Valenzuela, 1999, p. 22).

The trenza of authentic cariño incorporated many life strands—the spirit, mind, and body—the home, school, and community—and the social, economic, and political. Attention to these multiple life strands created safe and expansive spaces for students to engage in learning, reflection, healing, dreaming, and action. As documented in previous chapters, MHS students inhabited a learning ecology steeped in authentic cariño that offered cumulative opportunities to grow and glow. In Chapter 2, Letty's firewalks exemplified authentic cariño because they transpired within an intimate circle of supportive peers and adults, required metacognition to evaluate growth, and attended to her intersectional reality as a poor, college-bound, undocumented Latina. When her peers stood to celebrate her achievements and affirm her dream to become a pediatrician, Letty received a vote of confidence affirming her readiness to meet difficult challenges and undertake new ventures.

In a similar manner, Rafael's hour-long senior defense in Chapter 3 epitomized authentic cariño because it involved a cast of caring classmates and adults listening deeply and pushing him to elaborate the causes, symptomatology, societal costs, and remedies for Internet addiction—knowledge he had amassed during his year-long investigative project, a pursuit driven by his own struggles with Internet addiction. When the panel announced Rafael's honors distinction and his mother commended him in Spanish, a palpable sense of accomplishment, human connection, and joy engulfed the classroom. As Rafael's mother hugged her sobbing son, attendees witnessed the culmination of a 4-year high school journey in which authentic cariño had figured prominently.

Finally, authentic cariño surfaced powerfully in Chapter 4 as teams of students congregated after school in the library to argue the case of Ernesto Miranda. A judicial panel of volunteer teachers, eager to witness their advisees' performances, served as Supreme Court justices, pressing presenters to clarify reasoning and marshal evidence. Rising to the occasion with decorum and rhetorical flare, students consulted their legal teams, adopted lawyer personas, and demanded justice. These various activities (see Table 5.1) exemplify the way MHS repeatedly enveloped students in authentic cariño.

Although the metaphor of the trenza suggests a tidy process of separating equivalent bundles of familial, intellectual, and critical cariño and then methodically interweaving them, the process of braiding authentic

Table 5.1. Braided Strands of Authentic Cariño Across Featured Examples

	Familial	Intellectual	Critical
Firewalks (Chapter 2)	• Advisory circle • Personalized attention • Peer accountability • Reflection on identity, purpose, and growth	• Analysis of strengths and weakness • Posing and responding to thoughtful questions • Writing a speech/letter	• Contemplating how to give back to community • Reflecting on how to overcome barriers and inequitable systems
Senior Defenses (Chapter 3)	• Advisor as coach and panel chair • Advisory peers as audience • Biological family members in audience • Safe space to share personal experiences and emotions	• Rigorous investigative research paper • Assessment rubric that stresses Habits of Mind • Oral presentation and panel discussion	• Projects that address internships or issues faced by urban youth (e.g., asthma, pregnancy, addiction) • Interviews with experts that require community outreach • Community panels that promote real-world links, understanding of youth concerns, and problem solving
Miranda Moot Trial (Chapter 4)	• Students' collaboration in teams • Teacher emphasizing learning over competition • Teachers volunteering to serve so as to support advisees' success in another class	• Analysis of the Constitution, Bill of Rights, and precedent cases • Position papers on whether Miranda's rights were violated • Oral debate with on-the-spot rebuttals demanding logical reasoning and mastery of evidence	• Miranda's case that highlights the vulnerability of uneducated, poor Latinx immigrants • Unit exploration of abuse of power and how to protect constitutional rights

cariño into MHS's daily routines and cultural ethos enfolded organically and reflected the complexity of many weavers. As such, the strands of familial, intellectual, and critical cariño were not equally present in every setting or interaction. For example, in advisory, familial cariño prevailed. In classrooms, intellectual cariño prevailed. In EDP and town halls, critical cariño prevailed. And yet, even as a particular dimension of cariño eclipsed others in particular settings, all dimensions remained present. The net effect of these cariños being woven together across settings was a sense of balance, a sense that each was essential to sustaining MHS's institutional commitment to promoting students' success and well-being.

This chapter delves further into the institutionalization of authentic cariño. First, I examine how three interrelated and normalized social activities—boundary crossing, dialogue, and embodied action—facilitated the integration of familial, intellectual, and critical cariño. Next, I present an in-depth account of MHS's Peaceful City Campaign, a student-led crusade confronting violence. I devote considerable attention to this movement because it illustrates how MHS responsively wove together familial, intellectual, and critical cariño to push back against the toxicity and tragedy unfolding beyond its gates. Rather than allow students to succumb to hopelessness and victimhood, MHS educators steered youth toward critical awareness and robust civic engagement and in doing so demonstrated the healing power of authentic cariño. The chapter closes with reflections emphasizing how MHS's purposeful provision of authentic cariño dramatically transformed students' relationships with school, learning, and themselves.

WEAVING THE TRENZA OF AUTHENTIC CARIÑO: UNDERSTANDING AUTHENTIC CARIÑO'S PREVALENCE AT MHS

Prior chapters linked familial, intellectual, and critical cariño to particular formal and informal organizational structures that fostered authentic cariño schoolwide. Structures such as the social justice mission, the network of care, and the Habits of Life/Mind/Work all advanced by a deeply committed community of educators and community partners contributed to authentic cariño's robust presence at MHS. These structures, however, do not in and of themselves explain how authentic cariño managed to flourish across MHS's learning ecology. To understand how all three strands of cariño became interwoven, it is necessary to examine the social processes that occurred in conjunction with those structures. Three interrelated, normalized phenomena—boundary crossing, dialogue, and embodiment—emerged as important factors guiding MHS toward authentic cariño.

Weaving Worlds Together Through Boundary Crossing

Extensive boundary crossing promoted the integration of familial, intellectual, and critical cariño (Achinstein et al., 2014). As educators and students traveled regularly beyond the confines of academic classrooms, disciplinary silos, constricted roles, and school walls into neighborhoods, internships, and other settings, and as members of the outlying community (youth developers, community organizers, health clinicians, politicians, and families) regularly entered and inhabited the school, the insularity and compartmentalization of the egg crate school (Lortie, 1975) collapsed. The resulting inside-to-outside and outside-to-inside movement with its fluid, constant, and unpredictable dynamics unsettled longstanding grammars of school (Tyack & Cuban, 1995), prompting educators to expand their range of vision and develop new pedagogies. As the distinction between "out there" and "in here" blurred, students' full humanity—their membership in multiple communities and their location within particular sociohistorical contexts—became impossible to ignore. This shift pulled educators toward care that extended beyond academics to encompass students' development as bodymindspirit beings searching to find their way in the world.

Boundary crossing unfolded along myriad paths. When gathering in community circles for firewalks and sharing their experiences traversing the borderlands of home, school, and community, students like Letty crossed the psychic boundaries demarcating the academic self from the personal self. Likewise, educators facilitating these rituals extended themselves beyond occupational boundaries confining them to academics. Together teachers and students entered uncharted territory. In this manner, the firewalk ritual created what Anzaldúa (1987/2012) calls "nepantla" (a Nahuatl word meaning a space between two worlds). In this in-between space "you are not this or that but where you are changing. You haven't got into the new identity yet and haven't left the old identity behind either—you are in . . . transition. . . . It is very awkward, uncomfortable and frustrating" (p. 276). Despite the discomfort generated from becoming untethered from fixed roles and dualisms (e.g., student versus teacher, academic versus personal, school versus home), MHS firewalk participants once enmeshed in nepantla constructed new possibilities and relationships that allowed familial, intellectual, and critical cariño to synergistically commingle.

Boundary crossing also played a part in Rafael's senior defense. By selecting Internet addiction (IA) as the topic for his investigative project, Rafael carried his personal struggles with IA at home into school and transformed IA into a subject worthy of intellectual scrutiny. Drawing on his internship at a technology firm that delivered audio entertainment, Rafael gained insights into the marketplace driving IA. His advisor, Mr. Avila, stepped beyond his Spanish teacher role to coach Rafael through the year-long investigation, helping to deepen Rafael's understanding of the cognitive and social effects of IA. Finally, for Rafael's culminating oral defense, multiple community visitors—including a school district representative, two tech mentors, a city hall mentor from his junior year, one university professor, and his mother—crossed the MHS threshold to join teachers and peers witnessing and evaluating his performance. This mixed audience again illustrates how MHS engineered opportunities for people from multiple cultures, Discourses, economic classes, and ages to cross boundaries and converge for the purpose of supporting youth development. The presence of so many border crossers allowed Rafael to be connected with multiple worlds simultaneously and validated his right to exist in those worlds. This display of community support not only exemplified familial cariño, but also expanded the reach of Rafael's project beyond the borders of school.

Another glimpse of the multifaceted nature of border crossing emerged from Mr. Behari's Miranda Moot Court. Although this government class activity transpired within the spatial, geographic confines of school walls, this simulation pushed against normative school boundaries by occurring after school, outside a classroom, and with a heterogeneous group of volunteer educators holding no expertise in constitutional law and yet desiring to support their advisees during an intellectual challenge. In order for MHS students to argue the case, they needed to transverse temporal boundaries to understand the sociohistorical contexts shaping Ernesto Miranda's arrest in the 1960s. Students and teachers also had to cross over identity boundaries in order to comport themselves as legal experts carrying out the business of the U.S. Supreme Court. Attesting to the visceral intensity of stepping into these roles, Linda explained how the simulation "made us feel like lawyers . . . like we were actually gonna argue something that was real." These boundary crossings between the current day and the past, as well as between imagination and reality, unfolding as they did in a serious, but playful arena of exploration deepened authentic cariño by providing a venue for educators to enact familial, intellectual, and critical cariño.

These examples demonstrate how border crossing opened up *un mundo en donde caben muchos mundos* (a world within which many worlds can fit). By encouraging students and others to mindfully traverse physical, intellectual, psychic, political, economic, and social borders, MHS fashioned a trenza of authentic cariño that validated students' intersecting cultures and identities.

Weaving Robust, Human Relationships Through Dialogue

A second social process that enhanced authentic cariño was dialogue. Through conversations in classrooms, advisory, EDP, internships, field trips, defenses, firewalks, and post-sessions, MHS community members regularly and intentionally nurtured meaning, identity, and purpose. This trend distinguished MHS from most U.S. secondary schools in which sustained dialogue is rare (Applebee et al., 2003; Fine, 1987; Glazer, 2018; Nystrand & Gamoran, 1991). All too often, schools remain places where teachers talk and students passively listen. Even when conversations are pursued, they may get bogged down with academic procedures that make them feel contrived, rather than generative.

MHS students benefited from regular opportunities to listen, respond, and build meaning through conversation. In a schoolwide survey, three-quarters of faculty reported orchestrating small-group collaboration or extended student-to-student academic talk almost daily. Observations verified these self-reports as did the district literacy specialist, Ms. Buchanan, who highlighted dialogue's prominence:

> The kids are talking a lot at MHS. They're presenting a lot and they're doing activities where they're really able to produce ideas and get their ideas out. . . . They do a lot of group work to get the kids to talk to each other. . . . They can go back and forth between English and Spanish if they want. That's OK. The idea is what's important.

Teachers' efforts to promote dialogue surfaced in collaborative tasks such as the one chronicled in Mr. Tran's geometry class (see Figure 3.2), which encouraged students to ask teammates "What do you think?" "How do you see it?" "What do you want to try?" Teachers also confirmed the prevalence of dialogue. Mr. Tanaka shared his perception that MHS students "have a lot of interesting discussions in class." This emphasis tapped the oral traditions embedded within many MHS students' cultures. For youth comfortable with spoken words as the conduit for conveying and preserving knowledge, this dialogic emphasis represented another facet of authentic cariño (Hammond, 2014).

Not every conversation generated deep engagement and critical thinking, but the routine of being in dialogue compelled students to grapple with conflicting views, unpack ambiguity, judge the merits of evidence, and express themselves. These opportunities to engage in dialogue couched within MHS's Habits of Life and Mind frameworks fostered in students an "evaluative epistemology, in which all opinions are not equal and knowing is understood as a process that entails judgment, evaluation, and argument" (Kuhn, 1999, p. 22). The exchanges among students and adults during fire-walks, oral defenses, and the Miranda court simulation underscore how MHS educators used dialogue as a key lever to immerse students in authentic cariño.

This dialogic approach to coming to know and being known encouraged students to listen carefully to what others had to say, to contemplate multiple perspectives, and, in doing so, to travel into each other's worlds. Because such "world travelling" involves seeing others through the lens of empathy and sensing interdependence, Lugones (1987) asserts that it engenders "cross-cultural and cross-racial loving" (p. 3). She writes, "We are fully dependent on each other for the possibility of being understood and without this understanding we are not intelligible, we do not make sense, we are not solid, visible, integrated, we are lacking" (p. 8). In alignment with this view, dialogue at MHS became a process in which participants attended to the voice and presence of the bodymindspirit forming the words. Speaking to such exchanges, Parker Palmer (1983/1993) suggests that in true dialogue, "Our opening question should not be 'How logical is that thought?' but 'Whose voice is behind it? What is the personal reality from which that thought emerged?'" He recommends that participants in a learning dialogue ask themselves, "How can I enter and respond to the relation of that thinker to the world?" (p. 64). MHS educators modeled and encouraged these kinds of responsive conversations. Their emphasis on dialogue reflected a deep intention to nurture relationships in tandem with logical and critical thinking. The presence of both these impulses enabled dialogue to operate like a nimble hand intertwining familial, intellectual, and critical cariño into the braid of authentic cariño. Enveloped within this authentic cariño, students like Camila came away from school sensing that MHS adults "actually want us to show and express where we're coming from."

Weaving Healthy Connections to Self Through Embodiment

MHS's receptivity to the corporeal dimensions of learning and living was a third factor contributing to authentic cariño's prominence. Just as the act of braiding hair involves physical intimacy, movement, and coordination of bodies, the weaving of authentic cariño into the social fabric of MHS occurred as adults and youth interacted in ways that honored each other's flesh and body lived experiences. Given Western culture's enduring attachment to the Cartesian mind–body split, MHS's desire to feed students' bodies with "all their hungers" (Moraga, 1983/2000, p. 123)—especially their hunger to belong (familial), to learn (intellectual), and to live healthy and free (critical)—represented a radical praxis.

I consider it radical for three reasons. First, MHS educators refused to follow the mold of U.S. schools in which Brown and Black bodies have been (and continue to be) overly regulated to obtain obedience and conformity (Ferguson, 2000; Wacquant, 2011). The school gave students permission to dress as they pleased and practiced restorative discipline to heal students' psyches and bodies rather than punish them. In one notable instance, a student, whose distribution of marijuana-laced rice krispie treats caused a classmate's extreme allergic reaction, made amends by researching marijuana and making a presentation to every advisory in the school. This intervention allowed the "culture breaker" to learn from his transgression, take responsibility with an embodied apology, and regain community acceptance.

Second, MHS rejected the idea that "intelligence dwells only in the head" (Anzaldúa, 1987/2012, p. 59) and instead encouraged youth to trust their bodies as legitimate knowledge sources through which meaning could be intuited and constructed. In this regard, they understood that "all learning, as well as teaching, happens through responses and interactions of the body with texts, others, and the world" (Darder, 2011, p. 345). Grounded in this awareness, teachers optimized learning by taking into account students' somatic and affective responses to curricula; they paid attention and responded to how students' bodies expressed academic struggle, delight, doubt, excitement, confusion, confidence, desire, and disappointment. They also prompted students to notice these visceral sensations in their own bodies. Marisol, a junior, reported that three teachers noticed her stress and changed demeanor after her father lost his job and her family faced financial insecurity. Recalling those days, she said, "I felt like they [my teachers] were supporting me. . . . If you need help, they'll be there." Another student, Reina, who struggled mightily in and out of school, also received teachers' encouragement to tune into her body (Curry, 2016). Ms. Barrett coached Reina through a rough day by helping her to slow down and reflect. "I had to say to her, 'You're scared, and you feel weak right now. It is OK for you to show that.'" In a separate consultation, Ms. Clark counseled Reina, asking her, "What does it feel like to have that kind of anger inside? How do you negotiate that kind of anger? How do you not let that get in your way and be able to connect personally?" These compassionate responses signaled to Reina that teachers had her back and supported her personally and academically. By attending to how students like Marisol and Reina carried their bodies into school, MHS was able to envelop them in authentic cariño.

Third, rather than shunning bodies as dangerous, sexually transgressive, or illegal, MHS nurtured Brown and Black bodies by encouraging youth to viscerally feel their worth and importance through their bodies. Aware of how society has negatively racialized, sexualized, and traumatized the bodies of multiply marginalized youth in ways that have induced shame and internalized oppression (Cruz, 2001; Menakem, 2017), MHS adults recognized that many students entered school with "their safety-threat detection systems . . . cued to be on the alert for social and psychological threats based on past experience (Hammond, 2014, p. 45). To counteract alienation from the body, educators strove to cultivate positive *feelings* within students' bodies. Ms. Clark shared her intention "to make students feel important . . . feel confident in their abilities . . . [and] feel really smart." Ms. Barrett expressed her desire for "students to feel powerful" and in touch with "the passion and the drive" residing within them. Similarly, César spoke of helping students "experience success, experience triumph, experience accomplishment" so that they felt "what it's like to be praised . . . [and] connected to their abilities . . . [and] power." Echoing these colleagues, Mr. Tran stressed how making students "feel welcomed and loved . . . safe . . . and appreciated" supported their happiness and enjoyment of school. These educators' aspirations for students to *feel* important, connected, and powerful reflected a keen awareness that learning and growth depend on students feeling comfortable and grounded in their bodies.

This awareness came through in many ways. At the August retreat, when Luz trained teachers to facilitate advisory team-building activities, which involved students touching each other, she matter-of-factly informed new hires, "At this school, there's a culture of touching. . . . We have a sense of family, trust, empathy, loving and caring. Touching reinforces our culture of caring and affection." Against this backdrop, it was not uncommon to see teachers embrace students or students convene group hugs following an exhibition or challenge. Through respectful touch, students received assurance that they belonged. This affirmation was especially important for undocumented youth. Benicio, an undocumented junior, shared, "[At MHS] everyone knows I don't have papers, but I don't have to hide it. I am proud of being Mexican." Given the harsh reality of immigration raids, detentions, and deportations occurring nearby, it is noteworthy that Benicio felt sufficiently safe to inhabit his body without fear while on campus. Speaking to this security, Mr. Trung explained that, collectively, MHS educators "have an identity for advocating for recently arrived immigrants. . . . Our students feel safe and protected at our school."

This safety gave students permission to experience their bodies as conduits for joy. When students heeded César's invitation to "use what God has blessed us with" and joined one another in clapping and stomping out the unity clap, the positive energy created by their bodies was felt in the bones. When students and teachers flooded the gym floor during a FISTT assembly for a rowdy dance party in support of One Billion Rising's (www.onebillionrising.org) campaign to end violence against women, their jubilance was palpable. When students and teachers engaged in a lively game of basura ball and reveled in "sweat, laughter, and fun," their bodies occupied center stage. When students encircled firewalkers in "jelly roll hugs," they collectively felt the triumph of achievement in their bodies. Through these activities, MHS educators affirmed students' enfleshed aliveness and encouraged youth to embrace their bodies as powerful instruments to engage in learning, play, and resistance.

The Synchronicity of Border Crossing, Dialogue, and Embodied Action

The social processes elaborated often occurred simultaneously, and this convergence amplified authentic cariño. One especially powerful instance of this phenomenon transpired before Letty's sophomore firewalk (described in Chapter 2). Readers may have wondered how MHS engineered this rite of passage that allowed Letty to face struggles and receive support to persist in school. I think the answer lies in part in MHS's annual sophomore excursion to Yosemite. During that trip, Mr. Avila, Letty's firewalk facilitator, spent several days with her and her peers serving as their "pod" leader. Together they crossed borders, traveling far from home to explore a national park and engage in activities designed to tighten class bonds and strengthen students' Habits of Life and Mind. Mr. Avila facilitated a trust fall in which students stiffened their bodies while standing atop the massive trunk of a fallen tree and then fell backward. He guided pod members on the ground below, who were standing in two lines, to face one another and interlock their hands into a catching net. When it was Letty's turn, he whispered words of assurance to her in Spanish and counted down as he gently rocked her body preparing her for the moment of release and catch. As coached to do when ready, Letty asked her classmates, "Are you ready?" Her pod chorused, "Yes, we are!" And then she fell into the cradle of their arms. In the aftermath, Mr. Avila exclaimed, "I am proud of you! Give her a hug! Show the love!"

Once this sequence was repeated for everyone, Mr. Avila initiated a reflective debrief. As students dialogued about trusting others, falling down in life, and falling in love, they seized on the importance of having a community to catch you when you fall. This embodied experience of relational trust and familial cariño prepared Letty and her peers to approach the firewalk ritual a few days later with seriousness and receptivity. During Letty's emotional firewalk, her Yosemite pod pressed her to reflect on detrimental behaviors, while still assuring her that they "had her back." One peer explicitly reminded Letty that "We love you very much." This vignette offers one glimpse of how MHS harnessed border crossing, dialogue, and embodied action to immerse students in authentic cariño. Table 5.2 extends this analysis by summarizing how these three phenomena surfaced in this chapter's featured examples. In the next section, I take one final deep dive into authentic cariño's enactment to demonstrate its considerable power.

YA BASTA, ENOUGH IS ENOUGH:
AUTHENTIC CARIÑO CONFRONTS VIOLENCE

Seventy days into the 2011–2012 school year, Principal West emailed teachers to announce the shooting death of Lucho, a 2011 graduate. West grieved the loss of an "incredibly intelligent young man . . . [with] a huge heart" and laid out plans to offer counseling for students, especially Lucho's sister, a sophomore. That afternoon, the network of care sprang into action. Luz and Magdalena (MHS's parent liaison) visited Lucho's home to extend the school's condolences. Dolores from CCO assisted the family with burial costs by applying for aid from a city-sponsored victim fund. Meanwhile, Lucho's internship mentor helped coordinate funeral logistics. The next day, an altar adorned with santos candles, roses, and photos of Lucho appeared in an MHS hallway. In ensuing days, students added notes of remembrance to that altar.

Table 5.2. Social Processes Fostering Authentic Cariño Across Featured Examples

	Border Crossing	Dialogue	Embodied Action
Firewalks (FWs) (Chapter 2)	• To prepare for FWs, sophomores went to Yosemite National Park, where MHS educators led activities designed to deepen class solidarity, strengthen Habits of Life and Mind, and encourage reflection. Students shared their multiple worlds/selves. • Seniors reflected on the borders they had crossed for internships, field trips, classes, and post-sessions. They also contemplated future border crossings into college and career, reflecting on what parts of themselves would help them successfully navigate new terrains.	• Firewalks occurred in confidential, intimate community circles in which students and adults engaged in extended (30–60-minute) "brutally honest" conversations focused on an individual's growth and readiness to undertake new challenges/responsibilities. Facilitators encouraged the circle to ask thoughtful questions in order to push firewalkers toward deep reflection.	• Firewalks unfolded within a circle in which participants sat knee to knee with their bodies unobstructed by desks. The culminating moments of a successful firewalk involved participants collectively standing, speaking affirmations, and, finally, hugging the firewalker.
Senior Defenses (Chapter 3)	• Advisors acting as senior project coaches guided student investigations, often in areas outside their disciplinary expertise. • Student researchers crossed borders to interview experts and often wove internship experiences into their explorations. • Community panelists and family members entered the school to witness and evaluate defenses.	• A year-long dialogue between senior and advisor transpired around question formulation, research planning, progress monitoring, and revising and rehearsing defense presentations. • The defense presentation featured a substantial Q & A segment (usually 15–30 minutes) between presenter and panelists.	• Seniors dressed up for their defense presentations and stood in front of an audience beside a projector screen. Performance criteria included exhibiting control of body posture and gestures, eye contact, clear and audible voice, as well as maintaining a presence and energy capable of holding the audience's attention.

(continued)

Table 5.2. (Continued)

Miranda Moot Trial (Chapter 4)	• Teachers, administrators, and other staff stepped outside of disciplinary silos and normal roles to serve voluntarily as (pretend) Supreme Court justices. • Participants left their classrooms and convened in the library—a more public and formal space—to argue their case. • Participants traveled from the present into the past using their imaginations.	• Student legal teams worked cooperatively to build and present their respective arguments. • Teams dialogued with justices to explain, defend, and press claims.	• Students dressed in a professional manner appropriate for a courtroom. • Students strove for an inflected oral delivery and physical display of energy that grabbed justices' attention. • Students embodied their interest during cogent/responsive interactions with justices.

Figure 5.1. Roots of Violence Posters

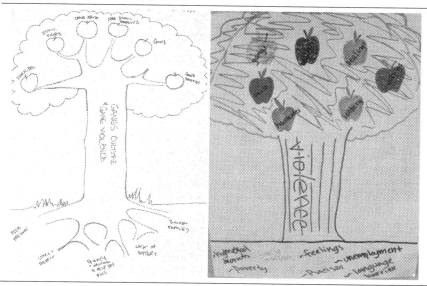

Within a week, advisory circles gathered to grieve and discuss how to interrupt "patterns of hood violence." As a community, they brainstormed how to prevent further suffering and promote safety for city residents. Guided by an ILT-designed lesson plan, advisories analyzed the "roots of violence" and crafted tree posters with roots labeling causes and branches displaying the effects of violence (see Figure 5.1). This activity focused students' attention on the interrelationships among gang violence, poverty, racism, and immigration.

The following day, the school convened a town hall. In advance, an ILT listserv post explained:

> This is more than a memorial. . . . It is a protest of the state of our society where young people are murdered by other young people and there is almost NO NEWS coverage and we find ourselves numb or trying to simply suck up our pain and move on with business as usual. . . . [This time] we have decided que YA BASTA, ENOUGH IS ENOUGH. (Capitalization in original)

César opened the event with a unity clap and decried the "broken system" and "brutal inequality" underpinning violence. Citing the Occupy Wallstreet movement, he implored students to rise up.[1] "In the name of the freedom fighters who gave their lives for a better world for working people, we must remember that it's up to us to carry on their legacy." Next, he invited Principal West to honor five MHS students slain by guns since 2005 by "giving their names real faces." First, West denounced the normalization of violence and observed how "In other communities, when a teenager dies, the world stops, but in our city, it just keeps going." Next, he shared memories of each victim while a slideshow scrolled photographs of the deceased engaged in home and school activities. At MHS, these victims were not permitted to become faceless statistics.

The town hall continued with a presentation from two parents whose son was murdered walking home from MHS in 2010. Next, a Navajo performer chanted a healing song. Asking the audience to stand and remove their caps, he explained how his ancestors believed that "when someone passes away through something tragic or violent, their spirit gets stuck on Earth. The only way to help that spirit go on is for the family to mourn and let that spirit go." He dedicated his chant to Lucho and all victims of violence. With his last drum stroke, a solemn silence enveloped the auditorium.

Luz stepped forward next to solicit volunteers to present tree posters. Students from two advisories detailed their analysis and proposals to confront violence. Praising volunteers and all students for seriously grappling with a complex problem that policy makers have spent years attempting to remedy, Luz finished with an impassioned speech:

> We know from history that people . . . who are poor . . . [and are from] ethnic communities usually get in distress. Blacks, Latinos, South East Asians, the undocumented, the war is on them. So this [town hall and advisory activity] was to wake you up. There's three things you can do. One, keep on talking to people about root causes [of violence]. We have to not stop talking about it. Two, they don't want us to graduate from high school but . . . we need to graduate with a 3.5 [GPA] or higher. . . . We have to go to college. Do you understand that? Because we can be the next mayor. . . . We need to be in charge of the police department and the health department, and you need to be the next boss! Do you understand that? [Audience claps.] You need to be the next boss! [Clapping gets louder.] Three, we need to change the social culture of the bling bling of the gangster. That we are homies. Violence only brings violence!

Not only did Luz stress a critical perspective connecting violence to macrosocietal structures oppressing marginalized populations, but she also emphasized the responsibility of youth to transform those structures through education and careers that would allow them to take charge of those structures. Additionally, her praise of students' analytic posters and her emphasis on academic excellence and college attainment were expressions of intellectual cariño.

Although the school day was officially over, students remained seated and attentive as more speakers—a mayoral policy advisor, Dolores from

CCO, and a Latino school board member—came forward to offer condolences, encouragement, and promises to work toward making students' proposed solutions a reality. Twenty-five minutes later, Big Dan, a rapper, closed the gathering by recounting his journey from being locked up in juvenile hall to graduating from UC Berkeley. Imparting life wisdom, Big Dan stressed, "It's important to have a positive outlet. How is it that you are going to release the frustration and anger? Pick up a camera, pen, paper, microphone, braid hair, go run, work out, and do positive things." He concluded with an original song entitled "Be the Change."[2] Ending on this positive note, the audience applauded and trickled out. Many students lingered to speak with presenters, purchase sweets at a bake sale benefiting Lucho's family, and light memorial candles placed on colorful altars erected by students in the Town Visionaries Club.

This Interrupting Patterns of Violence town hall demonstrated the vibrancy and healing power residing in a school steeped in authentic cariño. While some schools ignore the trauma and social toxins impacting students' lives (Camangian, 2015; Johnson, 1995), MHS as an organization responded to Lucho's murder with compassion, speed, and fervency. Even though Lucho was an alumnus, his death was not shrouded in silence; rather it became a vehicle for MHS to reflect and generate solutions to stem the violence plaguing the city.

The school's response illustrates how the three dimensions of familial, intellectual, and critical cariño braided themselves together to support students, build awareness of social oppression, and generate solidarity to solve a serious problem. Familial cariño surfaced when the network of care coordinated supports for Lucho's family and also when the ILT acknowledged collective trauma by convening advisory circles and a town hall. The Navajo healing chant, slideshow of victims, memorial altars, and unity clap tapped into spiritual impulses honoring the sacredness of life and community. Intellectual cariño emerged when teachers treated Lucho's death as a teachable moment and guided students to use HOM to deconstruct the root causes of violence. In advisory circles students grappled with the interconnectedness of social problems, theorized why violence occurs, and discussed remedies. Their tree posters, which were posted in hallways, photographed, and distributed to community stakeholders, became shared public texts promoting continued discussion. Finally, by framing the town hall as a protest and attracting media attention to ensure local newspaper coverage, critical cariño suffused the town hall. As Ms. Howard noted, "Our microphones, applause, tears, drums, songs, poems, candles, and posters made Lucho's death (and the senseless deaths of so many other young men and women) tangible, real, incapable of being ignored." By uniting to confront tragedy, MHS educators not only assured students that their lives and neighborhoods mattered, but they also raised community awareness and mobilized politicians to prioritize violence cessation. This commitment to authentic cariño radically transformed schooling for students and generated ripples of positive action beyond MHS.

Tragically, MHS suffered another loss 3 weeks later when Jorge, the 5-year-old sibling of an MHS junior, was shot and killed outside his parents' business. As students returned to campus after winter break, the theme of "Ya basta, enough is enough!" gained momentum. At the first staff collaboration meeting of 2012, four students from BEST, the young men's group, accompanied by their facilitator César, stepped forward in professional attire to present their plan for a CIP entitled the "Peaceful City Campaign."

César prefaced their presentation with his outrage over a recent, online comment to an article reporting Jorge's death. The post criminalized city youth, calling them "baby killers." Incensed, César discussed the matter with BEST and they decided to mobilize a campaign to show the world that they were peace-builders not violent criminals. Andres, a junior, spoke next to remind teachers that BEST was a group of 30 brothers dedicated to becoming responsible and respected men in school and out. Andres enumerated the "eight points of unity" BEST pledged to embody. "I'm respectful. I will honor my environment. I'm not indifferent. I will treat women with respect. I am honest and will follow through. I have self-control. I'll become organized and take care of business. I will achieve." He characterized the Peaceful City Campaign as BEST's refusal to be indifferent to the suffering caused by homicides.

His sophomore peer, Carlos, followed. Holding up his advisory's tree poster, Carlos explained how during his freshmen Our City project in Ms. Barrett's class, he and his classmates had "documented people's experiences in the neighborhood and heard many people express concerns about violence." (See Chapter 4 for project details.) Moved by these complaints the young men in BEST sought to increase people's awareness of the root causes of violence such as poverty and the warped notion of "street respect" that compels some misguided individuals to "act bad." Next was David, who described how BEST had renamed what is known as the Season of Nonviolence[3] to the Peaceful City Campaign. Reminiscent of Keating's (2013) advocacy for a post-oppositional politics of change, David maintained that "flipping the script" in this manner positioned students as being *for* peace rather than *against* violence. He argued that this orientation would focus community members' attention on building a healthy and vibrant community rather than one simply devoid of violence. Marco, the final speaker, outlined a calendar of activities aimed at achieving BEST's goal to "reunite the community." He distributed a press release emblazoned with the slogan, "If you want peace, work for justice!"

Afterward, faculty posed clarifying questions, pushing the young men to consider potential obstacles and additional strategies to advance peace-building. After 34 minutes of dialogue, students received the staff's endorsement. This presentation highlighted the generative power of authentic cariño. BEST—as a family of brothers within the broader MHS family—received familial cariño through peer–peer support, as well as through the encouragement of staff, who listened to their proposal with serious attention. In developing their CIP and figuring out how to organize a persuasive campaign pitch, BEST youth applied HOM and received intellectual cariño as teachers offered constructive feedback. Critical cariño surfaced in the school's willingness to devote limited staff collaboration time to discussing a grave problem wrenching the community and harming students' capacity to engage fully in school.

Over the next 74 days, the MHS community, led by BEST and FISTT members, became immersed in the Peaceful City Campaign. The campaign kick-off, filmed by Telemundo for the evening news, was a day of service held on the Martin Luther King holiday. Students, families, teachers, a school board representative, and several police officers gathered on campus to participate in beautification projects aimed at creating "safe, inspiring spaces for our students to learn every day." The volunteers installed a "healing garden," painted a mural, and cleaned the gym, auditorium, Teen Center, and a nearby neighborhood park. The event concluded with a ceremony in which several volunteers began a 24-hour fast relay to demonstrate their commitment to peace. From this day onward, the school held daily break-the-fast ceremonies at lunchtime in which several fasters and their supporters (a shifting cast of 12–20 students and adults) formed a sacred circle, shared insights, and passed armbands to the next fasters. Fasters, who numbered over 200 by the campaign's end, wrote reflections for the school newspaper. Their choice to abstain from food for 24 hours represented a profound example of embodiment because they were literally using their bodies to draw attention to an urgent issue and also taking time to re(member) themselves by focusing on their bodies' intuitions and sensations.

In addition to the fast relay, students developed a Peace Pledge, canvassed the neighborhood for signatures, and created a Facebook page. The pledge, which eventually garnered over 1,000 signatories, including the city mayor, city council members, and school board representatives, consisted of 10 declarative I-statements specifying ways to embody peace (e.g., I promise to not bring drama or discrimination into our community. I promise to find the beauty in and empathize with everyone. I promise to value the person I really am—physically, mentally, and emotionally. I promise to be mindful of my relationships and my actions. I promise to build up my beloved community to help build lasting peace.).

BEST and FISTT also created and facilitated a Peaceful City lesson for advisory. During a community circle, students discussed how violence affected them. In Ms. Howard and Mr. Keo's advisory, 14 students shared. Five students recounted losing a family member or friend to gun violence. Of these, one young woman wept openly and admitted her ongoing struggle with PTSD. Another five students reported that they or family members had been shot at or violently robbed. The remaining students highlighted the toxic effects of violence. "Nowadays you can't play outside because you're scared." "There's always gun shooting. You can't look at people in the eyes." "You can't walk around without worrying that you're going to get shot." This exchange allowed youth to open up and collectively examine the negative impact of violence on their bodymindspirits and broader community.

By making space for such conversations, MHS enacted authentic cariño. Students within supportive community circles dropped the "tough fronts" (Dance, 2002) worn to ensure survival and opted instead to reveal fear and pain with vulnerability. This communal truth telling not only ensured that the victims of violence were remembered, but enabled youth to shed silence and resist a society that too often erases or minimizes the trauma arising from gun violence. Boveda and Bhattacharya (2019) argue that the vulnerability involved in disclosing woundedness is essential for self-recovery and wholeness.

> *Vulnerability is a de/colonial move.* Since colonizers want and enact control, vulnerability allows for letting go of control-based narrative to expose tender, raw parts of ourselves. In exposing those parts, we invite others to do the same, and we connect in shared humanity that is not in the realm of superficial interest convergence, but in the realm of knowing and being agents of love for each other and ourselves. (p. 17, italics in original)

By facing the harsh reality of violence together and connecting with emotional intimacy, these students received comfort and strength from their advisory peers and adult mentors. In the spirit of authentic cariño, they became "agents of love for each other" and themselves. Ginwright (2010, 2016) contends that such vulnerability and communal truth telling catalyzes hope and empowers youth to exercise agency to build the kinds of communities in which they want to live.

As this student-led community circle continued, youth discussed the Peace Pledge, parsing its I-statements and identifying one that was especially resonant. One student, speaking of the statement "I pledge to not have negative feelings about myself," offered her view. "I think people struggle with that. I think if people liked themselves, there would not be so many gangs." Another student expressed doubts about the pledge to "not disrespect my community by trashing our environment," conjecturing that "even if the city is clean, there will still be violence." This ignited dialogue about how physical surroundings can generate a sense of safety and order and how trashed neighborhoods can communicate to their inhabitants that they too are trash. As one student put it, "We're expected to be trashy." Because this exchange prompted youth to ponder a high-interest topic relevant to their lived experiences, it illustrates how MHS cultivated students' HOM and community-mindedness simultaneously. Importantly, students were invited to move beyond reflection and select one I-statement to embody for the remainder of the campaign. To deepen commitment, the lesson culminated with students artistically rendering chosen pledges and writing reflections to explain their selections. These works were mounted in collages that were then posted in hallways and showcased at a FISTT town hall addressing dating violence (Chapter 3 describes that town hall).

Through community circle gatherings such as these, MHS imparted a "soft care" that nourished students' bodymindspirits and fostered "radical healing" (Ginwright, 2010). This soft care contrasts with the *pobrecito* syndrome of pity (Antrop-González & De Jesús, 2006) and instead entails providing safe, compassionate spaces for youth to acknowledge and attend to their raw/soft/real/authentic selves. This soft care is important because it suggests that authentic cariño requires teachers to be more than "warm demanders" (Ware, 2006) who offer "hard care" (Antrop-González & De Jesús, 2006) to support students' academic success. The soft care displayed in the Peaceful City community circle activity (and in other activities such as firewalks) provided students an opportunity to express themselves, release negative emotions, cultivate empathy, appreciate interrelatedness, and build solidarity. When adult mentors displayed soft care and supported youth to be socioemotionally vulnerable, they nurtured students' self-awareness, hope, and interest in building revitalized communities. MHS educators demonstrated how knowing and learning through dialogic interaction and interrelatedness might provide a blueprint for how to live meaningfully in the world. In this regard, MHS seeded new futures by showing youth that "the way we interact with the world in knowing it" can become "the way we interact with the world as we live in it" (Palmer, 1983/1993, p. 21), MHS seeded new futures.

The grand finale for the Peaceful City Campaign was a lively March for Peace attended by over 300 community members. Students (from MHS and other schools), family members, educators, community partners, and politicians walked and chanted through city streets for an hour and half en route to a rally in a park. Marchers assembled first on the school's front lawn where Aztec *danzantes* clad in full regalia with tall, fluttering feather headdresses and jangling *chachayotes* (rattle adorned ankle cuffs) danced a blessing ceremony. Student leaders, sporting matching T-shirts with the acronyms BEST and FISTT floating above intermingled gender symbols and the words "Peaceful City Campaign," held hands in a circle around the dancers. To commence the ceremony, the lead dancer joined by a student dancer ignited *copal* (an amber incense resin) in a *popoxcomitl* (an earthen chalice). As cleansing smoke billowed, an elder acknowledged the four directions and invoked the spirit of the ancestors to accompany marchers and strengthen their focus and purpose. This Indigenous ritual steeped the event in sacredness. Anzaldúa (2015), speaking of spiritual activism, explains that creative engagements (such as this Aztec dance) embed individuals within "a larger frame of reference," allowing them to connect their "personal struggles with those of other beings on the planet, with the struggles of the Earth itself" (p. 119). The presence of the danzantes heightened participants' sense of "radical interrelatedness" and "the possibility of planetary citizenship" (Keating, 2013, pp. 5 and 46).

As marchers linked arms, laughed, chanted, and waved to onlookers on balconies and in doorways, their camaraderie generated a celebratory energy. Some students exuberantly lifted and shook hand-drawn signs with hopeful slogans above their heads. "I am not part of the problem! I am part of the solution!" "I am a young person, not a statistic! I am not dangerous; I am just gifted!" "Peace is a verb!" "Peace = The right to be yourself." One marcher twirled an enormous, pole-mounted flag featuring a photo of planet Earth floating in space. Midway through the march, the throng paused at a plaza, where they placed flowers and candles on a shrine honoring the victims of violence. Speaking the names of MHS victims as well as Trayvon Martin and Oscar Grant, students invited the crowd and passersby to take a moment of silence.[4]

As the march continued, FISTT and BEST students acted as "culture keepers," security guards, and chant leaders. With the help of megaphones, the crowd followed call-and-response prompts. "Hey, hey, ho, ho! This senseless violence has got to go!" "What's this about? Building Peace!" "What do we want? Peaceful streets! When do we want it? Now!" "*Se puede? Si se puede!*" (Can it be done? Yes, it can!). "*Se ve, se siente . . . el pueblo está presente!*" (We see, we feel, the presence of the people is here!).

Once the throng arrived at the park, they were greeted by a serape-draped altar offering food and water and displaying pictures of Lucho, Jorge, Martin Luther King, César Chávez, and Gandhi. Student leaders and invited guests mounted a stage constructed for the occasion. A moving sequence of performances followed. Anthony Chávez, grandson of César Chavez, welcomed marchers and read a letter of praise sent by the United Farm Workers and the César Chavez Foundation. "We are inspired by your campaign to build peace. . . . We encourage you to continue to serve your communities. This is a lifelong challenge. Thank you students, staff, and teachers for your hard work and your patience." Next, representatives from FISTT and BEST presented over 1,000 signed pledges to MHS families who had lost children to gun violence. Several family members spoke, affirming the importance of building peace. The rally continued with the mayor, chief of police, two city council members, and the school board president offering remarks and commending students. Before a final fast-breaking ceremony, EDP coach César introduced his mother, a longtime union activist, and together they sang *De Colores*, the unofficial anthem of the UFW. The rally and 74-day campaign closed when the final fasters bit into apples and broke their fast.

Later that afternoon and into the next day, the staff listserv reverberated with accolades congratulating students and organizers for a logistically smooth, uplifting campaign. Ms. Buchanan gushed, "MHS is such an amazing school! I've never seen anything like it! These young people are truly empowered by events like the march yesterday. I feel so honored to be part of this school!" Mr. Behari praised students' leadership. "The young people really stepped up in an inspiring way. To see my little advisee Lucia, who came to our school having only been in the U.S. for eight months, with her fist in the air leading chants about peace made me proud to be her advisor." César wrote a long message of gratitude and described the march/rally as a life highlight. "I was wowed. . . . So many people in that park having fun together and being reverential! It was the best César Chávez event of my life—probably cuz it was purposeful! Real good energy to the very end." The exuberance evident in these posts demonstrates how the Peaceful City campaign transmuted tragedy into hopeful action. Through skillful organizing BEST and FISTT tapped into "the internal desire we all have for freedom, joy, restorative justice . . . and to matter to ourselves, our community, our family, and our country" (Love, 2019, p. 7). Their campaign "'demand[ed] the impossible' by refusing injustice and the disposability of dark children" (Love, 2019, p. 7). In doing so, the MHS community (re)membered its wholeness and showed others how authentic cariño can infuse joy and beauty into the struggle for community transformation.

Lest this tale read solely as a triumphant victory narrative, it is important to remind readers that 62 days after the march, MHS lost a third youth to a drive-by-shooting. (See Chapter 2 for the school's response to this tragedy.) The loss of Ernesto, an 11th-grade leader within the Peaceful City Campaign, shattered the community. Once again, staff and youth found themselves mourning, raising burial funds, and searching for meaning in the midst of profound grief. Although the community rose valiantly to meet the challenge and sustain its peace-building commitments, Ernesto's death highlighted how a school by itself, even if it embraces authentic cariño fullheartedly, must still contend daily with brutal macrostructural realities that oppress marginalized communities. Schools alone cannot transform communities, but they can incubate young, community-ready leaders who press forward to eradicate institutional violence by daring to imagine and build societies where justice, peace, and love prevail.

Following Ernesto's murder, MHS dug its heels in further to stand for peace. In extracurricular and academic settings, the community redoubled its efforts to end violence. Over the summer, 14 students, coached by Ms. Barrett and Ms. Howard, collaborated to publish a book of students' essays, poems, and reflections entitled *Our Lives and Voices Matter: 74 Days Striving for a Peaceful City*. They dedicated their volume to Ernesto, Jorge, and Lucho. Mr. Behari revised a local government unit, focusing it squarely on crime and violence prevention. He invited the school district's "organizational effectiveness" chief, a police sergeant, and a city council member into his classroom to dialogue with students about building peace in the city. That discussion explored housing segregation, community policing, graffiti, gun control, budget constraints, and immigration policy. Drawing from this conversation and other research, Mr. Behari's students wrote letters to local officials advocating promising policies. They also participated in an after-school panel to debate the efficacy of various crime mitigation measures before an audience of peers, parents, educators, and community members (Curry & Athanases, 2020). Given statistics showing that 69% of 12th-grade civics students graduate never having written an opinion letter to a newspaper or politician and similarly that 53% have never interacted with outside speakers in their classrooms (G. Wilburn, personal communication, December 23, 2020; U.S. DOE, 2010), Mr. Behari's violence prevention unit stands out as an outlier in the ways it wove together familial, intellectual, and critical cariño.

Perhaps most impressively, BEST and FISTT launched a second season of peace-building during which they resumed their fast-relay and peace pledge canvassing. At BEST's kick-off town hall, Principal West praised youth for embodying the Habits of Life and exhibiting courage, persistence, and dedication. Tugging gently at a handwoven bracelet worn to honor Ernesto, West tearfully acknowledged his ongoing grief, but he also highlighted the impact of the Peaceful City Campaign by displaying a police map indicating that crime in the neighborhoods adjacent to the school had declined in the last year. He credited students for being instrumental in this transformation. Quoting Martin Luther King, he closed by exhorting students "to hold back the flood of fear" and realize that "an eye for an eye leaves everyone blind. . . . The time is always right to do the right thing. . . . Peace is not a distant goal that we seek, but a means by which we arrive at that goal." This town hall once again featured advisories presenting proposals to promote peace. As they shared their humanizing vision for a world predicated on love, they displayed hope and willingness to solve community problems. Through these proposals, youth challenged institutional narratives and media images misrepresenting them as criminals, troublemakers, and freeloaders who endanger societal welfare and siphon away public resources. Their solidarity and commitment to peace resounded when the town hall ended with a rousing unity clap.

MHS's arduous and sustained efforts to confront violence and build peace (summarized in Table 5.3) demonstrated how the school braided together familial, intellectual, and critical cariño to create a learning environment saturated with authentic cariño. This cariño fortified members of the community as they faced unfathomable loss and the toxic fallout of social oppression and inequity.

CLOSING REFLECTIONS

Just as the intimacy of a parent braiding a child's hair involves connection, guidance, purpose, and love, the educators who wove the trenza of authentic cariño at MHS affirmed students' sense of belonging (familial cariño), intelligence (intellectual cariño), and agency (critical cariño). In delivering this

Table 5.3. Braided Strands of Authentic Cariño Across MHS's Peaceful City Campaign

Familial	Intellectual	Critical
• Sacred rituals to affirm wholeness, share personal reflections, and remember victims • Community circles in advisory to process tragedies • Whole school celebrations of life for victims and fundraising for burial • *Ofrendas* (offerings) and tributes to victims visibly displayed and maintained year-round	• Habits of Mind applied to press releases, blogs, campaign strategizing, logistics coordination, peace pledge development and dissemination, and book publication • Analysis of the root causes of urban violence • Policy analysis and advocacy in government class	• Public advocacy to highlight root causes of violence in order to flip media images and scripts criminalizing urban youth • Political organizing to mobilize protests and involve power brokers such as chief of police, school district superintendent, and mayor

Border Crossings	Dialogue	Embodied Action
• Door-to-door pledge canvassing • Protest march through city streets • Students at City Council and school board • Aztec dancers • Mayor, district superintendent, City Council members, school board representatives, CBO partners, UFW representatives, teachers, and families joined with students	• BEST and FISTT collaboration to orchestrate campaign • BEST vets CIP at staff meeting • Guest speakers in classrooms • Violence prevention panel • Fasting circles • Advisory circles • Summer book editing/publishing collaboration	• Fasting, protesting, marching, singing, dancing, and speaking • Wearing arm bands and solidarity T-shirts • Building altars • Fabricating braided memorial bracelets • Baking sweets and selling them

message and embracing authentic cariño, MHS rejected the idea of school as a bureaucratic organization and instead advanced a vision of school as an expansive homeplace. Mr. West highlighted the importance of this shift when he indicated that Latinx students' success hinged on making "kids feel like school is their home." This invocation of home surfaced repeatedly in my years at MHS. Students such as salutatorian Rosa (referenced in Chapter 1) considered MHS a "second home," and her teachers echoed this view. Mr. Trung and Ms. Dupont described advisory as a "home for kids to feel supported academically and emotionally." Mr. Avila, observing students' fondness for lingering on campus after hours, remarked, "They don't see the school as a school place; they see it as home. . . . I'm like, 'What are you doing here? Why don't you go home?' They give you the sense of, 'We *are* home.'" In a similar vein, Ms. Barrett, in her commencement address, characterized MHS as "home" and as a place of "comfort."

These ubiquitous references to home call to mind hooks' (1990) description of homeplace as the safe, healing space in which her family nurtured one another's wholeness and humanity. Recalling the affirmative ambiance of her grandmother's home, hooks writes about how her grandmother, along with countless other African American women, created homes in which "people could strive to be subjects, not objects, where we could be affirmed in our minds and hearts despite poverty, hardship, and deprivation, where we could restore to ourselves the dignity denied us on the outside in the public world." hooks credits this homespace with fortifying her to resist racist oppression and join liberation struggles. Her vision of homespace parallels the ways that authentic cariño fundamentally transformed schooling at MHS and equipped community members to engage in the Real Dream movement, the Futbolista's soccer field effort, the free college ballot initiative, and the Peaceful City Campaign.

Immersed in authentic cariño, MHS students received steady validation and support. In contrast to hostile educational settings marked by microaggressions (Sue et al., 2007; Yosso et al., 2009), MHS youth encountered a school saturated with microaffirmations (Powell et al., 2013; Rowe, 2008), which helped them feel welcome, worthy, and capable. This affirming environment fueled students' engagement in school. In this regard, MHS students corroborated Valenzuela's (1999) assertion that Latinx students view reciprocal relations with caring adults as "the basis for all learning" and a "precondition to caring about school" (p. 79). Knowing they mattered in the eyes of school adults and that they need not detach and compartmentalize their heritage identities to thrive academically, MHS students invested themselves in school. In return, MHS educators dedicated themselves to constructing transformative learning experiences that enhanced students' HOM and community cultural wealth (Yosso, 2005). In this manner, authentic cariño contributed to a culture of engaged learning in which students activated their bodymindspirits to deepen understanding, solve problems, and transform their communities (Curry & Athanases, 2020). It is through these endeavors that MHS students came to recognize learning in the world as a path toward personal growth, social uplift, and liberation. Ultimately, the trenza of authentic cariño allowed MHS to flourish and make headway toward its mission to interrupt inequity and injustice.

Seguir Adelante—Moving Forward

MHS's success enveloping students in authentic cariño represents a remarkable accomplishment, especially given the U.S. education system's history of underserving Latinx students, subtracting valuable cultural resources from them (Valenzuela, 1999), and, at worst, confining them to prison-like environments focused not on education, but on "custody and control" (Wacquant, 2011, p. 107). Through the portraits of authentic cariño highlighted in previous chapters, I demonstrated the possibilities that exist when a school tenaciously pursues social justice and cultivates a learning culture premised on authentic cariño. With familial cariño, MHS nurtured students' sense of belonging and imparted a holistic care that assured students that their lives and home communities mattered. With intellectual cariño, MHS sharpened students' Habits of Mind (HOM) and capacity to read the world and solve problems. And with critical cariño, MHS equipped youth to become change agents interested in joining the beautiful struggle for an equitable and just world. By offering glimpses of firewalks, digital immigration story festivals, Our City projects, Miranda trials, student-organized town halls, senior defenses, parent conferences, Basura Ball tournaments, post-session adventures, a new soccer field, and the Peaceful City campaign, this book illuminates how MHS's schoolwide enactment of authentic cariño involved compelling practices that transformed schooling. These glimpses are important because they unravel dominant, deficit-based narratives characterizing low-SES urban youth of color and the "city schools" they attend as beyond repair or redemption (Jacobs, 2015; Welsh & Swain, 2020). Additionally, these glimpses enrich our "images of the possible"—our "visions of what constitutes good education, or what a well-educated youngster might look like if provided with appropriate opportunities and stimulation" (Shulman, 1987, p. 10).

LESSONS FROM MHS

The MHS case offers important lessons to reinvigorate schooling for nondominant youth that can guide those wishing to cultivate authentic cariño in other settings.

The Importance of Institutionalizing Authentic Cariño

MHS prioritized institutional systems and procedures to ensure the presence and continuity of all three strands of authentic cariño across all settings of the school's learning ecology. Familial cariño was instantiated through the Habits of Life and the network of care, which enabled adult allies to collaborate and personalize students' learning and maintain robust, holistic, culturally affirming relations with youth. In stark contrast to the "fragile, incomplete, or nonexistent" social relationships Valenzuela (1999) documented at Seguín High, the proliferation of caring adult–youth relationships at MHS increased the odds that *every* student (not just those fortunate enough to have the "good" teacher or be enrolled in the "special" program) received the authentic cariño necessary to flourish in school. Intellectual cariño gained institutional traction through HOM, project-based curriculum, public exhibitions of learning, internships, town halls, and post-sessions. Finally, critical cariño achieved institutional salience through the social justice mission and intensive community partnerships. These various organizational structures and their ancillary components (e.g., advisory, restorative justice, professional development, and behavior-based staff hiring) demonstrated the school's awareness that authentic cariño's maintenance was not simply a technical endeavor, but one that demanded keen attention to students' humanity and wellness, as well as a willingness to experiment boldly and move beyond mere tinkering. This institutionalization unfolded in large part because educators relinquished adherence to long-standing, stultifying school grammars and audaciously invested themselves in the beautiful struggle.

The Importance of Engaged Learning and Intellectual Joy

Rejecting rote, scripted, skill-level work and test preparation, MHS educators embodying intellectual cariño strove to immerse youth in "transformative learning experiences" designed to kindle students' excitement about learning. Through interdisciplinary projects and expanded activities in the broader community, MHS provided students cumulative opportunities to engage in dialogue, discovery, debate, and problem solving. To engineer such activities, teachers invested considerable energy developing original curricula and thinking about how best to elicit student engagement and pleasure. Students recognized teachers' intensive efforts to make learning meaningful and fun as expressions of care; in repayment, they rose to meet academic challenges. As students argued over math problems, wrote personal narratives for public radio, published books, mobilized political campaigns, fielded probing questions from defense panelists, and undertook internships, their engrossment in learning showed up in lively conversation and investments of concerted effort into intellectual endeavors. In this manner, authentic cariño transformed school from drudgery and boredom to activity and life. This shift toward engagement and intellectual joy fueled students' investment in learning, allowing them to become active pensadoras accustomed to using their knowledge, skills, and creativity to pursue change in self and society.

The Importance of Inner Healing and Community Engagement

Committed to nurturing the holistic development of students' bodymind-spirits, authentic cariño extended beyond academics to support students' personal and social well-being. Given that many of MHS's nondominant students entered school worn down and often traumatized by harsh economic conditions, violence, and years of subtractive schooling, teachers understood that they could not ignore students' soul wounds. Through affirmative relations and advisor roles, educators exhibited profound familial cariño as they encouraged youth to engage in Socratic reflection, tap inner resources, and support each other. Educators paired this inner healing work with community-based activities that reflected critical cariño and connected youth to community cultural wealth and fostered students' sense of meaning and purpose. By encouraging inner healing and community engagement, MHS staff helped youth gain the confidence, equanimity, and capacity to enter classrooms ready to learn.

The Importance of College *and* Community Readiness

Through its mandatory college prep course sequence, advocacy for medical careers requiring postsecondary education, and active college counseling, MHS exemplified a "college going school" culture (Holland & Farmer-Hinton, 2009). Within this milieu, adults touted economic security and professional success as desirable and likely college outcomes, while also assuring students that college attendance need not pull them away from their heritage communities. Rather than focusing narrowly on college placement tests, college rhetoric, college symbols, and college admissions (Athanases et al., 2016), MHS in its embrace of both intellectual and critical cariño reified the importance of lifelong learning as a path to deepen meaning, purpose, and community transformation. This shift included explicit attention to ensuring that students graduated not only college ready, but "community ready." Community readiness meant encouraging students to develop the skills, knowledge, and inclinations necessary to participate in civic life and contribute to efforts to make communities and democracy function better. This broader focus proved essential to advancing MHS's mission to eradicate inequity and injustice, fostering engaged learning, and ensuring that youth understood the importance of lifting others.

These four lessons involve fundamental shifts in how we conceive and organize high schools. Most notably, they necessitate a transformation in community–school relations and demand substantive partnership with community organizations. Although these collaborations take time to develop, once established, they can prove generative and revitalizing. MHS's willingness to engage in this hard work of reculturing and reenvisioning school to ensure that education does not compound suffering, but rather liberates, demonstrates the positive outcomes that are possible when a school prioritizes authentic cariño.

CHALLENGES

Despite its successes and impressive track record supporting Latinx youth and other students of color, MHS faced ongoing challenges as it endeavored to fulfill its mission. Three of MHS's most daunting dilemmas are presented next, as well as possible responses to overcome these challenges.

Educators' Occupational Stress

Institutionalizing authentic cariño schoolwide involved a substantial expansion in educators' job responsibilities. The adults at MHS shouldered a heavy burden as teachers, advisors, professional developers, coaches, college counselors, curriculum developers, school leaders, therapists, fundraisers, and transformational mentors. Inadequate school funding (as evidenced in paper supply shortages, unreliable heat, low wages, limited computers, and scant technology supports) coupled with supporting students impacted by poverty, deportation, eviction, homelessness, gangs, violence, and drugs exacerbated this burden. Although MHS attempted to bolster educators' well-being through community-building activities, multiday retreats, and public appreciation rituals, the periodic departure of staff due to burnout exposed the limits of such efforts. Complicating matters, teacher attrition disrupted academic departments and the cohesion of student advisories, adding stress for the adults who remained at MHS.

Remunerating educators for their extra labor seems an obvious place to begin alleviating burnout because it symbolically conveys to teachers that their hard work is valued. Unfortunately, MHS's district's financial mismanagement and budgetary constraints made pay increases unlikely. During this study's most intensive year of data collection, the average teacher salary in the district was roughly $10,000 less than the statewide average. Without sufficient funds, salary increases were not an option. This shortfall suggests that state-level policy makers and citizens must do everything possible to reprioritize budgets to ensure that teachers are appropriately paid. Given surveys suggesting that 71% of Americans believe public school teachers are underpaid and that 66% would consent to paying higher taxes to increase salaries (Goldstein & Cassleman, 2018), there is sufficient public will to make our budgets reflect our values. Higher salaries will allow schools, especially hard-to-staff schools, better attract high-quality educators whose hearts are in the work. With better pay and favorable work conditions, teachers will perform better, remain in the profession, and students will benefit. These outcomes stand to positively impact all involved and society writ large. Reallocating budgets is a monumental undertaking, but with persistence, pressure, and moral conviction, we can and must prioritize spending that enables all children to discover their original genius and wholeness. Our future and liberation depend on this.

Beyond salary increases, MHS could experiment with other options to address stress and burnout. A few interventions that might help temper this menace include partnering with community businesses and organizations to provide access to secondary traumatic stress treatment and antiracist therapy (Love, 2020), self-care resources/opportunities, on-site childcare (staffed perhaps by MHS parents seeking employment), and annual "comadre" and "compadre" rewards to acknowledge educators for their authentic cariño. In order to gauge faculty morale and stress, MHS could conduct annual organizational surveys to assess teachers' professional well-being, satisfaction, and engagement coupled with collaborative processes for data analysis and intervention development. The educator version of the Maslach Burnout Inventory (MBI-ES) has proven a helpful tool for schools to evaluate organizational health and determine which conditions of educators' work (workload, control, reward, community, fairness, and values) deserve highest priority (Maslach et al., 1986). Above all, MHS and other schools seeking to sustain educators' commitment to authentic cariño must preserve and seek to expand educators' opportunities to benefit from the moral rewards generated from meaningful relationships with youth and their families, the intellectual joy of crafting and facilitating transformative educational experiences, and the satisfaction of advancing social justice. As they uphold these opportunities, though, leaders must never allow these intrinsic rewards to become justification for poor compensation.

Fostering Student Agency Rather Than Dependency

MHS envisioned graduates who would be change agents capable of transforming not only their lives and communities, but also the fields of bioscience and health. This goal meant instilling within students the conviction, confidence, and self-advocacy skills to fulfill their ambitious dreams. To foster these dispositions, MHS channeled authentic cariño toward creating an affirming "home" for students, assuming that with sufficient safety, youth would take risks to stretch themselves beyond comfort zones and become accustomed to overcoming obstacles. Some teachers, however, expressed concern that the school's intensive provision of familial cariño might handicap students. Mr. Behari, who conducted an informal investigation of graduates' college persistence from

2009–2011, found that only 45% of Latinx alums exhibited maximum college persistence (enrollment every semester following MHS graduation). Meanwhile, Ms. Clark reported that a faction of recently graduated students returned to MHS regularly for visits. She speculated that their ongoing presence on campus might be evidence of a "failure to launch." She worried that these alums lacked the skills and self-assurance needed to "jump [] into the real world . . . because we coddled them." Her apprehension suggested a shadow side to authentic cariño wherein zealous offerings of support habituate nondominant students to levels of peer and adult care that may be lacking in future settings.

To negotiate this dilemma, educators need to reflect on how their cariño enables students to chart their own futures and achieve independence. Although annual firewalk rituals facilitated such growth by requiring students to present "thoughtful plans for moving forward," students may need additional preparation of a more explicit, consistent, and applied nature to navigate real-world realities. Students need guidance about how to activate their *ganas* (desire) and *empeño* (determination) to contend with and prevail over wealth inequality, White supremacy, patriarchy, and other oppressive forces. Because of this, adult allies seeking to embody authentic cariño must assist students to self-advocate, handle setbacks, own their learning, and make concrete plans to achieve dreams. This cariño requires artistry and discernment to balance soft and hard care, support and pressure, and guidance and independence. To fine-tune these balances, educators may benefit from exploring the extent to which school structures, policies, and norms encourage (or hamper) students to exercise responsibility. Inviting alumni to join in such discussions could provide instructive feedback. Such deliberations may also generate insights into how teachers' roles could be reimagined to better support students' responsibility and competence. A fringe benefit may turn out to be that resulting alterations to practice could lighten teachers' excessive workload.

Confronting Oppressive Power Structures

The foregoing challenges—teachers' occupational stress and students' difficulty launching—have roots in broader socioeconomic contexts. The underfunding of public schools and the persistence of societal inequities that marginalize youth and limit their opportunities inevitably hampered MHS's capacity to optimize its good work. It is clear that schools alone cannot support student success and community development. As such, authentic cariño is a necessary but insufficient strategy to overcome institutional failures in housing, immigration, education, policing, health, and electoral politics. Ultimately, the hope is that youth who have been steeped in authentic cariño internalize new discourses, epistemologies, and practices that they carry into their future work as institutional/societal change agents. Viewed in this manner, authentic cariño holds transformative possibilities for interrupting and altering systemic inequities.

RECOMMENDATIONS FOR MOVING FORWARD

Although there is no recipe for institutionalizing authentic cariño because its provision must be responsive to particular community needs, this penultimate section offers a set of questions to ignite conversations that I hope might spur readers to infuse authentic cariño into their local settings (see Table C.1).

Table C.1. Reflection Questions to Promote Authentic Cariño

Cariño Domain	Guiding Questions
Familial	• How does our school nurture the bodymindspirits of students and teachers? • How can we build a network of care to ensure students' multiple hungers are met? • What habits or cultural values do we wish to instill in students to ensure that they become their best selves? How will we measure or track students' development in these areas?
Intellectual	• How does our school promote learning as a pleasurable and meaningful endeavor? • How does our curriculum and instruction prepare youth to be college and community ready? • How does instruction reflect the C's of connection, challenge, culture, communication, and collaboration? • How do assessments allow youth to demonstrate learning in academically and socially impactful ways?
Critical	• How does our mission explicitly advance social justice, and how can we ensure that we are mission-driven? • How does our school validate and tap the cultural wealth residing in students' families and communities? • How does our curriculum engage youth in activities to make the world better? • How can educators collaboratively examine and interrogate issues of race, power, and political consciousness among themselves and with students to ensure healthy enactments of authentic cariño?
Institutional	• How do we hire educators who have the capacity and willingness to embody authentic cariño? • How do we promote teachers' professional autonomy and relational trust to ensure that school systems maximize the moral rewards of teaching with authentic cariño? • How do we undertake serious self-evaluation of our work and school culture, and how do we do that in a manner that takes into the views of students, families, and educators?

CLOSING REFLECTIONS

Whenever I describe MHS to others at conferences or in chance encounters, I inevitably hear several responses. First, listeners are impressed by the school's accomplishments. Second, they ask questions of "scalability," expressing doubts about the replicability of MHS's institutionalization of authentic cariño. Third, they point out the limited power of schools to influence, much less fundamentally alter, the vast, entrenched structural forces underpinning social inequity. My reply to these skeptical admirers is to champion authentic cariño anyway. The images of the possible constructed by MHS educators, students, and families dare us as a society to imagine the vitality and joy that can exist in a world in which every member of the human family received authentic cariño. This kind of freedom dreaming (Kelley, 2002) is essential to advance the beautiful struggle. When we stop ourselves from contemplating bold and brave dreams, we resign ourselves to the status quo and abet the forces that oppress us. Such pessimism is crippling. Instead, I invite readers to pursue and celebrate the possibilities that emerge when educators collectively affirm students' humanity, when students love learning, and when all members of a school community embody empathy, courage, and integrity. The compelling counterstory offered by MHS demonstrates how schools can play a vital role in acquainting youth with humane ways to live in relation to one another. By immersing students in educational settings saturated with authentic cariño, MHS taught youth that they did not have to wait for some distant, better tomorrow for more enlightened humans to behave ethically and humanely. Rather, these youth and their adult allies, in defiance of violence, racism, xenophobia, and crushing material realities, constructed a more just and humane world in the *now*. Through this collaboration, MHS allowed youth to feel the transformative power of authentic cariño. This embodiment amplified community solidarity and fueled students' and teachers' commitment to "heal this world into what it might become" (Remen, 1999, p. 35).

A Reflexive Recap of Research

"Anthropology that will break your heart." This subtitle from Ruth Behar's book *The Vulnerable Observer* (1996) leaped off my qualitative methods syllabus and seized my attention. As a newly minted grad student, I noticed my peers dutifully flipping through their syllabi following Professor Gómez's course introduction, but my eyes remained fixed on Behar's title. Pondering its meaning, I wondered if my future as an educational researcher might ever break my heart. Would I be a vulnerable observer? Would my forays into K–12 classrooms reveal troubling scenes? Would relationships formed with "subjects" and co-researchers unearth unsettling truths about the world or about myself?

Fast forward 2 decades. I've crossed MHS's quad, passed the gymnasium's mural with its rainbow swirl of planets, celestial symbols, Aztec temples, Chinese dragons, and arrived at Principal West's office for our first interview. In the student-free calm of July, he relaxed quickly into conversation. When asked, "How does the school know if it is successful?" he replied, "The educational system is too narrow on this." He offered up the story of Ernesto. As a freshman, Ernesto arrived alienated from school and life, reeling from a violent episode that had left him scarred by a bullet and on probation. MHS's network of care—his teachers, mother, probation officer, and youth coaches—had united to support him. Ernesto was now a rising junior and promising leader, passing classes with mostly C's, but most importantly, engaged in MHS's community as an active participant in the young men's group and the student executive leadership team. According to West, Ernesto's transformation was an MHS "success story" because it demonstrated the school's ability to empower youth to become "agents of change in their own lives and their own communities." Thanks to MHS's interventions, Ernesto had escaped the school-to-prison pipeline and charted a new course. At home that evening, finalizing fieldnotes, I noted how humanizing it was to have a school measure its success not by quantitative metrics, but by the transformation of a student's life.

Fast forward again, 11 months later, to a somber Monday morning in June. The auditorium chairs are packed with students; community partners, district officials (including the superintendent), city officials, reporters, and parents stand crowded along the side walls. Students pass tissue boxes down the rows. Principal West begins to speak, "Never in my wildest dreams did I imagine that I would be standing here. . . . It just feels cruel. Our hearts are breaking." With his voice cracking and eyes moist, he recounts the Friday evening phone call informing him of Ernesto's death. Aware that most students already know that Ernesto was murdered while strolling to the corner store, Principal West skips the tragedy's details. Instead, he continues, "One of the pieces I love about this school is that we see each other as family. . . . The only thing we can do now is be with each other; we can't make sense of this. It just doesn't make sense." He shares memories of Ernesto. "I have all kinds of Ernesto stories. The one thing that really stays with me is, every morning, he would walk into school with a big smile on his face. He'd shake my hand and give me a hug." West chokes out his next words, "In 17 years of teaching, no one has treated me like that. He was truly a special man. So, we're here for each other. We're here for his teachers. Everyone who knew him is here. His family is here."

Throughout this town hall, I stood behind a video camera, wiping my eyes with a ratty, wet tissue. Documenting the memorial as requested for Ernesto's family, I tried to absorb the loss while watching those who loved Ernesto most—his family, Mr. West, Luz, his advisors, César, and his classmates—mourn. As I watched a commemorative slideshow set to the spirited, ranchera-style song "Un Puño De Tierra" (A fistful of dirt), sadness engulfed me. There was Ernesto smiling and dissecting a frog, Ernesto wearing a garbage bag on a rainy day in Yosemite, Ernesto enlacing his arms with peers in an icebreaker activity, Ernesto cradling Ms. Barrett's baby.

Seeing his face reminded me of my own encounters. I remembered entering the front office and finding Ernesto chatting with Ms. Garcia, the secretary. They would smile and greet me. I remembered him in the teen center playing pool with friends. I remembered him setting up sound equipment for town halls. I remembered him in a sacred circle of students gathered to protest gun violence. I remembered him analyzing a Diego Rivera mural and pointing at the brand marks conquistadors had burnt into Indigenous flesh. I remembered, too, how on Saturday—less than 24 hours after Ernesto's slaying—I had attended an impromptu memorial in the teen center, where the air, aromatic with purifying sage, was punctuated with sobs. Gathered together to grieve, we had enacted a ritual, spontaneously choosing a nearby neighbor, exchanging hand-woven bracelets, and uttering in unison the words "You are not alone." We pledged to keep Ernesto's legacy alive.

Behind the tripod, I felt a raw ache press against my insides. I kept imagining my own sons in Ernesto's place—what would it be like to never again hear their voices or see their faces? I imagined Ernesto's mother's dark, all-consuming despair. At this moment, it dawned on me how much I loved these people, this school, this community. How could I not after so many months of being enmeshed in the authentic cariño saturating MHS's classrooms, hallways, and grounds? I had become a vulnerable observer. Sequestered behind the camera, I dropped my educational researcher identity and surrendered to sorrow.

Days later, at the Catholic church, we assembled for Ernesto's funeral. Honoring the family's request, mourners arrived clad in all white to symbolize peace. Outside, while waiting for the hearse, César led a smudging ceremony. He fanned smoking sage around our bodies to "empower the spirit, restore balance, and release negativity." Enfolded within this circle, I felt connected to MHS and grounded before entering the sanctuary. During the mass, the priest urged attendees to overcome pain and find inspiration in Ernesto's capacity to love and his commitment to transforming his life. As the priest pressed us to find the courage to "make a difference in the community," I thought of Gloria Anzaldúa's words: "May we do work that matters. Vale la pena, it's worth the pain" (2015, p. 22).

After all these years, the priest's exhortations still linger. Driven by "duty memory" (Nora, 1989), I have attempted to render MHS's story faithfully. By capturing this school and its inhabitants in rich texture, I hope to spur conversations, reforms, and transformations that make a difference for youth like Ernesto. Viewing this book as a "repayment of an impossible debt" (p. 16), I've written it with profound gratitude for those who allowed me inside the school, for those who sat for interviews, for those who endured the presence of a video camera documenting their classrooms and town halls, for those who worked so hard to create and sustain a school steeped in authentic cariño, and for those whose scholarship guided my way.

This responsibility has weighed heavily on me at times and spawned internal *choques* (collisions) and confusion. I have found myself doubting whether I, as a White, U.S.-born, English-dominant, economically privileged, doctorate-holding woman, should be the one to tell this story. I have wrestled with how to responsibly share my findings in ways that will benefit nondominant communities and how to avoid interpretations that could perpetuate domination. I have interrogated my language, motives, frameworks, and methods attempting to ensure that unconscious biases and cultural blinders did not contaminate and undermine my project. I have debated weaving Spanish into my prose, fearing that I might be viewed as a *gringa* "culture vulture" clumsily misappropriating a language that is not my mother tongue. Wary of simplistic victory or pain narratives, I have attempted to temper impulses to romanticize or sensationalize, to portray educators as heroic saviors or depleted warriors. Cautioned by some colleagues to tone down emotion-laden, florid prose and eschew spirituality in conformance with "scientific reporting," I've often retreated, fearing that I will not be taken seriously. And yet afterward, I have scolded myself for yielding and lacking courage. I've squirmed under the penetrating glares of scholars at conferences whom I sense are questioning my legitimacy—my right to narrate this account of youth and educators whose lives and histories bear little resemblance to mine. Niggling internal critics have taunted me, asking, "What can a gringa like you bring to this conversation? Is all this transparency necessary? Why are you exposing yourself like this? To what extent is your scholarship actually interrupting oppressive power relations and educational inequities?"

When rattled and unsure, I meditated, I journaled, I procrastinated, I gardened, I cooked, I walked the dog. Futilely, I tried to escape, but the book still percolated, still haunted me, still called. I took refuge in the works of Gloria Anzaldúa. I read and reread her accounts of writing in *nepantla*—the chaotic, uncomfortable, creative space where she as a Chicana lesbian navigated the clash of multiple worlds and her insider/outsider identities (Anzaldúa, 2002/2013, 2015). Her metaphors for the writing process—of composition choices tormenting her like an aching tooth, of stalled drafts becoming stillborn corpses, of overworked drafts transformed into fields of dead bones, and of missed deadlines gnawing on her insides like rats—resonated. Moved by her journey to bridge psychic, spiritual, and emotional borderlands and usher forth transformation for herself and others, I attempted to walk in her footsteps. Ultimately, Anzaldúa's fear of not doing her subject matter justice left me feeling less alone and encouraged me to reach out to others.

When confused and adrift, I reached out to Luz, whose cheerful *saludo* (greeting) "¡Hola doctora!" and queries about the book's progress energized me. Patiently listening to me ramble about writer's blocks and inner turmoil, Luz dismissed my worries. "Marnie, forget that bullshit. I am counting on you to tell the story. You were there. You shared our cultura. You are the one that has the time, the skills, the resources, the understanding, the heart to do this work." Buoyed by her faith, I resumed writing, determined to not let her down.

Now, as I write this appendix and gaze at the bracelet memorializing Ernesto, I recognize how my multiples selves—my professional and personal selves, my spiritual-intuitive self, and academic-thinking self—have all contributed to this project in ways that I pray make it compelling, rigorous, and hopeful. One byproduct of the years spent grappling with the importance of authentic cariño has been my deepening conviction of the necessity of conducting research from a stance of authentic cariño. Now more than ever, I believe research undertaken *con corazón y razón* (with heart and intellect) is an ethical imperative. If we want our research to matter, we must build relationships of trust and care with those in the field and fellow collaborators (familial cariño), harness our intellects and Habits of Mind to carefully select methodologies and methods that enable deep, rigorous, and respectful investigations into the world and people's lived realities (intellectual cariño), and anchor ourselves in political *conocimiento* (knowledge/awareness) to ensure that we interrogate oppressive structures and dedicate ourselves wholeheartedly to social, economic, and political justice (critical cariño). Although my theorization of authentic cariño emerged from grounded analysis of MHS, I believe that, in many ways, our methods reflected its core commitments. I outline those methods in the next section.

STUDY DESIGN

The Authentic Cariño (AC) study arose from a larger project led by principal investigators (PIs) Betty Achinstein and Rod Ogawa. The original study, known as Schools Organized for Latinos' Educational Success (SOLES), was a multimethod, comparative, critical case study (Flyvbjerg, 2001) examining how high schools serving predominantly Latinx youth organized themselves to promote students' engagement in academically challenging work. Because the Authentic Cariño study drew heavily on data gathered during the SOLES study, I briefly outline this parent study. The SOLES study pursued two research questions.

1. How and to what extent do instructional interactions within innovating high schools engage Latina/o youth in academically challenging work?
2. How and to what extent is the organization of high schools associated with promoting instructional interactions that engage Latina/o youth in academically challenging work?

Motivated by a desire to improve educational opportunities for Latinx youth, SOLES's choice to investigate schools with promising track records represented a conscious effort to uncover images of the possible (Shulman, 1987) and avoid "damage-centered research" (Tuck, 2009). Tuck explains that the latter pathologizes the "other" by documenting brokenness, suffering, and pain, and thereby perpetuates stereotypes of urban schools, of the youth within these settings, and of surrounding communities as being "depleted, ruined, and hopeless" (p. 409). Such research reinforces views of "real urban schools" as deficient places where "poverty, lack, or chaos" prevent any chance of success (Jacobs, 2015, p. 27).

The SOLES study challenged such deficit orientations by embracing an asset/strength orientation and investigating three high schools recognized for achieving some measure of success. SOLES's theoretical framework concentrated on the interplay among two key elements of school organizations—normative social structures (values, norms, and roles) and resource allocation—and classroom instruction. Because organizations may shape instruction by expanding successful practices or curtailing those that prove lacking, we anticipated dynamic flows of influence among these elements.

At the instruction level, SOLES originally emphasized four C's (challenge, culture/language, collaboration/community, and code-breaking with academic language scaffolding) that prior research had associated with Latinx students' academic engagement. Professional development was also predicted to influence organization and/or classroom contexts. SOLES examined the ways in which the coordination of the organization and instruction impacted student learning.

When the SOLES study concluded and authentic cariño emerged as a salient theme garnering strong enthusiasm from MHS educators, I decided to explore authentic cariño further. I embarked on a constructivist, grounded, qualitative study (Charmaz, 2006) that investigated four questions: (a) How does the school promote authentic cariño? (b) How do youth experience authentic cariño? (c) What organizational tensions arise in the pursuit of authentic cariño? and (d) What organizational, individual, and/or community outcomes flow from schoolwide authentic cariño?

DATA COLLECTION

As the SOLES researcher appointed to be the MHS case expert, I spent several days on campus each month during our year of intensive data collection (August 2011 through June 2012). Thereafter, I made monthly visits through February of 2015 depending on events of interest. Data collection spanned 4 years. During my first official appearance at the 2011 summer faculty retreat, I introduced myself as a former high school English teacher turned educational researcher. I attempted to connect with educators as an individual first and as a researcher second. In the spirit of reciprocity, I offered my assistance and at various points served as a student writing coach, National Board Teacher Certification assistant, library organizer, field trip chaperone, community panelist for student exhibitions, security monitor for a protest march, and documentary videographer. Through these overtures, I gained the *confianza* (trust) of staff. Ms. Clark even remarked in one interview that I had penetrated the "veil" of MHS. "You spend way too much time at our school! Everybody on the outside sees one version of us, but you know how we actually work."

My rapport with staff substantially aided data collection, which proceeded along two paths reflecting our bi-level focus on organization and instruction. UC-Santa Cruz's Institutional Review Board approved our study, and we negotiated access to MHS through its district's Research and Evaluation office. Our human subject agreements stipulated confidentiality for all parties, required parental permission for focal student participation, and further specified that students would lose no instructional time as a consequence of participation.[1]

School Organization

To answer questions regarding MHS as an organization, we achieved triangulation by gathering data from five sources: (a) semi-structured interviews with administrators and key stakeholders; (b) focus groups with parents, students, and teachers (the latter undertaken within subject matter departments); (c) observations of professional collaboration sessions and other school activities (town halls, field trips, internships, advisories, EDP, etc.); (d) archival documents (flyers, newsletters, student handbooks, reports, accreditation self-studies, listserv, etc.); and (e) a schoolwide faculty survey. The administrator interviews explored a range of topics, including personal and professional background; school history and mission; organizational roles and expectations for teachers, students, and families; school norms, policies, curricula, and resources; connections between school organization and classroom interactions; the role of subject matter departments; the school's vision for ideal instruction; and home–school–community relationships.

The two 90-minute parent focus group interviews (one in English and one in Spanish) explored families' choices to send their children to MHS, their perceptions of the school's strengths and weaknesses, and home–school connections and/or tensions. Students from each focal classroom (described in the next section), representing a range of academic performance and English language proficiency, convened during lunch and advisory for hour-long focus groups. Of focal students, 87% spoke Spanish at home, 67% were born in the United States, and 83% planned to attend college. Conversations with students explored their views on MHS, focal teachers and classrooms, schoolwide learning opportunities, support structures, and home–school relations. (See Curry and Athanases [2020] for student focus group interview questions.) All student interviews were recorded, transcribed, and conducted in English. This latter choice proved problematic with Ms. Clark's reading students, who seemed reticent to speak and may have been more forthcoming in Spanish.

The two teacher focus groups covered a range of topics, including work conditions and norms, schoolwide efforts/structures to promote Latinx students' success, school and department instructional visions/ideals/practices, schoolwide attention to Latinx students' cultural capital, organizational obstacles to or supports for Latinx students' academic achievement, teachers' professional culture, and curricular tracking. These interviews allowed us to explore trends uncovered in our survey and observations and determine if our six focal teachers were representative of the broader faculty. (Appendix F provides the teacher focus group interview protocol.)

We documented school observations with fieldnotes as events unfolded using laptop computers and/or notebooks depending on our perception of participants' comfort with our presence. Most observations were audio

Table A.1. Constructs Measured by SOLES Faculty Survey

Survey Foci	Number of Items
Norms and Values	38
School's Definition of Success	11
Teachers' Roles and Work Satisfaction	12
Principal's Role	9
Physical Capital (resources and time)	6
Social Capital (teacher/teacher, student/teacher, parents/teachers)	19
Human Capital (teacher knowledge, teacher collaboration, and professional development)	19
Teaching and Learning Practices (4 of 5 C's—challenge, culture, communication/collaboration)	14
Multicultural Capital (supports for navigating dominant and heritage communities)	5
Respondents' Demographic/Biographic Info	18

recorded. Some were videotaped. Following each observation, researchers completed a post-observation summary reflection memo. [See Appendix A in Athanases et al. (2016) for this template.] These memos heightened our attention to research questions and core constructs within our conceptual framework. Finally, the schoolwide survey elicited teachers' responses to 151 items. (See Table A.1 for an overview of the survey's foci.) While only a sliver of survey data found its way into the book, the results increased my confidence in the validity of findings.

Instruction

To examine instruction, we identified six focal teachers, selected to reflect diversity of subject areas (English and math as gatekeeper subjects for college-going, as well as Spanish), ethnicity/race, gender, and experience. Participating teachers received a $300 honorarium. We aimed to observe and videotape six class sessions (two consecutively in fall, winter, and spring) per focal teacher and eventually logged 39 hours of video- and audio-recorded instruction, roughly 6.5 hours per teacher. We instructed teachers to not put on a "dog and pony" show and to simply teach as normally as possible despite the presence of researchers. In conjunction with each lesson, researchers recorded detailed fieldnotes, which included timestamps, segmentation of instructional activities/topics, and scanned handouts and/or photos. Final notes also included responses to the previously referenced post-observation summary reflection template. When it was available, we collected focal students' work (essays, journals, problem sets, projects, etc.). Additionally, we conducted three 90-minute, semi-structured interviews with each focal teacher (two post-observation sessions in fall and spring and a member-check a year later). These conversations addressed personal biographies; instructional philosophies, training, and practices; perceptions of the school (mission, values, structures, etc); school–home connections; staff relations, collaboration, professional development, retention, and diversity; student outcomes; and reflections on observed lessons. Audio-recordings of focal teacher interviews totaled 30 hours.

We broadened our understanding of MHS instruction through faculty focus groups (one for humanities and another for math/science), observations of culminating student exhibitions (expos, mock trials, debates, community panels, defenses, film festivals, etc.), and open-ended responses from the faculty survey.

Table A.2 summarizes the data. In the aggregate, this book draws on over 300 hours of formal observations and interviews. This tally does not include countless hours of informal interactions that transpired as I waited between class periods or lingered after an event to help clean up or socialize with MHS educators.

DATA ANALYSIS

In a multiyear project such as this, accounting for the myriad analytic procedures undertaken during various phases and with different collaborators is a daunting enterprise. In all honesty, our iterative and layered analyses have yielded a cumulative understanding that defies tidy parsing. For this reason, I highlight a few generative strategies.

While collecting data, our team conducted preliminary analysis in weekly 3-hour meetings in which we debriefed observations and discussed emerging insights. Given the UCSC team's diversity (Betty and me, White; Rod, Asian; and five university students research assistants, four of whom were Latinx), these were lively conversations surfacing multiple questions, themes, and interpretations. Because our study involved three schools, we often made comparisons across sites, analyzing how different structures and practices reflected distinctive values and yielded different results. We consulted with collaborators (Steve Athanases at University of California-Davis and Luciana C. de Oliveira now at Virginia Commonwealth University), as well as a critical friend (Ana María Villegas, Montclair State University, NJ) via Skype to engage in cross-case analysis. Throughout the project, we held several multiday retreats to undertake deep, sustained, collaborative analysis.

Table A.2. Summary of Data

Data Source	# of Participants	# of Events	Total Hours
Interviews			
Individual Focal Teacher Interviews	7	19	30
Department Focus Groups (math/science and humanities)	17	2	2
Student Focus Groups	30	7	6
Parent Focus Groups	18	2	3
Principal	1	6	8
Others (literacy coach, EDP staff, health clinician, college counselors, community partners, etc.)	9	9	11
Observations			
Focal Classrooms	7	38	39
Student Project Exhibitions/Community Defenses	–	18	36
Teacher Collaboration/Professional Development/Retreats	–	19	74
Family Events (Back-2-School Nite, parent–teacher conferences, graduation, meetings)	–	11	20
Other (field trips, town hall assemblies, advisory, principal shadow, internships, restorative justice, firewalks, etc.)	–	36	87
Survey			
Schoolwide Faculty Survey (100% response)	17	–	–

Coding

During the SOLES study's 1st year, we developed an a priori coding scheme aligned with our conceptual framework. (Appendices B and C in Athanases et al., 2016, elaborate the SOLES coding scheme.) We periodically updated our codes to reflect emerging patterns and themes. We utilized NVivo, a qualitative data analysis software, to systematize analysis of interview transcripts and open-ended survey responses. Following training from software developers, our team participated in intensive interrater calibration (Athanases et al., 2016) until we achieved a Kappa coefficient of .68. According to Landis and Koch (1977), this score indicates "substantial" interrater agreement. From this point onward, we coded transcripts independently, and team members became case experts on different informants.

During the coding process, we periodically drafted theorizing memos within the NVivo project. These memos served as sense-making tools, helping us conceptualize relationships between various codes and formulate provisional claims. By the project's end, we had 22 such memos related to MHS.

During the Authentic Cariño study, I extended our 35-item coding scheme, adding 18 new codes (e.g., familial/intellectual/critical cariño, student affective engagement, full-service community school, expanded teacher role, and student civic awareness). In addition, I incorporated all observation fieldnotes into the NVivo project before rereading and recoding the entire data corpus. This process heightened my familiarity with the entire data set and sharpened my focus on authentic cariño. I also continued to theorize while coding, adding another 20 memos to the project. At the end of these coding phases (SOLES and AC), we generated code reports, which compiled all "raw" data associated with a particular code. From these reports, we identified salient patterns and themes, summarizing them into synthesis memos that included frequency calculations indicating the number of times a theme surfaced across participants as well as illustrative quotes. (See Athanases and Curry, 2020, p. 26 for a memo sample.) From these various analyses, we developed a summative, holistic school case memo that examined connections between organization and instruction and identified MHS's successes and tensions.

Organization Analyses

While NVivo coding generated substantial insights into MHS's organizational structures and practices, additional analyses further amplified our understandings. In some instances, these efforts involved segmenting observation data by event type (e.g., professional development, firewalk, and community events), cataloguing and scrutinizing them, and generating synthesizing memos. In other instances, we elaborated on themes from NVivo coding by doubling back to data to explore relationships and antecedents more fully. Together, these forays enabled us to unpack phenomena that we regarded as especially promising or unusual.

Take, for example, the sphere of professional collaboration. As a former teacher, inquiry group facilitator, and researcher specializing in teachers' professional communities, I knew that many schools had pockets of innovation within which a few enterprising teachers collaborated to offer students exceptional academic and personal support. At MHS, this expectation was upended by the vibrancy of *schoolwide* professional community. Noting that MHS teachers as a collective engaged in community-building activities and pedagogies among themselves that they then employed in classrooms with their students, Rod Ogawa suggested that MHS bore the hallmarks of a holographic organization in that every organizational element at every organizational level (e.g., individual participant, organizational role, subunit) reflected every characteristic of the whole (Morgan & Ramirez, 1984). Spurred by this insight, we subjected our 19 observations of professional collaboration events totaling 74 hours to more detailed examination. This systematic process involved holistically reviewing fieldnotes, faculty minutes of these sessions, and materials distributed during these events and compiling inventories of (a) agenda items, (b) instructional issues (topics covered, total minutes devoted to teaching, and four C references), (c) instances in which staff explicitly discussed Latinx students raising issues of race, equity, culture, and language, (d) evidence of professional community (norms, collaboration, and culture of professionalism), and (e) specific interactions deemed "juicy" and deserving closer inspection. We then considered how the features of teachers' collaborative work identified by these inventories resurfaced in classrooms and other settings within the MHS learning ecology. By examining the degree of correspondence among various settings, we came to appreciate the cohesion of MHS as a mission-driven school. These analyses revealed how authentic cariño pervaded the entire organization and yielded findings related to the faculty's robust internal accountability reported in Chapter 3.

A second fruitful organization-focused analysis concentrated on how school–community boundary-crossing practices facilitated Latinx students' enrichment from and contribution to community wealth (Yosso, 2005). Seeking to make sense of the dense data we had related to social capital, we looked across interviews with community partners and observations of community events to identify the community resources (EDP, health care, college counseling, mentors) flowing into the school, as well as how the school reciprocated by offering resources outward (interns and political mobilization for the Free College Ballot Initiative, Peaceful City Campaign, Dream Act, and new soccer field). We developed a meta-matrix (Miles & Huberman, 1994) that listed all school–community observations and charted the ways in which each event involved "inside out" and/or "outside in" resource flows of physical, social, human, and multicultural capital. Scanning down the meta-matrix columns, we were able to identify specific elements and examples of boundary-crossing practices. These analyses undergird Chapter 5's claims about how boundary crossing facilitated the braiding of familial, intellectual, and critical cariño.

A third and unexpected line of analysis emerged from MHS's novel tradition of rites of passage rituals known as firewalks in which students demonstrated their embodiment of the Habits of Life/Mind/Work. These rites intrigued me because they transgressed rigid separations between the spiritual and secular, as well as between the private and public usually evident in U.S. public schools. Curious about how these rituals influenced MHS's organizational capacity and student learning, I sought permission to document and analyze these events in greater detail even though this line of inquiry fell outside our grant-approved research design. My analyses of 11 firewalks involved discourse analysis (delineating the questions posed to firewalkers, audience contributions, turn-taking patterns, and adult facilitator roles) and content analyses. These reviews enabled me to understand how firewalks reinforced organizational values and strengthened authentic cariño at MHS.

Instruction Analyses

Our instruction analysis involved two distinct approaches—a holistic, qualitative review coupled with a standardized, instrument-driven review. The former, spearheaded by co-investigators Steve Athanases and Luciana C. de Oliveira, yielded detailed teacher case profiles that wove together teacher history and reflections on practice derived from interviews and discourse analytic reviews of focal teachers' lesson videos. Using the four C's as filters, meta-matrices mapped each lesson's topic, duration, purpose, student engagement (listen, read, speak), academic challenge, and use of culture and language as support. Additionally, because so many learning opportunities at MHS occurred beyond classrooms, we subjected our 18 observations of students' culminating exhibitions to similar four C's analyses. These efforts involved repeatedly reviewing fieldnotes and audio and video records, parsing salient interactions, drafting memos, and mapping meta-matrices.

To complement these qualitatively, we utilized and adapted two research-based observation instruments, the Classroom Assessment Scoring System-Secondary (CLASS-S) (Pianta et al., 2006) and the Center for Research on Education, Diversity, and Excellence's Standards Performance Continuum (CREDE/SPC) (Hilberg et al., 2003). Premised on the idea that student–teacher interactions are the primary mechanism of students' learning, these instruments (previously elaborated in Chapter 3) provided common metrics to assess teaching quality. Appendix E identifies the instructional constructs measured by these instruments.

To undertake the CLASS-S and CREDE/SPC analyses, the SOLES team received 4 days of training from instrument developers. The CLASS training culminated with an online test and all coders obtained certificates of reliability. For CREDE/SPC reliability, we identified a lead coder, then conducted several calibration rounds to ensure that other coders achieved agreement of 85% or higher. For each MHS focal teacher, we scored three randomly selected lessons (one per each 2-day observation cycle) for an average of 3 hours of instruction per teacher. Because the CREDE/SPC instrument relied on a 4-point scale (0 to 3), we adapted it to align with CLASS-S's 7-point scale. Each construct was scored at timed intervals of 20 minutes. Because block scheduling yielded varied lesson lengths, we scored between two to five instructional segments per observation with an overall total average of nine segments per focal teacher across the three lessons. For each construct, we tabulated mean rater scores per focal teacher for each instructional segment, for each class observation, and for cross-lesson summaries.

We then tallied mean scores per construct across all focal teachers. From this body of scores, we tracked trends in the data.

Given the SOLES study's multisite design, these instruments facilitated analysis across schools, classrooms, and teachers. Additionally, the use of these instruments in other studies enabled comparisons between MHS and national samples, allowing me to speculate about the school's relative instructional efficacy. Drawing on both the qualitative and instrument-based analyses in conjunction with teacher focus group responses and survey results, we then created schoolwide tables and memos elucidating themes that surfaced across lessons and classes.

MEMBER CHECK

Twenty-eight months after the start of our research at MHS and 8 months following our last interview, the SOLES team returned to campus to present our findings to staff. Using PowerPoint, we highlighted three "headline" themes, stressing how MHS's mission-driven ethos empowered youth, how the full-service community school model promoted boundary crossing that enhanced community wealth (Achinstein et al., 2014), and how an environment of authentic cariño fostered a culture of engaged learning. We concluded with reflection questions to uncover areas for growth. The audience shared how our findings resonated with their experiences, and we engaged in open-ended dialogue. Attendees completed written reflections that we compiled and reviewed.

Overall, the faculty indicated that we had gotten MHS's story right. Their feedback recommended attention on four topics for future research, specifically the human costs and sustainability of MHS's programs given educators' intensive work, the experiences of Black and Asian students within a Latinx-dominated culture, the experiences of emergent bilinguals and special education students, and the staff's decreasing ethnic/racial diversity. This member check provided a gratifying sense of closure to the SOLES study. In subsequent years, I have shared MHS-focused publications with administrators and on the listserv to maintain transparency, enact reciprocity, and underscore how MHS's investment in the research process helped generate scholarship that was potentially helping other educators to enact equitable and transformative schooling for Latinx youth. Given MHS's expressed desire to become a national model, our publications constituted an important avenue to advance the school's agenda.

WRITING

In *The Vulnerable Observer*, Behar (1996) describes writing up findings as a researcher's "hardest work." She speaks to the effort it takes "to bring the ethnographic moment back, to resurrect it, to communicate the distance, which too quickly starts to feel like an abyss, between what we saw and heard and our inability, finally, to do justice to it in our representations" (pp. 8–9). Behar's account aptly captures the challenges I faced writing years after field work. Countless times, I found myself revisiting data, sifting through transcripts and fieldnotes, watching videos, and emailing informants to resuscitate the vibrancy and truth of what I witnessed. Often, I felt swamped by details and minutiae, unable to chart a clear path. When overwhelmed, I retreated into the scholarship of others in search of guidance. As I stewed in data and my pile of marked-up journal articles mounted, I endured bouts of anxiety and writers' block. At some point, I discovered that my preoccupation with obtaining some perfect (but maddeningly elusive) rendition of MHS was actually distancing me from the ethnographic moment and paralyzing me. To stay grounded, I developed a regular practice of revisiting photos of students, staff, and campus. These images became a stimulated recall device fueling my duty memory and reconnecting my bodymindspirit to the work at hand. Anchored in this awareness, I was able to resume and recommit to writing.

As I completed chapters, I shared drafts with a small circle of readers. Rod Ogawa and Betty Achinstein drew on their familiarity with MHS through the SOLES project to offer insight. Anand Behari, an MHS focal teacher turned educational researcher, helped me ensure accuracy and consider additional interpretations. Cate Sundling, a longtime English teacher pal, acted not only as an editor, but as a "generic" teacher reader. Armida Valencia, my Spanish-speaking *cuñada* (sister-in-law), who is also a respected ELD coach, reviewed my Spanish and shared her reactions. These readers and a few others helped me sharpen my analysis and prose and maintain momentum. Even though I struggled with isolation, uncertainty, and discouragement, the work has proven fulfilling. Ultimately, I feel I have answered Anzaldúa's entreaty to "do work that matters."

LIMITATIONS

No research proceeds without complications or missed opportunities. This project was no exception. The cultural mismatch between SOLES's lead researchers and Latinx youth stands out as a significant limitation. Although we benefited enormously from the participation of seven Latinx assistant researchers, it is likely that lead researchers' cultural frames introduced biases undermining the robustness and cultural sensitivity of findings. I was acutely aware of this limitation in regard to our shallow Spanish–English bilingual capacity. Within the core UCSC team, we relied on two fluent bilinguals, a graduate student and an undergraduate, who conducted and translated interviews with Spanish speakers. While Paulina and Adriana did an excellent job, I wonder what we might have learned had we always offered the option to conduct interviews in respondents' preferred language. I suspect, for example, that the focus group with Ms. Clark's reading students would have been more animated and informative had it transpired in Spanish.

Personally, I found myself in numerous settings in which Spanish was spoken without translation. My then rudimentary Spanish allowed me to puzzle out these exchanges in broad strokes, but nuances were lost. My shame over my poor Spanish propelled me to live in Perú from 2015 to 2017 and intensively study Spanish as I began writing this book. While this interlude afforded me the opportunity to revisit data with fresh perspectives, I "graduated" from my language studies still very much an emergent bilingual. My improved Spanish aided my analysis and writing, but I recognize more fully now the importance of conducting research projects such as this one with a deeper bench of bilingual–bicultural investigators. To minimize the negative effects of this limitation, our team listened closely to Latinx research assistants, undertook extensive member checks, enlisted the feedback of accomplished Latina scholars (Patricia Gándara, Ana Maria Villegas, and Peggy Estrada), and strove to develop genuine relationships with MHS community members that reflected personalismo.

A second limitation related to my role within the SOLES team. Because I started after the grant proposal process, I had little control over the study's design. While the project was well conceived and I enjoyed ample opportunities to contribute to instrument development and analytic procedures, my capacity to pursue my own emergent interests was limited. Thankfully, the project introduced me to MHS and I was able to continue my research from 2013 to 2015. This second phase, however, lacked the benefit of extramural funding and was squeezed into moments when I could carve out free time. The resulting data often came to me in serendipitous ways, for example, during hallway conversations with teachers when I volunteered as a writing coach or in classroom exchanges with students when I videotaped a lesson for Mr. Behari, who was pursuing National Board certification. After such encounters, I scribbled notes in my fieldwork journal or recorded voice memos on my cell phone, but time constraints often prevented me from systematically documenting these occasions. As a result, my account of MHS is shaped by accumulated layers of experience that are not all tidy "official" bits of data.

Another limitation involved confidentiality. Since the original project's human subjects agreement promised anonymity to MHS and all participants, our team struggled repeatedly with how to contextualize the site and characterize certain practices without risking confidentiality breaches. In an era when Google searches of mission statements, school mottos, and neighborhood entities can easily reveal a site's identity, we were forced to modify the language used at the site and omit details in ways that prevented optimal verisimilitude. Additionally, several school-level participants indicated wanting public recognition for MHS as a national model; however, the anonymity agreements established at the outset prevented such acknowledgment. These same agreements thwarted co-written articles or presentations with MHS educators because such activities would also have compromised confidentiality. Similarly, acknowledgments of research participants had to be cast in generic terms. In short, confidentiality guarantees circumscribed our work in unanticipated ways.

Given the chance to reconceive this study, I would pursue additional lines of inquiry. Rather than focus principally on students' engagement in "academically challenging work," I would expand the frame to incorporate students' experiences of intellectual joy and community engagement and drastically increase classroom observations. With regard to authentic cariño, I would explore students' perceptions of support and engagement more directly, investigating their experiences of authentic cariño within different settings and more actively seeking disconfirming cases. I would also attend to the issues raised during the MHS member check (i.e., sustainability, emergent bilinguals, non-Latinx youth, special education students, and staff diversity). Methodologically, I would engage educators and youth in a co-research methodology (de los Ríos et al., 2015; Oakes & Rogers, 2006) to elevate their concerns and center their voices.

RETROSPECTIVE REFLECTIONS

This appendix documents the emergence of this book from the "borderland between passion and intellect, analysis and subjectivity" (Behar, 1996, p. 174) and demonstrates how my theorizing unfolded in tandem with substantial bodymindspirit growth. Being a researcher at MHS has deepened my capacity to love and absorb sadness and also fortified my commitment to actively participate in the beautiful struggle. In the end, I view my readers as traveling companions deserving the kind of authentic cariño I witnessed at MHS. For me, this means offering a transparent report of my research and inviting readers to join me in thinking deeply about authentic cariño in ways that may generate action in the world—action that transforms institutional structures to ensure that culturally and linguistically diverse youth who have suffered for too long in subtractive schools truly thrive. Knowing that this journey is ongoing and demands more conversation, I welcome comments and constructive feedback.

Appendix B: Roster of MHS Certificated Staff With Biographic Detail

STAFF PSEUDONYM

Last Name	First Name	Self-identified Race/ Ethnicity/Nationality	Spanish/ English Bilingual	Masters Degree	Subject Area(s)	Total Yrs Teaching as of 2011/12	Yrs @ MHS as of 2011/12	Last year at MHS	Total Yrs @ MHS
Avila	Leonardo	Latino/El Salvador	Y	N	Spanish	8	8	2015–2016	12
Barrett	Sylvia	White	Y	Y	Humanities	7	7	2013–2014	9
Behari	Anand	White & East Indian	Y	Y	Humanities	6	4	2014–2015	7
Chin	Julia	Asian	N	Y	Math	0	0	2016–2017	4
Clark	Audrey	Black & Latina/Mexican	Y	Y	Humanities & Spanish	6	6	2014–2015	9
Dupont	Lillian	White	N	Y	Special Ed	3	2	2014–2015	5
Glass	Jean	White	N	Y	Math	3	3	2011–2012	3
Grace	Jennifer	White	N	Y + PhD	Multiple subjects	15	1	2011–2012	1
Howard	Vera	White	N	Y	Humanities	1	1	2019–2020	9
Keo	Edward	Asian/Cambodian	N	Y	Math	7	7	2011–2012	7
Romano	Ashley	White	N	Y	Science	7	6	2018–2019	13
Schmidt	Madeline	White		Y	Humanities	2	2	2014–2015	5
Simmons	Paul	White	N	N	Math	20	11	2019–2020	19

(continued)

Tanaka	Kaito	Asian/Japanese	N	Y	Humanities & PE	4	2	N/A	10
Tran	Marcus	Asian	N	Y	Math	1	1	2017–2018	7
Trung	Wei	Asian/Vietnamese	N	N	Science & PE	13	13	N/A	21
Wang	Kay	Asian	Y	Y	Science	2	2	2018–2019	9
Ward	Tim	White & Native American	N	Y	Special ed	1	1	2014–2015	4
Whitmore	Eliza	White	Y	N	Science	2	2	2015–2016	6
West	Braxton	White/Czech	N	Y	Science	16	13	2014–2015	16

Note: Shading indicates focal teachers. Jennifer Grace held a temporary 1-year position. Braxton West became principal in 2009 but continued to teach a course until 2011–2012. Jean Glass departed mid-2011–2012; Edward Keo, an MHS veteran, who was on a leave of absence, replaced her.

Appendix C: Roster of Prominent MHS Staff and Community Partners

First Name	Last Name	Role/Position	Organization	Spanish/English Bilingual?	Details
Andrea	Baranoski	Health clinic coordinator	Indigenous Health Advocates	N	Raised in OH. Graduated from Marquette University in Wisconsin. Came to IHA as a part of the Jesuit Volunteer Corps and ended up staying on. Spearheaded Peer Health Advocates.
Wanda	Buchanan	Literacy specialist	School district	Y	ELD coach responsible for teaching two sections of Read 180.
Carmen	Garcia	Front office secretary	MHS	Y	Credited by teachers for being the "lifeblood" of MHS and keeping staff unified as a "big family to support kids." Translator for IEP meetings. Mother of several MHS graduates.
César	Castro	EDP coach	Community Action	Y	Chicano rap artist. Son of United Farm Worker activists/leaders. Raised in Delano, CA. Former MHS college counselor. Leader of BEST (Brothers Excelling and Striving Together), the young men's empowerment circle.
Desirée	Campos	EDP coach	Community Action	Y	Self-proclaimed sports liberation educator and city culture keeper. Former professional soccer player. Parents exiled from Chile.
Diego	Gonzales	EDP director	Community Action	Y	Argentine youth developer. Succeeded Luz. Assisted with Dream Act advocacy, boxing, soccer club, and computer literacy for parents.
Dolores	Reyes	Community organizer	City Community Organization	Y	Faith-based community organizer and MHS founder. Born and raised in Guadalajara, Mexico.

(continued)

Appendix C: Roster of Prominent MHS Staff and Community Partners (continued)

Jasmine	Mahelona	Administrative assistant	MHS	N	Affectionately called "Mama Jasmine" by students. Advisor to FISTT (Fearless, Intelligent Sisters Thriving Together). Born and raised in Hawaii. Deeply anchored in her faith to God (Akua).
Luz	Lopez	Director of EDP & community programs	Community Action	Y	Lesbian, Colombian youth advocate. Lived undocumented for decades and obtained U.S. citizenship in 2019. Attended seminary.
Magdalena	Gutiérrez	Parent liaison	Community Action/MHS	Y	Mother of two MHS grads. Started as an MHS volunteer in 2008 and was hired in 2010 to promote family engagement. "The students are all our kids. I see them as my kids, because I love them all."
Nayeli	Ruiz	College counselor	College & Beyond Support Consortium	Y	Second-generation Mexican American. First college graduate in her family. Served as a college counselor while attending University of CA and became director of MHS's College Center in 2005.
Ricardo	Delgado	College counselor and MHS graduate	College & Beyond Support Consortium	Y	Mexican American 2007 MHS graduate served as a college counselor while attending University of CA. Currently works as academic counselor at MHS.

Course Assessment Summary Sheets Distributed to Students

9th-Grade English Course Assessment Summary Sheet

Molina High School

9th-Grade English Standards and Certifications for Fall (F) and Spring (S) Semesters

Standard/Unit Name	Certification Assignment	Score
1. Literary Response and Analysis I can analyze textual themes and character motivations by making inferences from and connections to a work of fiction. *Habit of Mind: Logical reasoning and Analysis*	Must pass: • Autobiographical poem inspired by *True Diary* (F) Must earn a 3 or better: • *To Kill A Mockingbird (S)*	
2. Effective Communication I can support my ideas verbally using sentence starters to present evidence selected from the text. *Habit of Mind: Evidence/logical reasoning and analysis*	Must earn at least a 3 on 1 fishbowl discussion: • L.A. Riots fishbowl (F) • N-Word fishbowl (S)	
3. Assertion Paragraph I can support my thesis with at least three pieces of evidence that are explained in a well-developed assertion paragraph. *Habit of Mind: Evidence*	Must earn at least a 3 on 1 assertion paragraph: • L.A. Riots paragraph (F) • N-Word paragraph (S)	
4. Research-based Project I can gather and use anecdotal and statistical data to support my claim about an issue of concern in Oakland. *Habit of Mind: Inquiry and investigation*	Must earn a 3 or better: • Our City Project (F)	

(continued)

Molina High School
9th-Grade English Standards and Certifications for Fall (F) and Spring (S) Semesters

Standard/Unit Name	Certification Assignment	Score
5. Persuasive Writing I can use rhetorical devices like concession to persuade my audience to see the point of view of my stated thesis. *Habit of Mind: Perspective*	Must earn a 3 or better: • *Chew On This* persuasive essay (S)	
6. Vocabulary Strategies I can use vocabulary strategies to figure out the meaning of a word I don't know, and I can explain my process for applying these strategies. *Habit of Mind: Reflection and metacognition*	Must pass the following: • Metacognitive writing portion of vocabulary test (S)	
7. Writing Growth I can demonstrate and reflect on my growth as a writer by improving my Process Writing Assessment (PWA) score from the pre-assessment to the post-assessment. *Habit of Mind: Reflection and metacognition*	Must *complete* all: • PWA (F) • PWA (S) • Portfolio with reflective letter on writing growth	

12th-Grade Government/Economics Course Assessment Summary Sheet

Molina High School
12th-Grade Government/Economics Standards and Certification

Standard/Unit Name	Certification Assignment *(Must pass both assignments to be certified for a standard)*	Score
1. Persuasive Argumentation: Logic and Evidence. I can evaluate the success of various policies aimed at addressing violence/crime in my community. (Writing 1.3)	**Public Policy Proposal on Crime** An essay that analyzes a variety of anticrime policies and arrives at a plan for tackling crime in my city. **Panel Presentation** Students will be required to attend an after-school panel on crime and present prepared questions or participate on the panel.	

Habits of Mind: Logical reasoning and analysis, evidence

Molina High School
12th-Grade Government/Economics Standards and Certification

Standard/Unit Name	Certification Assignment (*Must pass both assignments to be certified for a standard*)	Score
2. Persuasive Argumentation: Perspectives, Evidence. I can demonstrate knowledge of the role of Congress and the president and evaluate their roles in the sphere of current events (Reading 2.6)	**Political Pundit Roundtable** A televised CNN-style roundtable in which students debate whether or not Barack Obama has been an effective president. The television program will need to be shown to a variety of people in the students' lives.	

Habits of Mind: Logical reasoning and analysis, evidence

Standard/Unit Name	Certification Assignment	Score
3. Persuasive Argumentation: Evidence. I can use the Bill of Rights and evidence from a court case to assess whether the police violate an individual's constitutional rights. (Writing 1.3)	**Miranda Essay** Use evidence from the case of Ernest Miranda to assess whether his rights were violated. **Miranda Mock Trial** Use evidence from the case of Ernest Miranda to assess whether his rights were violated. Present arguments in front of the Supreme Court	

Habits of Mind: Evidence, Logical Reasoning and Analysis

Standard/Unit Name	Certification Assignment	Score
4. Cause and Effect: Supply and Demand. I can explain how supply and demand work to influence the decisions made in an economy. (Econ 12.2)	**Supply and Demand Exam** Students must pass a thorough multiple-choice and short-answer test on various economic concepts involving supply and demand.	

Habits of Mind: logical reasoning and analysis

Standard/Unit Name	Certification Assignment	Score
5. Persuasive Argumentation: Poverty. I can use logical/graphical reasoning, evidence and analysis to support a claim about to what extent government should play a role in addressing poverty in the United States. (Writing 1.4, Econ 12.3)	**Poverty Essay** Use evidence and logic to create a plan that will help alleviate poverty in America. **Presidential Panel on Poverty** With a team, present and defend your poverty plan in a discussion with President Obama in hopes that he accepts your plan.	

Habits of Mind: Logical reasoning/analysis, evidence, perspectives, reflection/metacognition

(*continued*)

Molina High School
12th-Grade Government/Economics Standards and Certification

Standard/Unit Name	Certification Assignment *(Must pass both assignments to be certified for a standard)*	Score
6. Personal Finance. I can develop a responsible financial plan for my future that ensures I am protected from future financial downturns. (Writing 1.3)	**Personal Finance Exam** Students must be able to be financial advisors by giving advice to teachers and give sound, professional advice.	
	First-Year of College Financial Plan Students present a budget poster to their advisor that explains their financial plan for their 1st year of college.	

Habits of Mind: Logical reasoning, metacognition/reflection

Classroom Observation Analysis Instruments and Their Constructs

5 C's	Instruction Dimension (Abbrev/Source)	Description
Connection (Familial cariño in the classroom)	Absence of a negative climate (NC/CLASS)	NC reflects the overall level of negativity among teachers and students in the class; the frequency, quality, and intensity of teacher and student negativity are important to observe.
	Positive climate (PC/CLASS)	PC reflects the emotional connection and relationships among teachers and students and the warmth, respect, and enjoyment communicated by verbal and nonverbal interactions.
	Teacher sensitivity (TS/CLASS)	TS reflects the teacher's responsiveness to the academic and social/emotional needs and developmental levels of individual students and the entire class and the way these factors impact students' classroom experiences.
	Behavior management (BM/CLASS)	BM encompasses the teacher's use of effective methods to encourage desirable behavior and prevent and redirect misbehavior.
Challenge (High expectations and rigor)	Content understanding (CU/CLASS)	CU refers to both the depth of lesson content and the approaches used to help students comprehend the framework, key ideas, and procedures in an academic discipline. At a high level, this refers to interactions among the teacher and students that lead to an integrated understanding of facts, skills, concepts, and principles.

(continued)

	Analysis and problem solving (APS/CLASS)	APS assesses the degree to which the teacher facilitates students' use of higher level thinking skills such as analysis, problem solving, reasoning, and creation through the application of knowledge and skills. Opportunities for demonstrating metacognition (i.e., thinking about thinking) are also included.
	Productivity (P/CLASS)	P considers how well the teacher manages time and routines so that instructional time is maximized. This dimension captures the degree to which instructional time is effectively managed and down time is minimized for students; it is not a code about student engagement or about the quality of instruction or activities.
Culture (Lived contexts)	Regard for adolescent perspective (RAP/CLASS)	RAP focuses on the extent to which the teacher is able to meet and capitalize on the social and developmental needs and goals of adolescents by providing opportunities for student autonomy and leadership. Also considered are the extent to which student ideas and opinions are valued and content is made useful and relevant to adolescents.
	Contextualization (CNTX/SPC)	CNTX focuses on how the teacher integrates new activity/information with what students already know from home, school, or community.
Communication and Collaboration (Language-rich activity)	Quality of feedback (QF/CLASS)	QF assesses the degree to which feedback expands and extends learning and understanding and encourages student participation. In secondary classrooms, significant feedback may also be provided by peers. Regardless of the source, the focus here should be on the nature of the feedback provided and the extent to which it "pushes" learning.

Language and literacy development[a] (LLD/SPC)	LLD focuses on both (a) teachers' assistance with student language expression and development through questioning, listening, rephrasing, or modeling throughout much of instruction and (b) instructional activities generating language expression and development of content vocabulary.
Instructional learning formats (ILF/CLASS)	ILF focuses on the ways in which the teacher maximizes student engagement in learning through clear presentation of material, active facilitation, and the provision of interesting and engaging lessons and materials.
Student engagement (SE/CLASS)	SE is intended to capture the degree to which all students in the class are focused and participating in the learning activity presented or facilitated by the teacher. The difference between passive engagement and active engagement is of note in this rating.

a. LLD overlaps considerably with a more recently added CLASS dimension of instructional dialogue (Hafen et al., 2015) that "captures the purposeful use of dialogue—structured, cumulative questioning and discussion that guide and prompt students—to facilitate students' understanding of content and language development." (p. 656).

Note: This table displays CLASS (Pianta et al., 2006) and selected SPC instruction dimensions (Hilberg et al., 2003) clustered by their relationship to the 5 C's—connection, challenge, culture, communication, and collaboration.

Teacher Focus Group Protocol (Department)

1. Please introduce yourselves.
2. What's it like to be a teacher at MHS?
3. What, if anything, is done on a schoolwide basis to support Latinx student success? What, if at all, is unique about how your school organizes itself to support Latinx student success?
4. Does MHS have a common vision of ideal instructional interactions that engage Latinx youth in academically challenging work? If so, what is it? How does the school and district promote this kind of instruction? To what extent does your department embrace that ideal and how, if at all, does it show up across the department's practice?
5. How does MHS support or inhibit *you* to teach in ways that engage Latinx students in academically challenging work?
6. Describe how your department typically functions. How do you interact with one another?
7. Does your department have a common vision of ideal instructional interactions that engage Latinx youth in academically challenging work? If so, what is it? How, if at all, does your department support or inhibit you to teach in ways that engage Latinx students in academically challenging work?
8. How, if at all, does MHS help students achieve academic success within the dominant culture while also affirming their home cultures and communities? Are there any tensions between these two goals?
9. Please describe if there is any academic grouping or tracking at MHS? Provide examples. What is the impact of this on Latinx student opportunities to engage in academically challenging work? How, if at all, is tracking discussed among staff?
10. This school has some unique structures (defenses, post-session, EDP, etc.). What are the benefits and challenges of having these structures? To what degree are they working to support Latinx student academic success?

Notes

Chapter 1

1. I have assigned pseudonyms to all people, places, groups, organizations, and school publications. The pseudonym "Molina High" honors Mario José Molina-Pasquel Henríquez, a Nobel Prize–winning Mexican American chemist who discovered how chlorofluorocarbon gas damages the Earth's ozone.

2. While some may recognize the phrase "beautiful struggle" from Talib Kiweli's (2004) eponymous rap album, Martin Luther King spoke these words in a 1967 speech condemning the Vietnam War. He urged listeners to dedicate themselves "to the long and bitter, but beautiful, struggle for a new world."

3. I first encountered the term *authentic cariño* in an article by Lilia Bartolomé (2008). She linked authentic cariño to Valenzuela's (1999) exploration of authentic care and argued that "caring for and loving one's subordinated students is insufficient unless the love and care are informed by authentic respect and a desire to equalize unequal learning conditions in school" (p. 2). I humbly embrace this terminology and in doing so seek to honor Bartolome's and Valenzuela's scholarship.

4. Appendix B lists MHS certificated staff, indicating ethnicity/race, bilingualism, educational attainment, credential, and years of service. Appendix C lists EDP coaches, noncertificated staff, and community partners.

5. See Yosso (2006) and Yosso and Solórzano (2006) for more on Latinx students' attrition along the educational pipeline. See Shange (2019) for a critique of the pipeline metaphor (pp. 53–56).

6. I use the term "Latinx" to decenter the patriarchal heritage of "a," "o," and "@" endings (Latina, Latino, Latin@). The Spanish custom of referring to mixed gendered groups with the term "Latino" erases the existence of women, as well as individuals identifying as lesbian, gay, bisexual, transgender, and queer. Latinx is more inclusive and signals the complexity of identities that go beyond gender and racial norms. Given the heterogeneity of ethnic and national subgroups hailing from Latin America, Latinx is a classification of convenience denoting some measure of shared experience with colonization, Catholicism, immigration, and discrimination. While I use Latinx as a shorthand, I recognize the unique social, political, and cultural contexts shaping the lives of individuals and communities. Additionally, I would be remiss if I did not mention that many MHS educators initially balked at interview questions exclusively focused on Latinx youth. Ms. Whitmore shared, "I feel really awkward. I understand that the focus is Latino students, but . . . all these strategies we're using are for *all* the students." Finally, I acknowledge that the term Latinx has its own drawbacks and is continually evolving (Salinas, 2020; Salinas & Lozano, 2019).

7. For readers' unfamiliar with the U.S. education system, GPA refers to grade point average, a standard metric reflecting students' overall academic achievement across courses. GPA is based on a letter grade system: A (4 points), B (3 points), C (2 points), D (1 point), or F (0 points).

8. I capitalize White, Black, and Brown to acknowledge their common usage as labels for U.S. ethnoracial groups. I view homogenizing labels as problematic, but I wish to underscore how these groups share particular "group" histories in relation to oppressive societal structures. For me, capitalization is a way to avoid color-blindness and the simplistic erasure of ethnoracial difference by asserting that we are all really "the same."

9. The use of "Hispanic" reflects NCES and ACT classifications.

10. Readers familiar with care theory may be surprised that I refrain from using "aesthetic care." Scholars (including myself in past publications) often note Valenzuela's (1999) distinction between authentic and aesthetic care. Valenzuela borrowed these terms from Noddings (1984), who characterized "aesthetical care" as a "caring about things and ideas" that manifests in "passionate involvement with form and nonpersonal content" (p. 21). Noddings argued that because aesthetical caring "distracts us from caring about persons" (p. 21), it leads us away from ethical caring. Drawing from Noddings, Valenzuela contrasted her ideal of authentic care with aesthetic care, characterizing the latter as an "abstract . . . commitment to ideas and practices that purportedly lead to achievement" but that ultimately "shape and sustain a subtractive logic" (pp. 61–62). Articulated in these ways, aesthetic caring is inhuman, impersonal, and harmful.

The problem is that in common vernacular "aesthetic" is most often associated with an appreciation for beauty and an attention to the appealing features of artistic works. The disconnect between this common usage and Noddings' and Valenzuela's use of "aesthetic" generates confusion, especially since Noddings in later work (1992/2005) urged educators to foster students' aesthetic appreciation for the design elements of houses, living environments, and social ceremonies. Similarly, Valenzuela's (1999) work includes mixed messages pertaining to aesthetic care. She rails against aesthetic care, decrying it as "devastating," "superficial," and "culturally chauvinistic" (p. 263). Yet elsewhere she notes how "aesthetic and authentic caring are not mutually exclusive" (p. 63) and mentions one exemplary Seguín teacher who exhibited a "near perfect mix of aesthetic and authentic caring" (p. 101), implying that some measure of aesthetic caring is desirable and necessary. Aside from the alliterative appeal of pairing "aesthetic" with "authentic," this terminology has confused rather than clarified our understanding of educative care. My model redresses this confusion by offering new constructs to refine our understanding of authentic care.

11. Noddings (1988) herself acknowledged the limits of the mother–child caring model, noting that not "all relations must approach that of the prototypical mother–child relation in either intensity or intimacy. On the contrary, an appropriate and particular form of caring must be found in every relation, and the behaviors and feelings that mark the mother–child relation are rarely appropriate for other relations" (p. 219). In my view, some critics have ignored the evolution of Noddings' (1988, 1990, 1992/2005, and 1999) thinking and have simply recycled critiques of her initial book *Caring: A Relational Approach to Ethics and Moral Education* (1984).

12. These critical scholars theorize within the traditions of critical theory (Apple, 1982/2012) and critical race theory (Bell, 1995), both of which interrogate and condemn oppressive structures and racism in U.S. society.

13. Vexed by the failure of economically and educationally privileged Anglo feminists to account for the intersectionality of gender, race, and class, many women of color identify as womanists (Walker, 1993) and mujeristas (Isasi-Diaz et al., 1992) to highlight their particular struggles against oppression.

14. Lara (2002) introduced this term to convey a holistic integration of body, mind, and spirit. See also Facio and Lara (2014).

15. Although educational researchers rarely address spirituality, Anzaldúa's emphasis on the spiritual self deserves recognition. Anzaldúa criticized the expunction of spirit from mainstream academic discourse. "We're supposed to ignore, forget, kill those fleeting images of the soul's presence and of the spirit's presence. . . . We're supposed to forget that every cell in our bodies, every bone and bird and worm has spirit in it" (Anzaldúa, 1987/2012, p. 58). Chagrined that many scholars eagerly embraced the "safe" elements of her borderland theory but avoided the "unsafe" elements such as "the connection between body, mind, and spirit—anything that has to do with the sacred, anything that has to do with the spirit," Anzaldúa insisted that matters of the spirit be taken seriously (p. 247). Readers who have difficulty with my attention to the spiritual may find hooks' (2001) clarification helpful. hooks views "spiritual" as that "dimension of our core reality where mind, body, and spirit are one." She contends that "an individual does not need to be a believer in a religion to embrace the idea that there is an animating principle in the self—a life force (some of us call it soul) that when nurtured enhances our capacity to be more fully self-actualized and able to engage in communion with the world around us" (p. 13).

16. Appendix A provides a chapter-length, reflexive account of the study's design, data, procedures, and limitations.

17. Interested readers may wish to consult these SOLES publications: Achinstein et al. (2013); Achinstein et al. (2014); Achinstein et al. (2015); Athanases (2018); Athanases & de Oliveira (2014); Athanases & Curry (2018); Athanases et al. (2016); Curry (2013); Curry (2016); and Curry & Athanases (2020).

18. These requirements include receiving a C or higher grade in 15 courses (4 years of English, 3 years of math, and 2 years of history, laboratory science, and foreign language, and 1 year of a performing/fine art and other college preparatory elective).

19. MHS expanded to offer a middle school in 2012–2013, adding new cohorts of 6th graders over 3 years until reaching a full 6–12 grade configuration.

20. These students have been previously classified as English language learners (ELLs), limited English proficient (LEPs), and English learners (ELs). These terms imply English monolingualism as the standard, cast those acquiring a second language as lacking, and ignore the cognitive and social advantages of bilingualism. For these reasons, I prefer the term Emergent bilinguals (EBs) (García, 2009).

Chapter 2

1. Achinstein et al. (2014) provide a fuller account of MHS's history. The substantial involvement of parents in MHS's creation echoes other counterstories of parents of color who have advocated for equitable schools (Chapman, 2006; Warren & Mapp, 2011; Yosso, 2006). Critical race theory scholars document these ex-

amples to push back against unfounded stereotypes of parents of color being unconcerned with education and too "disadvantaged" to participate fully.

2. Love (2019) critiques the term "ally." Observing how Whites within intersectional social justice groups have adopted the mantel of allyship in performative and self-glorifying ways, she instead lauds "coconspirators" who interrogate Whiteness and leverage privilege "to stand in solidarity and confront anti-Blackness" (p. 117). Along a continuum of ally to coconspirator, MHS educators leaned toward the coconspirator end even though they used the language of "allies."

3. Translanguaging involves using two languages flexibly in a bilingual arrangement to promote bilingualism and biliteracy (Bartlett & García, 2011).

4. Slater (2017) chronicles this crime with journalistic complexity in *The 57 Bus*.

5. Prior to Yosemite, upper grade advisees, teachers, families, and youth coaches wrote affirming letters called *palancas* (a Spanish word meaning "lever") to lift up sophomores. Each student received at least two palancas; some received up to six. These letters were a surprise, secretly delivered while students were at an activity.

Chapter 3

1. I use the etic term "pensadoras" rather than the English word "thinkers" to draw attention to how educators who embody intellectual cariño move away from the limiting gaze of Eurocentric, dominant lenses to see students not generically as thinkers, but as social beings shaped by cultural, political, and economic contexts.

2. The phrase "using one's mind well" originated with Sizer (1984, 1992), the founder of the Coalition of Essential Schools (CES). MHS modeled itself in part on CES principles and periodically received technical support from a CES affiliate.

3. School reform has been an ongoing project in U.S. schools (Tyack & Cuban, 1995). While cases of successful restructuring exist (Antrop-Gonzáles & De Jesús, 2006; Bartlett & García, 2011; Casanova, 2010; Conchas & Rodriguez, 2008; Meier, 1995; Mehan, 2012), high school reforms overall "have been widely attempted, highly visible—and largely disappointing" (Siskin, 2011, p. 11).

4. The Power of Food project examined the essential questions "Who is negatively affected by fast food and how?" and "What actions can we take to lessen fast food's impact?" During this unit, students read *Chew on This* (Schlosser & Wilson, 2006); created public service announcements; studied the impact of fast food on the environment and human biology; examined the distribution of fast-food restaurants, grocery stores, and green space in local contexts; and calculated correlations between fast-food restaurant location/density with population demographics. The Political Pundit unit involved producing a newscast with student commentators analyzing the policies of presidential candidates; the resulting video was aired schoolwide during advisory and used to spur discussion.

5. The SOLES team concentrated on the 4 C's of Challenge, Culture/language, Collaboration/community, and Code-breaking with academic language scaffolding (Athanases et al., 2016). My analyses related to authentic cariño led me to add Connection as a fifth C and subsume code-breaking into Culture.

6. Anzaldúa's haunting memory of being punished for speaking Spanish at school underscores the importance of Camila's freedom to speak Spanish. Anzaldua (1987/2012) recounts, "I remember being caught speaking Spanish at recess—that was good for three licks on the knuckles with a sharp ruler. I remember being sent

to the corner of the classroom for 'talking back' to the Anglo teacher when all I was trying to do was tell her how to pronounce my name. 'If you want to be American, speak 'American.' If you don't like it, go back to Mexico where you belong'" (p. 75).

7. "Race to the Top" was a 2009 U.S. federal initiative intended to "turn around our lowest-achieving schools" (https://www2.ed.gov/programs/racetothetop/factsheet .html). My conceptualization of Pillar 4 benefited from Marshall's (1988, 1990) examinations of how classroom metaphors of work, play, and learning powerfully shape instruction and perceptions of schooling. Langer's (2000) experiment in which subjects evaluated cartoons also shed light on work versus play metaphors. For half the subjects, Langer labeled the activity as work; for the other half, play. "Even though the task . . . could seem inherently fun to some people, when we called it work, subjects did not enjoy it, and their minds tended to wander while they were doing it" (p. 222).

8. Popularized by Dweck (2008), a growth mindset involves the belief that intelligence is not fixed but can be developed. This orientation, which encourages learners to "grow their brains" through hard work, good strategies, and input from others, is associated with improved performance.

9. Horn (2005) describes group-worthy tasks as having four distinct properties: "They illustrate important mathematical [or other disciplinary] concepts; include multiple tasks that draw effectively on the collective resources of a [student] group; allow for multiple representations; have several possible solution paths" (p. 219).

10. Ms. Howard and Mr. Tran's positive views reflected their status as 1st-year teachers eager to expand their professional acumen. The survey revealed variation in teachers' perceptions of professional development. Some veterans expressed disappointment in inadequate opportunities and funds to enhance skills/pedagogy /knowledge.

11. The reference to Discourses (Gee, 2015) captures how participation within different settings demands particular sociocultural ways of being and communicating. Discourses with a capital "D" encompass language as well as the ways in which humans embody and present themselves to signify group membership.

12. Our categorization differed from CLASS-S's scheme, which grouped constructs into four domains: emotional support, classroom organization, classroom support, and student outcome. We relied on the 2009 CLASS-S. The instrument has subsequently added a dimension of instructional dialogue that overlaps considerably with SPC/CREDE's language and literacy/development.

13. Read 180, published by Scholastic, features small-group direct instruction, computer-based reading skills practice, and independent reading. A meta-analytic review of the program (U.S. DOE, 2016) found positive effects on comprehension and general literacy.

14. I requested these data but never obtained them, probably because intensive workloads made answering my request a low priority. The absence of data leaves Read 180's impact on achievement unverified. Given MHS's focus on literacy across the curriculum, other facets of instruction may account for reported gains.

15. On CLASS-S's 7-point scale, Ms. Clark's instructional interactions averaged 5.8 for the connection cluster, 3.6 for the challenge cluster, 3.5 for the culture/ contextualization cluster, and 3.8 for the communication/collaboration cluster.

16. In their qualitative study of four EBs, Wu and Coady (2010) reached similar findings and concluded that Read 180 was "unable to respond to the unique cultural

needs and background knowledge of each ELL to facilitate reading development" (p. 153).

Chapter 4

1. Rubin (2007) and Solorzano and Delgado Bernal (2001) inspired this conceptualization.

2. MHS humanities teachers expressed ambivalence about the bioscience emphasis. Ms. Barrett noted that her "curriculum doesn't really connect to the health thing." Instead, she indicated that "social inequality . . . [is the] primary theme in my class—injustice and what we can do about it." Ms. Clark went so far as to say, "I hate science, but I love the school." Finally, Mr. Behari characterized the "magnety, health and science focus as an interesting model for public education," but also shared his dream to open "a school with a social science focus, where instead of building doctors, we're building lawyers and politicians."

3. In the United States, the n-word is a highly offensive, ethnic slur for Black people, but it has also been reappropriated and used either humorously or as a term of affection among some African Americans. Its use is highly contested (Wellington, 2008).

4. The unit, developed with a colleague from another school, featured *Texas v. Johnson* (1989), *Tinker v. Des Moines* (1969), *Florida v. Bostick* (1991), *Escobedo v. Illinois* (1961), and *Spano v. NY* (1959). These cases addressed free speech, unlawful search and seizure, and judicial due process.

5. MHS's mandatory EDP accustomed students to staying after school. When teachers scheduled after-school assessments/exhibitions, students simply skipped regular enrichment activities and joined their academic teacher.

6. Mr. Behari attributed his love for debate to childhood family dinner conversations. He stressed that political argumentation need not be grim and combative. "I don't think debate has to be rigid. This is the way you do it over coffee in college. You have conversation, you laugh, you talk. That's how you learn. It should be pleasurable." This reference to pleasure reprises Chapter 3's fourth pillar emphasizing learning as fun.

7. Bryk and Driscoll (1988) found that teachers within high schools operating with high levels of communal interdependence and relational trust reported high levels of efficacy, job satisfaction, and morale and less absenteeism. These same schools also had lower incidences of student discipline problems and dropouts, as well as higher levels of student academic engagement. Bryk's subsequent research replicated these findings in other settings (Bryk et al., 1998; Bryk & Schneider, 2002).

8. These included *Autobiography of Malcolm X, Twilight Los Angeles* by Anna Deavere Smith, *Our America: Life and Death on the South Side of Chicago* by LeAlan Jones and Lloyd Newman, *To Kill a Mockingbird* by Harper Lee, *Native Son* by Richard Wright, *Cops and Robbers* by Jinho Ferreira, *Why Are All The Black Kids Sitting Together in the Cafeteria* by Beverly Tatum, and excerpts from *The New Jim Crow* by Michelle Alexander. Ms. Barrett characterized her 9th-grade English curriculum as "much more African American-centric than Latino-centric" and mentioned that on a few occasions "a couple of students actually have said aloud, 'Why are we always reading about Black people?'"

Chapter 5

1. Launched in 2011, the Occupy movement protested against social and economic inequality and the lack of "real democracy" around the world. See Chomsky (2012) for an overview of the movement's concerns and goals.

2. Free track at https://brwnbflo.bandcamp.com/track/12-be-the-change.

3. An annual observance running from January 30th, the date of Mahatma Gandhi's assassination, to Martin Luther King Jr.'s assassination on April 4th. See http://www.seasonofnonviolence.com/.

4. Trayvon Martin was an unarmed, African American, Florida teen fatally shot by a self-appointed neighborhood watchman in 2012. Oscar Grant was a 22-year-old African American man killed by a transit police officer in 2009 in Oakland, California. Both killings sparked national outrage and controversy regarding racial injustice.

Appendix A

1. By protecting instructional time, we endeavored to support students' academic success. During the SOLES study, MHS also participated in another study. I was chagrined when our counterparts obtained no parental consent for minors and pulled students out of class for focus groups. While it is certainly true that parental consent requirements limited our student recruitment, obtaining such permissions seemed ethically responsible.

References

Abelmann, C., Elmore, R., Even, J., Kenyon, S., & Marshall, J. (1999). *When accountability knocks, will anyone answer?* Consortium for Policy Research in Education.

Achinstein, B. (2002). *Community, diversity, and conflict among schoolteachers: The ties that blind.* Teachers College Press.

Achinstein, B., Athanases, S. Z., Curry, M. W., Ogawa, R. T., & de Oliveira, L. C. (2013, May/June). These doors are open: Community wealth and health as resources in strengthening education for lower-income Latina/o youth. *Leadership, 30*–34.

Achinstein, B., Curry, M. W., & Ogawa, R. T. (2015). (Re)labeling social status: Promises and tensions in developing a college-going culture for Latina/o youth in an urban high school. *American Journal of Education, 121*(3), 311–345.

Achinstein, B., Curry, M. W., Ogawa, R. T., & Athanases, S. Z. (2014). Organizing high schools for Latina/o youth success: Boundary crossing to access and build community wealth. *Urban Education, 51*(7), 824–854.

ACT. (2016). *The condition of college & career readiness 2015: Hispanic students.* http://www.act.org/content/dam/act/unsecured/documents/06-24-16-Subcon -Hispanic-Report.pdf

Allen, J. P., Pianta, R. C., Gregory, A., Mikami, A. Y., & Lun, J. (2011). An interaction-based approach to enhancing secondary school instruction and student achievement. *Science, 333*(6045), 1034–1037.

Ancess, J. (2003). *Beating the odds: High schools as communities of commitment.* Teachers College Press.

Andrés-Hyman, R. C., Ortiz, J., Añez, L. M., Paris, M., & Davidson, L. (2006). Culture and clinical practice: Recommendations for working with Puerto Ricans and other Latinas(os) in the United States. *Professional Psychology: Research and Practice, 37*(6), 694–701.

Antrop-González, R., & De Jesús, A. (2006). Toward a theory of critical care in urban small school reform: Examining structures and pedagogies of caring in two Latino community-based schools. *International Journal of Qualitative Studies in Education, 19*(4), 409–433.

Anzaldúa, G. (1987/2012). *Borderlands/la frontera: The new mestiza.* Aunt Lute.

Anzaldúa, G. (2015). *Light in the dark/Luz en lo oscuro: Rewriting identity, spirituality, reality.* Duke University Press.

Anzaldúa, G. E. (2002/2013). Now let us shift . . . the path of conocimiento . . . inner work, public acts. In G. E. Anzaldúa & A. Keating (Eds.), *This bridge we call home* (pp. 554–592). Routledge.

Apple, M. W. (1982/2012). *Education and power*. Routledge.

Applebee, A. N., Langer, J. A., Nystrand, M., & Gamoran, A. (2003). Discussion-based approaches to developing understanding: Classroom instruction and student performance in middle and high school English. *American Educational Research Journal, 40*(3), 685–730.

Ashton, P., Webb, R. B., & Doda, N. (1982). *A study of teachers' sense of efficacy.* http://files.eric.ed.gov/fulltext/ED231834.pdf

Athanases, S. Z. (2018). Locked in sequence and stuck on skills in a college-for-all culture for urban Latinx youth. *Urban Education.* https://doi-org.oca.ucsc.edu/10.1177/0042085918806944

Athanases, S. Z., & Curry, M. W. (2018). Framing literacy as "revolutionary": Creating transformative learning opportunities in a predominantly Latinx-serving high school. In A. M. Lazar & P. R. Schmidt (Eds.), *Schools of promise for multilingual students: Transforming literacies, learning, and lives* (pp. 70–86). Teachers College Press.

Athanases, S. Z., Achinstein, B., Curry, M. W., & Ogawa, R. T. (2016). The promise and limitations of a college-going culture: Towards cultures of engaged learning for low-SES Latina/o youth. *Teachers College Record, 118*(7), 1–60.

Athanases, S. Z., & de Oliveira, L. C. (2014). Scaffolding versus routine support for Latina/o youth in an urban school: Tensions in building toward disciplinary literacy. *Journal of Literacy Research, 46*(2), 263–299.

Bailey, T. (2009). Challenge and opportunity: Rethinking the role and function of developmental education in community college. *New Directions for Community Colleges, 145*, 11–30.

Bartlett, L., & García, O. (2011). *Additive schooling in subtractive times: Bilingual education and Dominican immigrant youth in the heights*. Vanderbilt University Press.

Bartolomé, L. I. (2008). Authentic cariño and respect in minority education: The political and ideological dimensions of love. *International Journal of Critical Pedagogy, 1*(1), 1–17.

Beauboeuf-Lafontant, T. (2002). A womanist experience of caring: Understanding the pedagogy of exemplary Black women teachers. *The Urban Review, 34*(1), 71–86.

Behar, R. (1996). *The vulnerable observer: Anthropology that breaks your heart*. Beacon.

Bell, D. A. (1995). Who's afraid of critical race theory. *University of Illinois Law Review*, 893–910.

Betts, J. R., Reuben, K. S., & Danenberg, A. (2000). *Equal resources, equal outcomes? The distribution of school resources and student achievement in California*. Public Policy Institute of California. https://www.ppic.org/content/pubs/report/R_200JBR.pdf.

Boveda, M., & Bhattacharya, K. (2019). Love as de/colonial onto-epistemology: A post-oppositional approach to contextualized research ethics. *The Urban Review, 51*(1), 5–25.

Bridges, M., Cohen, S. R., McGuire, L. W., Yamada, H., Fuller, B., Mireles, L., & Scott, L. (2012). Bien educado: Measuring the social behaviors of Mexican American children. *Early Childhood Research Quarterly, 27*, 555–567.

Bruna, K. R., Vann, R., & Escudero, M. P. (2007). What's language got to do with it?: A case study of academic language instruction in a high school "English learner science" class. *Journal of English for Academic Purposes, 6*(1), 36–54.

Bryk, A. S., & Driscoll, M. E. (1988). *The high school as community: Contextual influences and consequences for students and teachers.* https://files.eric.ed.gov/fulltext/ED302539.pdf

Bryk, A., & Schneider, B. (2002). *Trust in schools: A core resource for improvement.* Russell Sage Foundation.

Bryk, A. S., Sebring, P. B., Kerbow, D., Rollow, S., & Easton, J. Q. (1998). *Charting Chicago school reform: Democratic localism as a lever for change.* Westview.

California State University. (2016). *Systemwide CSU first-time freshmen remediation.* http://asd.calstate.edu/performance/remediation/16/index.shtml

Camangian, P. (2010). Starting with self: Teaching autoethnography to foster critically caring literacies. *Research in the Teaching of English,* 179–204.

Camangian, P. R. (2015). Teach like lives depend on it: Agitate, arouse, and inspire. *Urban Education, 50*(4), 424–453.

Cammarota, J., & Fine, M. (2010). *Revolutionizing education: Youth participatory action research in motion.* Routledge.

Cariaga, S. (2019). Towards self-recovery: Cultivating love with young women of color through pedagogies of bodymindspirit. *The Urban Review, 51*(1), 101–122.

Carmen, S. A. S., Domínguez, M., Greene, A. C., Mendoza, E., Fine, M., Neville, H. A., & Gutiérrez, K. D. (2015). Revisiting the collective in critical consciousness: Diverse sociopolitical wisdoms and ontological healing in sociopolitical development. *The Urban Review, 47*(5), 824–846.

Carter, P. L. (2005). *Keepin' it real: School success beyond Black and White.* Oxford University Press.

Casanova, Ú. (2010). *¡Sí se puede! Learning from a high school that beat the odds.* Teachers College Press.

Cauce, A. M., & Domenech-Rodriguez, M. (2002). Latino families: Myths and realities. In J. M. Contreras, K. A. Kerns, & A. M. Neal-Barnett (Eds.), *Latino children and families in the United States: Current research and future directions* (pp. 3–25). Praeger.

Cervantes-Soon, C. G. (2012). Testimonios of life and learning in the borderlands: Subaltern Juárez girls speak. *Equity & Excellence in Education, 45*(3), 373–391.

Chapman, T. K. (2006). Pedaling backward: Reflections of Plessy and Brown in Rockford public schools' de jure desegregation efforts. In A. D. Dixson & C. K. Rousseau (Eds.), *Critical race theory in education: All god's children got a song* (pp. 67–88). Routledge.

Charmaz, K. (2006). *Constructing grounded theory: A practical guide through qualitative analysis.* SAGE.

Chomsky, N. (2012). *Occupy.* Zuccotti Park Press.

Cohen, E. G. (1994). *Designing groupwork: Strategies for the heterogeneous classroom* (2nd ed.). Teachers College Press.

Cohen, E. G., Lotan, R. A., Scarloss, B. A., & Arellano, A. R. (1999). Complex instruction: Equity in cooperative learning classrooms. *Theory Into Practice, 38*(2), 80–86.

Conchas, G. Q. (Ed.) (2016). *Cracks in the schoolyard: Confronting Latino educational inequality.* Teachers College Press.

Conchas, G. Q., & Rodríguez, L. F. (2008). *Small schools and urban youth: Using the power of school culture to engage students.* SAGE.

Cooper, K. S. (2013). Safe, affirming, and productive spaces: Classroom engagement among Latina high school students. *Urban Education, 48*(4), 490–528.

Cooper, K. S. (2014). Eliciting engagement in the high school classroom: A mixed-methods examination of teaching practices. *American Educational Research Journal, 51*(2), 363–402.

Cousins, E. (1998). *Reflections on design principles.* Kendall Hunt.

Cruz, C. (2001). Toward an epistemology of a brown body. *International Journal of Qualitative Studies in Education, 14*(5), 657–669.

Cruz, C. (2012). Making curriculum from scratch: Testimonio in an urban classroom. *Equity & Excellence, 45*(3), 460–471.

Cuban, L. (1982). Persistent instruction: The high school classroom, 1900–1980. *Phi Delta Kappan, 64*(2), 113–118.

Curry, M. W. (2012). In pursuit of reciprocity: Researchers, teachers, and school reformers engaged in collaborative analysis of video records. *Theory Into Practice, 51*(2), 91–98.

Curry, M. W. (2013). Being the change: An inner city school builds peace. *Phi Delta Kappan, 95*(4), 23–27.

Curry, M. W. (2016). Will you stand for me? Authentic cariño and transformative rites of passage in an urban high school. *American Educational Research Journal, 53*(4), 883–918.

Curry, M. W., & Athanases, S. Z. (2020). In pursuit of engaged learning with Latinx students: Expanding learning beyond classrooms through performance-based engagements. *Teachers College Record, 122*(8), 1–49.

Dabach, D. B., Suárez-Orozco, C., Hernandez, S. J., & Brooks, M. D. (2017). Future perfect?: Teachers' expectations and explanations of their Latino immigrant students' postsecondary futures. *Journal of Latinos and Education, 17*(1), 38–52.

Dance, L. J. (2002). *Tough fronts: The impact of street culture on schooling.* Psychology Press.

Darder, A. (2011). Unfettered bodies: Forging an emancipatory pedagogy of the flesh. *Counterpoints, 418,* 343–359.

Darder, A. (2020). Critical pedagogy. *Rethinking Critical Pedagogy, 1*(2), 19–34. http://mjura41.net/rethinking-critical-pedagogy-rcp/

Delgado Bernal, D. (1998). Using a Chicana feminist epistemology in educational research. *Harvard Educational Review, 68*(4), 555–583.

Delgado Bernal, D. (2006). Learning and living pedagogies of the home: The mestiza consciousness of chicana students. In D. Delgado Bernal, C. A. Elenes, F. E. Godinez, & S. Villenas (Eds.), *Chicana/Latina education in everyday life: Feminista perspectives on pedagogy and epistemology.* SUNY Press.

Delgado Bernal, D. (2008). La trenza de identidades: Weaving together my personal, professional, and communal identities. In K. P. González & R. V. Padilla (Eds.), *Doing the public good* (pp. 135–148). Stylus.

Delgado Bernal, D., Elenes, C. A., Godinez, F. E., & Villenas, S. (Eds.). (2006). *Chicana/Latina education in everyday life: Feminista perspectives on pedagogy and epistemology.* SUNY.

Delgado-Gaitan, C. (1994). Consejos: The power of cultural narratives. *Anthropology & Education Quarterly, 25*(3), 298–316.

Delpit, L. (1988). The silenced dialogue: Power and pedagogy in educating other people's children. *Harvard Educational Review, 58*(3), 280–299.

de los Ríos, C., V., López, J., & Morrell, E. (2015). Toward a critical pedagogy of race: Ethnic studies and literacies of power in high school classrooms. *Race and Social Problems, 7*(1), 84–96.

DeNicolo, C. P., González, M., Morales, S., & Romaní, L. (2015). Teaching through testimonio: Accessing community cultural wealth in school. *Journal of Latinos and Education, 14*(4), 228–243.

DeNicolo, C. P., Yu, M., Crowley, C. B., & Gabel, S. L. (2017). Reimagining critical care and problematizing sense of school belonging as a response to inequality for immigrants and children of immigrants. *Review of Research in Education, 41*(1), 500–530.

Doherty, R. W., & Hilberg, R. S. (2007). Standards for effective pedagogy, classroom organization, English proficiency, and student achievement. *The Journal of Educational Research, 101*(1), 24–35.

Doherty, R. W., Hilberg, R. S., Pinal, A., & Tharp, R. G. (2003). Five standards and student achievement. *NABE Journal of Research and Practice, 1*(1), 1–24.

Dryfoos, J. (2002). Full-service community schools: Creating new institutions. *Phi Delta Kappan, 83*(5), 393–399.

Duncan, G. A. (2002). Beyond love: A critical race ethnography of the schooling of adolescent Black males. *Equity & Excellence in Education, 35*(2), 131–143.

Duncan-Andrade, J. M. R. (2009). Note to educators: Hope required when growing roses in concrete. *Harvard Educational Review, 79*(2), 181–194.

Dweck, C. S. (2008). *Mindset: The new psychology of success.* Random House.

Ellsworth, E. (1989). Why doesn't this feel empowering? Working through the repressive myths of critical pedagogy. *Harvard Educational Review, 59*(3), 297–325.

Engström, Y. (1991). Non scolae sed vitae discimus: Toward overcoming the encapsulation of school learning. *Learning and Instruction, 1*, 243–259.

Facio, E., & Lara, I. (Eds.). (2014). *Fleshing the spirit: Spirituality and activism in Chicana, Latina, and Indigenous women's lives.* University of Arizona Press.

Faircloth, B. S. (2012). "Wearing a mask" vs. connecting identity with learning. *Contemporary Educational Psychology, 37*(3), 186–194.

Farrell, G. (2000). Introduction. In E. Cousins (Ed.), *Roots: From outward bound to expeditionary learning* (pp. 1–7). Kendall Hunt.

Ferguson, A. (2000). *Bad boys.* University of Michigan Press.

Fine, M. (1987). Silencing in public schools. *Language Arts, 64*(2), 157–174.

Flores-Gonzáles, N. (2002). *School kids/ street kids: Identity development in Latino students.* Teachers College Press.

Flyvbjerg, B. (2001). *Making social science matter: Why social inquiry fails and how it can succeed again.* Cambridge University Press.

Fox, M., Mediratta, K., Ruglis, J., Stoudt, B., Shah, S., & Fine, M. (2010). Critical youth engagement: Participatory action research and organizing. In L. R. Sherrod, J. Torney-Purta, & C. A. Flanagan (Eds.), *Handbook of research on civic engagement in youth* (pp. 621–649): John Wiley & Sons.

Freire, P. (1970/2005). *Pedagogy of the oppressed.* Continuum.

Fuentes, E. H., & Pérez, M. A. (2016). Testimonio as radical story-telling and creative soulful resistance. *Association of Mexican American Educators Journal, 10*(2), 5–14.

Gándara, P., & Contreras, F. (2009). *The Latino education crisis: The consequences of failed social policies.* Harvard University Press.

García, O. (2009). Emergent bilinguals and TESOL: What's in a name? *Tesol Quarterly, 43*(2), 322–326.

Gee, J. P. (2015). Discourse, small d, big D. In K. Tracy, C. Ilie, & T. Sandel (Eds.), *The international encyclopedia of language and social interaction* (pp. 418–422). Wiley-Blackwell.

Gilligan, C. (1982). *In a different voice: Psychological theory and women's development.* Harvard University Press.

Ginwright, S. A. (2010). *Black youth rising: Activism and radical healing in urban America.* Teachers College Press.

Ginwright, S. (2016). *Hope and healing in urban education: How urban activists and teachers are reclaiming matters of the heart.* Routledge.

Ginwright, S. (2019, March 21). *Webinar on healing centered engagement.* Flourish Agenda, Inc.

Glazer, J. (2018). The power of hmm . . . : Bringing life (back) to words in the classroom. *Phi Delta Kappan, 99*(5), 56–60.

Godinez, F. E. (2006). Haciendo que hacer: Braiding cultural knowledge into educational practices and policies. In D. Delgado Bernal, C. A. Elenes, F. E. Godinez, & S. Villenas (Eds.), *Chicana/Latina education in everyday life: Feminist perspectives on pedagogy and epistemology* (pp. 25–38). SUNY.

Goldstein, D., & Casselman, B. (2018, May 31). Teachers find public support as campaign for higher pay goes to voters. *The New York Times.* https://www.nytimes.com/2018/05/31/us/politics/teachers-campaign.html

Gonzalez, F. E. (1998). Formations of Mexicananess: Trenzas de identidades multiples. *International Journal of Qualitative Studies in Education, 11*(1), 81–102.

Gonzales, R. G., Chavez, L. R., Boehm, D. A., Brettell, C. B., Coutin, S. B., Inda, J. X., . . . Sigona, N. (2012). "Awakening to a nightmare" abjectivity and illegality in the lives of undocumented 1.5-generation Latino immigrants in the United States. *Current anthropology, 53*(3), 255–281.

Gonzales, R. G., Heredia, L. L., & Negrón-Gonzales, G. (2015). Untangling Plyler's legacy: Undocumented students, schools, and citizenship. *Harvard Educational Review, 85*(3), 318–341.

Gramlich, J. (2017, September 29). *Hispanic dropout rate hits new low, college enrollment at new high.* http://pewrsr.ch/2x2wyy1

Gutiérrez, K. D. (2008). Developing a sociocritical literacy in the third space. *Reading Research Quarterly, 43*(2), 148–164.

Gutiérrez, K. D., & Larson, J. (2007). Discussing expanded spaces for learning. *Language Arts, 85*(1), 69–77.

Gutiérrez, K. D., Morales, P. Z., & Martinez, D. C. (2009). Re-mediating literacy: Culture, difference, and learning for students. *Review of Research in Education, 33*, 212–245.

Gutiérrez, R. (2012). Embracing Nepantla: Rethinking" knowledge" and its use in mathematics teaching. *REDIMAT—Journal of Research in Mathematics Education, 1*(1), 29–56.

Gutiérrez, R. (2013). Why (urban) mathematics teachers need political knowledge. *Journal of Urban Mathematics Education, 6*(2), 7–19.

Hafen, C. A., Hamre, B. K., Allen, J. P., Bell, C. A., Gitomer, D. H., & Pianta, R. C. (2015). Teaching through interactions in secondary school classrooms:

Revisiting the factor structure and practical application of the Classroom Assessment Scoring System—Secondary. *Journal of Early Adolescence, 35*(5–6), 651–680.

Hafiz. (1996). Tripping over joy (D. Ladinsky, Trans.). In *I Heard God Laughing: Poems of Hope and Joy* (p. 127). Mobius Press.

Hammond, Z. (2014). *Culturally responsive teaching and the brain: Promoting authentic engagement and rigor among culturally and linguistically diverse students.* Corwin.

Hess, D. E. (2009). *Controversy in the classroom: The democratic power of discussion.* Routledge.

Hidalgo, N. D., & Duncan-Andrade, J. M. R. (2009). When stepping to college is stepping to consciousness: Critical pedagogy, transformational resistance, and community building with urban Latin@ and African American youth. In E. G. Murillo, S. Villenas, R. T. Galván, J. S. Muñoz, C. Martínez, & M. Machado-Casas (Eds.), *Handbook of Latinos and education: Theory, research and practice* (pp. 262–275). Routledge.

Hilberg, R. S., Doherty, R. W., Tharp, R. G., Estrada, P., & Lee, V. (2003). *Standards performance continuum (SPC) manual for classroom observation.* UC-Santa Cruz: Center for Research on Education, Diversity & Excellence (CREDE).

Hirsch, L. (2011). *Bully.* http://www.thebullyproject.com/

Holland, N. E., & Farmer-Hinton, R. L. (2009). Leave no schools behind: The importance of a college culture in urban public high schools. *The High School Journal, 92*(3), 24–43.

hooks, b. (1989). *Talking back: Thinking feminist, thinking black.* South End Press.

hooks, b. (1990). *Yearning: Race, gender, and cultural politics*: South End Press.

hooks, b. (1994). *Sisters of the yam: Black women and self-recovery.* South End Press.

hooks, b. (2001). *All about love: New visions.* Harper Perennial.

hooks, b. (2003). *Teaching community: A pedagogy of hope.* Routledge.

Horn, I. S. (2005). Learning on the job: A situated account of teacher learning in high school mathematics departments. *Cognition and Instruction, 23*(2), 207–236.

Irizarry, J. G. (2007). Ethnic and urban intersections in the classroom: Latino students, hybrid identities, and culturally responsive pedagogy. *Multicultural Perspectives, 9*(3), 21–28.

Isasi-Díaz, A. M., Olazagasti-Segovia, E., Mangual-Rodriguez, S., Berriozábal, M. A., Machado, D. L., Arguelles, L., & Rivero, R. (1992). Roundtable discussion: Mujeristas who we are and what we are about. *Journal of Feminist Studies in Religion, 8*(1), 105–125.

Jacobs, K. B. (2015). "I want to see real urban schools": Teacher learners' discourse and discussion of urban-based field experiences. *Perspectives on Urban Education, 12*(1), 18–37.

Jimenez, R. M. (2020). Community cultural wealth pedagogies: Cultivating autoethnographic counternarratives and migration capital. *American Educational Research Journal, 57*(2), 775–807.

Johnson, D. W., & Johnson, R. T. (1988). Critical thinking through structured controversy. *Educational Leadership, 45*(8), 58–64.

Johnson, J. A. (1995). Life after death: Critical pedagogy in an urban classroom. *Harvard Educational Review, 65*(2), 213–230.

Kahne, J., & Middaugh, E. (2008). High quality civic education: What is it and who gets it? *Social Education, 72*(1), 34–39.

Kane, T. J., & Staiger, D. O. (2012). *Gathering feedback for teaching: Combining high-quality observations with student surveys and achievement gains*. MET Project. http://files.eric.ed.gov/fulltext/ED540960.pdf

Keating, A. (2013). *Transformation now!: Toward a post-oppositional politics of change*. University of Illinois Press.

Keefe, S. E. (1984). Real and ideal extended familism among Mexican Americans and Anglo Americans: On the meaning of "close" family ties. *Human Organization, 43*(1), 65.

Kelley, R. D. (2002). *Freedom dreams: The Black radical imagination*. Beacon.

King, M. L. (1967). Beyond Vietnam—A time to break silence. Paper presented at the Riverside Church, New York. http://www.americanrhetoric.com/speeches/mlkatimetobreaksilence.htm

Kiweli, T. (2004). *The beautiful struggle*. Rawkus Records and Geffen Records.

Kuhn, D. (1999). A developmental model of critical thinking. *Educational Researcher, 28*(2), 16–46.

Ladson-Billings, G. (1994). *The dreamkeepers: Successful teachers of African American children*. Wiley.

Ladson-Billings, G. (1995). But that's just good teaching! The case for culturally relevant pedagogy. *Theory Into Practice, 34*(3), 159–165.

Ladson-Billings, G. (2006). From the achievement gap to the education debt: Understanding achievement in US schools. *Educational Researcher, 35*(7), 3–12.

Ladson-Billings, G. (2014). Culturally relevant pedagogy 2.0: Aka the remix. *Harvard Educational Review, 84*(1), 74–84.

Landis, J. R., & Koch, G. G. (1977). The measurement of observer agreement for categorical data. *Biometrics*, 159–174.

Langer, E. J. (2000). Mindful learning. *Current Directions in Psychological Science, 9*(6), 220–223.

Lara, I. (2002). Healing sueños for academia. In G. E. Anzaldúa & A. Keating (Eds.), *This bridge we call home: Radical visions for transformation* (pp. 433–438). Routledge.

Lawson, H. A., Caringi, J. C., Gottfried, R., Bride, B. E., & Hydon, S. P. (2019). Educators' secondary traumatic stress, children's trauma, and the need for trauma literacy. *Harvard Educational Review, 89*(3), 421–447.

Levinson, M. (2010). The civic empowerment gap: Defining the problem and locating solutions. *Handbook of Research on Civic Engagement in Youth*, 331–361.

Little, J. W. (2006). *Professional community and professional development in the learning-centered school*. http://www.nea.org/assets/docs/HE/mf_pdreport.pdf

Lortie, D. C. (1975). *Schoolteacher: A sociological study*. University of Chicago Press.

Love, B. (Feb. 6, 2020). White teachers need anti-racist therapy. *EdWeek*. Retrieved from https://mobile.edweek.org/c.jsp?cid=25919971&bcid=25919971&rssid=25919961&item=http%3A%2F%2Fapi.edweek.org%2Fv1%2Few%2Findex.html%3Fuuid%3DD705DBC6-490A-11EA-AAD8-8AF258D98AAA

Love, B. L. (2019). *We want to do more than survive: Abolitionist teaching and the pursuit of educational freedom.* Beacon.

Lugones, M. (1987). Playfulness, "world"-travelling, and loving perception. *Hypatia, 2*(2), 3–19.

Malcolm, X. (June 28, 1964). *Speech at the founding rally of the Organization of Afro-American Unity.* https://www.blackpast.org/african-american-history/1964-malcolm-x-s-speech-founding-rally-organization-afro-american-unity/

Marshall, H. H. (1988). Work or learning: Implications of classroom metaphors. *Educational Researcher, 17*(9), 9–16.

Marshall, H. H. (1990). Beyond the workplace metaphor: The classroom as a learning setting. *Theory Into Practice, 29*(2), 94–101.

Maslach, C. (1999). Progress in understanding teacher burnout. In R. Vandenberghe & A. M. Huberman (Eds.), *Understanding and preventing teacher burnout: A sourcebook of international research and practice* (pp. 211–222). Cambridge University Press.

Maslach, C., Jackson, S. E., & Schwab, R. L. (1986). *Maslach burnout inventory: Educator survey.* https://www.mindgarden.com/316-mbi-educators-survey

Maslach, C., & Leiter, M. P. (1997). *The truth about burnout: How organizations cause personal stress and what to do about it.* Wiley.

McCarty, T., & Lee, T. (2014). Critical culturally sustaining/revitalizing pedagogy and Indigenous education sovereignty. *Harvard Educational Review, 84*(1), 101–124.

McLaren, P., & Jaramillo, N. (2007). Critical pedagogy Latino/a education and the politics of class struggle. In A. Darder & R. D. Torres (Eds.), *Latinos and education: A critical reader* (pp. 91–120). Routledge.

McNeil, L. (1986). *Contradictions of control: School structure and school knowledge.* Routledge.

McNeil, L. M. (2005). Faking equity: High-stakes testing and the education of Latino youth. In A. Valenzuela (Ed.), *Leaving children behind: How "Texas-style" accountability fails Latino youth* (pp. 57–111). SUNY.

Mehan, H. (2012). *In the front door: Creating a college-going culture of learning.* Paradigm.

Mehan, H., Hubbard, L., & Villanueva, I. (1994). Forming academic identities: Accommodation without assimilation among involuntary minorities. *Anthropology and Education Quarterly, 25*(2), 91–117.

Meier, D. (1995). *The power of their ideas: Lessons for America from a small school in Harlem.* Beacon.

Menakem, R. (2017). *My grandmother's hands: Racialized trauma and the pathway to mending our hearts and bodies.* Central Recovery Press.

Menjívar, C. (2006). Liminal legality: Salvadoran and Guatemalan immigrants' lives in the United States. *American Journal of Sociology, 111*(4), 999–1037.

Meyer, J. W., & Rowan, B. (1977). Institutional organizations: Formal structures as myth and ceremony. *American Journal of Sociology, 83*(2), 340–363.

Meyer, J. W., & Rowan, B. (1978). The structure of educational organizations. In M. W. Meyer (Ed.), *Environments and organizations* (pp. 78–109). Jossey-Bass.

Michaels, S., O'Connor, C., & Resnick, L. B. (2007). Deliberative discourse idealized and realized: Accountable talk in the classroom and in civic life. *Studies in Philosophy and Education, 27*(4), 283–297.

Middaugh, E., & Kahne, J. (2013, August 27). Technology can help get kids "community ready." *Oakland Tribune.* https://www.civicsurvey.org/press-blogs/technology-can-help-kids-get-community-ready

Miles, M. B., & Huberman, A. M. (1994). *Qualitative data analysis*. SAGE.

Mohan, B., & Slater, T. (2006). Examining the theory/practice relation in a high school science register: A functional linguistic perspective. *Journal of English for Academic Purposes*, 5(4), 302–316.

Moje, E. B. (2015). Doing and teaching disciplinary literacy with adolescent learners: A social and cultural enterprise. *Harvard Educational Review*, 85(2), 254–278.

Moll, L. C., Amanti, C., Neff, D., & Gonzalez, N. (1992). Funds of knowledge for teaching: Using a qualitative approach to connect homes and classrooms. *Theory Into Practice*, 31(2), 132–141.

Montoya, M. E. (1994). Mascaras, trenzas, y grenas: Un/masking the self while un/braiding Latina stories and legal discourse. *Chicano-Latino Law Review*, 15, 1–37.

Moraga, C. (1983/2000). *Loving in the war years: Lo que nunca pasó por sus labios*. South End Press.

Moraga, C., & Anzaldúa, G. (1983). *This bridge called my back: Writings by radical women of color*. Kitchen Table Press.

Morgan, G., & Ramirez, R. (1984). Action learning: A holographic metaphor for guiding social change. *Human Relations*, 37(1), 1–27.

Nasir, N. S., & Hand, V. (2008). From the court to the classroom: Opportunities for engagement, learning, and identity in basketball and classroom mathematics. *Journal of the Learning Sciences*, 17(2), 143–179.

National Center for Educational Statistics. (2016). Status and trends in the education of racial and ethnic groups. https://nces.ed.gov/pubs2016/2016007.pdf

National Center for Education Statistics. (2018). Table 203.70: Percentage distribution of enrollment in public elementary and secondary schools, by race/ethnicity and state or jurisdiction: Fall 2000 and fall 2016. *Digest of Education Statistics*. https://nces.ed.gov/programs/digest/d18/tables/dt18_203.70.asp?current=yes

Newmann, F., King, M. B., & Rigdon, M. (1997). Accountability and school performance: Implications from restructuring schools. *Harvard Educational Review*, 67(1), 41–75.

Noddings, N. (1984). *Caring: A relational approach to ethics and moral education*. University of California Press.

Noddings, N. (1988). An ethic of caring and its implications for instructional arrangements. *American Journal of Education*, 96(2), 215–230.

Noddings, N. (1990). A response to Card, Hoagland, Houston. *Hypatia*, 5(1), 120–126.

Noddings, N. (1992/2005). *The challenge to care in schools: An alternative approach to education*. Teachers College Press.

Noddings, N. (1999). Care, justice, and equity. In M. S. Katz, N. Noddings, & K. A. Strike (Eds.), *Justice and caring: The search for common ground in education* (pp. 7–20). Teachers College Press.

Nora, P. (1989). Between memory and history: Les lieux de mémoire. *Representations*, 26, 7–24.

Nystrand, M. (1997). Dialogic instruction: When recitation becomes conversation. In A. Gamoran, R. Kachur, M. Nystrand, & C. Prendergast (Eds.), *Opening dialogue: Understanding the dynamics of language and learning in the English classroom* (pp. 1–29). Teachers College Press.

Nystrand, M., & Gamoran, A. (1991). Instructional discourse, student engagement, and literature achievement. *Research in the Teaching of English*, 261–290.

Nystrand, M., Gamoran, A., & Carbonaro, W. (2001). On the ecology of classroom instruction. In P. Tynjala, L. Mason, & K. Londa (Eds.), *Writing as a learning tool* (pp. 57–81): Kluwer Academic Publishers.

Oakes, J. (1985). *Keeping track: How schools structure inequality.* Yale University Press.

Oakes, J., & Rogers, J. (2006). *Learning power: Organizing for education and justice.* Teachers College Press.

Orfield, G., Kucsera, J., & Siegel-Hawley, G. (2012). *E pluribus . . . separation: Deepening double segregation for more students.* Harvard Civil Rights Project. https://escholarship.org/uc/item/8g58m2v9

Page, R. N. (1998). Moral aspects of curriculum: "Making kids care" about school knowledge. *Journal of Curriculum Studies, 30*(1), 1–26.

Palmer, P. J. (1983/1993). *To know as we are known: Education as a spiritual journey.* HarperCollins.

Papay, J. P., Bacher-Hicks, A., Page, L. C., & Marinell, W. H. (2017). The challenge of teacher retention in urban schools: Evidence of variation from a cross-site analysis. *Educational Researcher, 46*(8), 434–448.

Paris, D. (2012). Culturally sustaining pedagogy: A needed change in stance, terminology, and practice. *Educational Researcher, 41*(3), 93–97.

Paris, D., & Alim, H. S. (2014). What are we seeking to sustain through culturally sustaining pedagogy? A loving critique forward. *Harvard Educational Review, 84*(1), 85–100.

Pekrun, R., & Linnenbrink-Garcia, L. (2012). Academic emotions and student engagement. In S. L. Christenson, A. L. Reschly, & C. Wylie (Eds.), *Handbook of research on student engagement* (pp. 259–282). Springer.

Perry, A. (2016, May 2). Black and Brown boys don't need to learn grit; They need schools to stop being racist. *The Root.* https://www.theroot.com/black-and-brown-boys-don-t-need-to-learn-grit-they-nee-1790855155

Phillippo, K. (2012). "You're trying to know me": Students from nondominant groups respond to teacher personalism. *The Urban Review, 44*(4), 441–467.

Pianta, R. C., Hamre, B. K., & Allen, J. P. (2012). Teacher–student relationships and engagement: Conceptualizing, measuring, and improving the capacity of classroom interactions. In S. L. Christenson, A. L. Reschly, & C. Wylie (Eds.), *Handbook of research on student engagement* (pp. 365–386). Springer.

Pianta, R. C., Hamre, B. K., Haynes, N. J., Mintz, S., & La Paro, K. M. (2006). *CLASS classroom assessment scoring system: Manual middle secondary version pilot.* University of Virginia.

Pianta, R. C., Hamre, B. K., & Mintz, S. (2012). *Upper elementary and secondary CLASS technical manual.* http://cdn2.hubspot.net/hubfs/336169/Technical_Manual.pdf

Pierce, K. (2005). Posing, pretending, waiting for the bell: Life in high school classrooms. *The High School Journal, 89*(2), 1–5.

Powell, A., Farrar, E., & Cohen, D. (1985). *The shopping mall high school.* Houghton-Mifflin.

Powell, C., Demetriou, C., & Fisher, A. (2013). Micro-affirmations in academic advising: Small acts, big impact. *The Mentor: Innovative Scholarship on Academic Advising, 15.* https://journals.psu.edu/mentor/article/view/61286/60919

Putnam, R. D. (1995). Bowling alone: America's declining social capital. *Journal of Democracy, 6*(1), 65–78.

Quiñones, S. (2016). (Re)braiding to tell: Using trenzas as a metaphorical–analytical tool in qualitative research. *International Journal of Qualitative Studies in Education, 29*(3), 338–358.

Remen, R. N. (1999). Educating for mission, meaning, and compassion. In S. Glazer (Ed.), *The heart of learning: Spirituality in education* (pp. 33–49). Tarcher.

Resnick, L. B. (2010). Nested learning systems for the thinking curriculum. *Educational Researcher, 39*(3), 183–197.

Ritchhart, R. (2002). *Intellectual character: What it is, why it matters and how to get it.* Jossey-Bass.

Rodriguez, L. F. (2018). The educational journeys of students of color across the educational pipeline: A pedagogy of storytelling or a struggle for freedom? *Diaspora, Indigenous, and Minority Education, 12*(4), 214–229.

Rogers, J., Franke, M., Yun, J.-E. E., Ishimoto, M., Diera, C., Geller, R. C., Berryman, A., & Brenes, T. (2017). *Teaching and learning in the age of Trump: Increasing stress and hostility in America's high schools.* UCLA IDEA. https://files.eric.ed.gov/fulltext/ED580203.pdf

Rolón-Dow, R. (2005). Critical care: A color(full) analysis of care narratives in the schooling experiences of Puerto Rican girls. *American Educational Research Journal, 42*(1), 77–111.

Rose, M. (1985). The language of exclusion: Writing instruction at the university. *College English, 47*(4), 341–359.

Rowan, B. (1990). Chapter 7: Commitment and control: Alternative strategies for the organizational design of schools. *Review of Research in Education, 16*(1), 353–389.

Rowe, M. (2008). Micro-affirmations and micro-inequities. *Journal of the International Ombudsman Association, 1*(1), 45–48.

Royal, C., & Gibson, S. (2017). They schools: Culturally relevant pedagogy under siege. *Teachers College Record, 119*(010306), 1–25.

Rubin, B. C. (2007). There's still not justice": Youth civic identity development amid distinct school and community contexts. *Teachers College Record, 109*(2), 449–481.

Salinas, C. (2020). The complexity of the "x" in Latinx: How Latinx/a/o students relate to, identify with, and understand the term Latinx. *Journal of Hispanic Higher Education, 19*(2), 149–168.

Salinas, C., & Lozano, A. (2019). Mapping and recontextualizing the evolution of the term Latinx: An environmental scanning in higher education. *Journal of Latinos and Education, 18*(4), 302–315.

Santiago-Rivera, A. (2003). Latinos values and family transitions: Practical considerations for counseling. *Counseling and Human Development, 35*(6), 1–12.

Sarason, S. (1990). *The predictable failure of educational reform.* Jossey-Bass.

Scheffler, I. (1977). In praise of the cognitive emotions. *Teachers College Record, 79*(2), 171–186.

Scherman, T. (1997). The great debaters. *American Legacy,* 40–42.

Schlosser, E., & Wilson, C. (2006). *Chew on this: Everything you don't want to know about fast food.* Houghton Mifflin Harcourt.

Scott, W. R. (1997). *Organizations: Rational, natural, and open systems* (4th ed.). Prentice Hall.

Sepúlveda, E. (2011). Toward a pedagogy of acompañamiento: Mexican migrant youth writing from the underside of modernity. *Harvard Educational Review, 81*(3), 550–572.

Shanahan, T., & Shanahan, C. (2008). Teaching disciplinary literacy to adolescents: Rethinking content area literacy. *Harvard Educational Review*, 78(1), 40–59.

Shange, S. (2019). *Progressive dystopia: Abolition, antiblackness, and schooling in San Francisco*. Duke University Press.

Shulman, L. S. (1987). Knowledge and teaching: Foundations of the new reform. *Harvard Educational Review*, 57(1), 1–22.

Siskin, L. S. (2011). Changing contexts and the challenges of high school reform in New York City. In J. A. O'Day, C. S. Bitter, & L. M. Gomez (Eds.), *Education reform in New York City: Ambitious change in the nation's most complex school system* (pp. 181–198). Harvard Education Press.

Sizer, T. R. (1984). *Horace's compromise: The dilemma of the American high school*. Houghton Mifflin Harcourt.

Sizer, T. R. (1992). *Horace's school: Redesigning the American high school*. Houghton Mifflin Harcourt.

Slater, D. (2017). *The 57 bus*. Farrar Straus Giroux.

Solórzano, D. G., & Delgado Bernal, D. (2001). Examining transformational resistance through a critical race and LatCrit theory framework: Chicana and Chicano students in an urban context. *Urban Education, 36*(3), 308–342.

Sosa-Provencio, M. A. (2019). A revolucionista ethic of care: Four Mexicana educators' subterraneous social justice revolution of fighting and feeding. *American Educational Research Journal, 56*(4), 1113–1147.

Stanton-Salazar, R. D. (2001). *Manufacturing hope and despair: The school and kin support networks of U.S.-Mexican youth*. Teachers College Press.

Sue, D. W., Capodilupo, C. M., Torino, G. C., Bucceri, J. M., Holder, A. M. B., Nadal, K. L., & Esquilin, M. (2007). Racial microaggressions in everyday life: Implications for clinical practice. *American Psychologist, 62*(4), 271–286.

Sullivan, F., & Godsay, S. (2014). Electoral engagement among young Latinos. *In* The Center for Information and Research on Civic Engagement (Ed.), *Fact sheet*. Tufts University.

Thomas, M. S., Crosby, S., & Vanderhaar, J. (2019). Trauma-informed practices in schools across two decades: An interdisciplinary review of research. *Review of Research in Education, 43*(1), 422–452.

Thompson, A. (1998). Not the color purple: Black feminist lessons for educational caring. *Harvard Educational Review, 68*(4) 522–554.

Thompson, A. (2003). Four feminist theories on gender and education. *Curriculum Inquiry, 33*(1), 9–65.

Torre, M. E. (2009). Participatory action research and critical race theory: Fueling spaces for nos-otras to research. *Urban Review, 41*(1), 106–120.

Toshalis, E. (2012). The rhetoric of care: Preservice teacher discourses that depoliticize, deflect, and deceive. *Urban Review, 44*(1), 1–35.

Tuck, E. (2009). Suspending damage: A letter to communities. *Harvard Educational Review, 79*(3), 409–428.

Tuck, E., & Yang, K. W. (2014). R-words: Refusing research. In D. Paris & M. T. Winn (Eds.), *Humanizing research: Decolonizing qualitative inquiry with youth and communities* (Vol. 223, pp. 223–247). SAGE.

Turner, E. O., & Mangual Figueroa, A. (2019). Immigration policy and education in lived reality: A framework for researchers and educators. *Educational Researcher, 48*(8), 549–557.

Tyack, D. B., & Cuban, L. (1995). *Tinkering toward utopia*. Harvard University Press.

U.S. Census Bureau. (2017). *National population projections: Race and Hispanic origin by selected age groups*. https://www2.census.gov/programs-surveys/popproj/tables/2017/2017-summary-tables/np2017-t6.xlsx.

U.S. Department of Education, Institute of Education Sciences, What Works Clearinghouse. (2016, November). *Adolescent literacy intervention report: READ 180*. https://ies.ed.gov/ncee/wwc/EvidenceSnapshot/665

U.S. Department of Education, National Center for Education Statistics (2010). *National Assessment of Educational Progress (NAEP) 2010 civics assessment*. https://nces.ed.gov/nationsreportcard/pdf/main2010/2011466.pdf

Valdés, G. (1998). The world outside and inside schools: Language and immigrant children. *Educational Researcher, 27*(6), 4–18.

Valdés, G., Bunch, G., Snow, C., Lee, C., & Matos, L. (2007). Enhancing the development of students' language(s). In L. Darling-Hammond & J. Bransford (Eds.), *Preparing teachers for a changing world: What teachers should learn and be able to do* (pp. 126–168). John Wiley & Sons.

Valenzuela, A. (1999). *Subtractive schooling: U.S.-Mexican youth and the politics of caring*. SUNY.

Valenzuela, A. (2005). *Leaving children behind: How "Texas-style" accountability fails Latino youth*: SUNY.

Villenas, S., & Moreno, M. (2001). To valerse por si misma between race, capitalism, and patriarchy: Latina mother–daughter pedagogies in North Carolina. *International Journal of Qualitative Studies in Education, 14*(5), 671–688.

Vygotsky, L. S. (1987). *The collected works of L. S. Vygotsky, Volume 1: Problems of general psychology*. Plenum Press.

Wacquant, L. (2011). Deadly symbiosis: When ghetto and prison meet and mesh. *Punishment and Society, 3*(1), 95–134.

Walker, E. V. S. (1993). Interpersonal caring in the "good" segregated schooling of African-American children: Evidence from the case of Caswell County Training School. *Urban Review, 25*(1), 63–77.

Walker, E. V. S., & Snarey, J. R. (Eds.). (2004). *Race-ing moral formation: African American perspectives on care and justice*. Teachers College Press.

Ward, J. V. (2000). *The skin we're in: Teaching our children to be emotionally strong, socially smart and spiritually connected*. The Free Press.

Ware, F. (2006). Warm demander pedagogy: Culturally responsive teaching that supports a culture of achievement for African American students. Urban Education, *41*(4), 427–456.

Warren, M. R., & Mapp, K. L. (2011). *A match on dry grass: Community organizing as a catalyst for school reform*. Oxford University Press.

Weissberg, R. P., & Cascarino, J. (2013). Academic learning+ social-emotional learning= national priority. *Phi Delta Kappan, 95*(2), 8–13.

Weiston-Serdan, T. (2017). *Critical mentoring: A practical guide*. Stylus.

Wellington, D. L. (2008). History, amnesia, and the N word. *Dissent, 55*(1), 112–115.

Welsh, R. O., & Swain, W. A. (2020). (Re)defining urban education: A conceptual review and empirical exploration of the definition of urban education. *Educational Researcher, 49*(2), 90–100.

Williams, P. (1987). Spirit-murdering the messenger: The discourse of fingerpointing as the law's response to racism. *University of Miami Law Review, 42*, 1273–1158.

Wu, C., & Coady, M. R. (2010). "The United States is America?": A cultural perspective on READ 180 materials. *Language, Culture and Curriculum, 23*(2), 153–165.

Yazzie-Mintz, E., & McCormick, K. (2012). Finding the humanity in the data: Understanding, measuring, and strengthening student engagement. In S. L. Christenson, A. L. Reschly, & C. Wylie (Eds.), *Handbook of research on student engagement* (pp. 743–761): Springer.

Yosso, T. J. (2005). Whose culture has capital? A critical race theory discussion of community cultural wealth. *Race Ethnicity and Education, 8*(1), 69–91.

Yosso, T. J. (2006). *Critical race counterstories along the Chicana/Chicano educational pipeline.* Taylor & Francis.

Yosso, T. J., & Solórzano, D. G. (2006). *Leaks in the Chicana and Chicano educational pipeline.* Latino Policy & Issues Brief, no. 13. https://files.eric.ed.gov/fulltext/ED493404.pdf

Yosso, T., Smith, W., Ceja, M., & Solórzano, D. (2009). Critical race theory, racial microaggressions, and campus racial climate for Latina/o undergraduates. *Harvard Educational Review, 79*(4), 659–691.

Index

Page numbers followed by *t* indicate tables and *f* indicate figures.

About the Author

Marnie W. Curry is a researcher at the University of California, Santa Cruz. A former middle school and high school teacher, she is committed to bridging the world of academia and K–12 schools in order to advance educational equity for historically underserved youth. Her areas of expertise include urban schooling, teaching and learning to support culturally and linguistically diverse learners, and teacher professional communities. Previously, she directed Project IMPACT, a collaborative teacher inquiry initiative sponsored by the University of California, Berkeley. Her research has been featured in *Teachers College Record, Phi Delta Kappan, American Educational Research Journal,* and *Urban Education.*